# Programming with GitHub® Copilot

## Write Better Code–Faster!

## Kurt Dowswell

# WILEY

# Acknowledgments

Creating this book has been a collaborative effort that would not have been possible without the guidance, support, and encouragement of many people.

First, I want to express my gratitude to Kenyon Brown for believing in my vision and providing me with the opportunity to bring this book to life.

A heartfelt thanks to Satish Gowrishankar for keeping everything on track with meticulous planning, organization, and dedication to deadlines. Your oversight ensured the process remained smooth and effective.

I am deeply grateful to Janet Wehner for coordinating the content and guiding the production through each step with keen attention to detail and precision.

Special appreciation goes to T.J. Corrigan for offering invaluable expertise and meticulously reviewing the technical aspects. Your assistance helped shape this book into what it is today.

To my wife, Paige Lord-Dowswell, thank you for your encouragement, insights, and acumen. You were instrumental in helping me get this book across the finish line.

—Kurt Dowswell

# About the Author

**Kurt Dowswell** is a seasoned software architect with more than 13 years of industry experience. Kurt has spent the larger part of his career leading teams of developers in building, deploying, and maintaining large-scale enterprise software solutions for the U.S. government. He graduated with a BS in computer science from James Madison University.

## About the Technical Editor

**T.J. Corrigan** has worn many hats in his career, including scientist, developer, architect, platform engineer, and engineering lead. Throughout this time, he has always been passionate about improving developer productivity through standardization, automation, self-service, and, most recently, generative AI. T.J. holds a bachelor's degree in computational biology from Carnegie Mellon University. Currently he works as a principal cloud solutions engineer at GitHub, where he helps joint GitHub/Microsoft customers achieve more.

# Contents at a Glance

# Contents

# Introduction

Welcome to *Programming with GitHub Copilot*, your comprehensive guide to GitHub Copilot. As programming evolves, the tools and techniques at your disposal must adapt to meet the increasing complexity of projects and the demand for faster, more efficient development cycles. GitHub Copilot represents a monumental shift in how code is written, offering you an exceptional partner in your coding journey.

GitHub Copilot is not just a tool; it's transforming the concept of pair programming. Traditionally, pair programming involves two programmers working together at one workstation, continuously collaborating to write better code. However, finding a human partner for this task isn't always feasible. Enter GitHub Copilot, your ever-present AI companion, ready to assist by suggesting code, helping debug, and even writing blocks of code autonomously.

This book is designed to give you practical applications of GitHub Copilot. From setting up your environment to advanced topics like enhancing code security and accelerating DevSecOps practices, each chapter dives deep into real-world applications and provides insights into making the most of this powerful tool.

On the book's website (`https://www.wiley.com/go/programminggithubcopilot`), you will find code files for the starter projects discussed in select chapters. These companion files are designed to help you follow along with the practical examples provided throughout the book.

Whether you're a seasoned developer or just starting out, this book will enable you to harness the capabilities of GitHub Copilot to enhance your programming skills, learn new languages, refactor code, and much more.

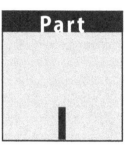

Part

I

# Getting Started with
# GitHub Copilot

## In This Part

# Get Started with GitHub Copilot

Software development is full of challenges to overcome. For years, it has been known that programming with a partner can help you learn more, produce better work, and gain more satisfaction while accomplishing your tasks. Although the benefits of pair programming are known, it isn't always possible to have a pair programming partner with you—until now.

GitHub Copilot is your artificial intelligence (AI) pair programming partner, always ready to assist and eager to help you learn! This book will walk you through how to best utilize GitHub Copilot to help you write better code and do it faster.

In this chapter, we will focus on the required steps for getting started with GitHub Copilot. Let's begin!

- Learn Why GitHub Copilot Matters to You
- Create a GitHub Account
- Acquire a GitHub Copilot License
- Install an IDE Extension
- First Run: Test Copilot

## Learn Why GitHub Copilot Matters

GitHub Copilot is your AI pair programmer that can assist you in every phase of your software development lifecycle. Whether you are defining your next great feature or configuring a complex continuous integration/continuous delivery (CI/CD) pipeline for an enterprise-grade deployment, GitHub Copilot will be by your side every step of the way, giving you bespoke insights into your business needs. Get ready to take your development productivity and joy of programming to the next level.

You will find your favorite new AI-powered pair programmer, GitHub Copilot, in an ever-growing number of places within your integrated development environment (IDE) and beyond. This book will teach you how to use each Copilot feature in the different license options. We will also explore case studies with best practices that will help to extend your use of Copilot into all areas of your development lifecycle.

To prove the effectiveness of Copilot, a team at GitHub has conducted qualitative and quantitative research to test their hypothesis of improved developer productivity and happiness. One large-scale survey resulted in some amazing results: 88% indicated they were more productive, 74% said they were able to focus on more satisfying work, 96% indicated they were faster with repetitive tasks, and 73% of survey participants indicated they had more time in a flow state [1].

In addition to the survey, the GitHub team conducted a qualitative experiment by having developers create a web server in JavaScript. Individuals using Copilot finished the exercise on average 55% faster [1]! The team used GitHub Classroom to score submissions for correctness and completeness automatically.

## Create a GitHub Account

Before you can start using Copilot, you need to have a valid GitHub account. Head to the following web page and ensure that you have access to your account before getting started:

```
https://github.com/login
```

## Acquire a GitHub Copilot License

With a valid GitHub account, we can now review the available licenses for GitHub Copilot. You will need to pick the license that is best for you. There are three GitHub Copilot plans available.

- Copilot Individual
- Copilot Business
- Copilot Enterprise

There are several factors to consider when choosing the correct plan. If you are a student or a maintainer of a popular open-source project, you might be eligible for a free Copilot Individual license.

You can get more information on licenses on this web page:

```
https://docs.github.com/enterprise-cloud@latest/billing/
managing-billing-for-github-copilot/about-billing-for-github-copilot
```

## Install an IDE Extension

GitHub Copilot runs as an extension in the following IDEs:

- Azure Data Studio
- JetBrains IDEs (IntelliJ, PyCharm, Rider, and so on)
- Vim/Neovim
- Visual Studio
- Visual Studio Code

**NOTE**  In this book, we will be using the Visual Studio Code IDE for most of the examples. If you use one of the other supported IDEs as your preferred development platform, the information shared in these examples will be transferrable. We will be covering these additional IDEs later in the book when we detail how to set up and configure them to work with GitHub Copilot.

**NOTE**  Support for the JetBrains IDEs is currently in beta.

## Download Visual Studio Code

You can download Visual Studio Code (VS Code) from the following page:

```
http://code.visualstudio.com
```

Once you have installed VS Code on your computer, you should see a welcome screen (see Figure 1.1).

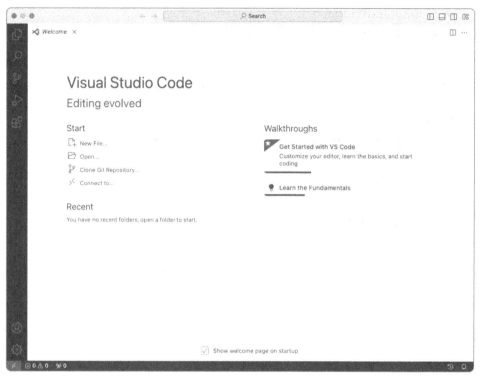

**Figure 1.1:** VS Code welcome screen

## Install the GitHub Copilot Extension

Now that you have the VS Code IDE installed and open, let's navigate to the Extensions panel on the Action Bar. You will find the Extensions panel identified by the "squares" icon.

Now follow these steps:

1. Open the Extensions panel.
2. Search for "GitHub Copilot."
3. Within the GitHub Copilot extension result, click Install (see Figure 1.2).

**Figure 1.2:** VS Code Extensions panel

## Configure the IDE Settings for Copilot

After successfully installing the Copilot extension, you are ready to ensure you are authenticated to your GitHub account within VS Code. You should see a pop-up in the lower-right corner of VS Code prompting you to sign in to GitHub (see Figure 1.3). Please use this option to sign in.

If you don't see this prompt after installing the extension, you can also authenticate using the profile menu on the Action Bar (see Figure 1.4).

After completing the sign-in process via the GitHub authentication pages, you can verify your authentication status within VS Code via the bottom-right Copilot icon. Click this icon to bring up the Copilot status menu (see Figure 1.5).

Within the status menu you have access to your status, chat, settings, logs, documentation, and forums.

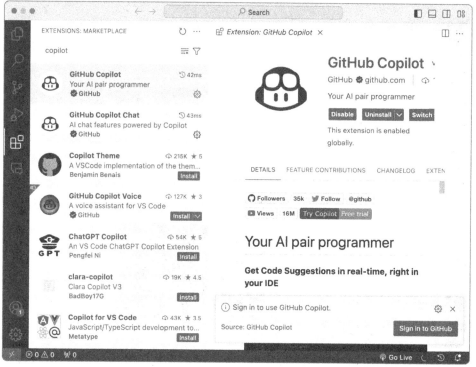

**Figure 1.3:** Sign-in prompt

**Figure 1.4:** Signing in via the Action Bar

**Figure 1.5:** Copilot status menu

## Install Node.js

Lastly, Node.js will need to be installed to run the example. Node.js is an open-source, cross-platform, back-end JavaScript runtime environment. It allows us to execute JavaScript outside of the web browser.

The easiest way to install Node.js is to go to the website:

```
https://nodejs.org/en/download.
```

Based on your operating system and computer hardware, select the appropriate download, and follow the installation steps.

After installing Node.js, run the following command in your terminal to confirm that you have installed it successfully.

```
node -v
```

This command will output the node version you have installed.

# First Run: Test Copilot

As mentioned, this book will be showcasing the features of GitHub Copilot primarily in Visual Studio Code. There are dedicated chapters later in the book to detail all the other GitHub Copilot IDE experiences.

While most of the code completion features are universal between IDEs, there are differences in the menus, the keyboard shortcuts, and the availability of Copilot Chat (which is available only in Visual Studio and VS Code).

## Get the Prerequisites

As mentioned, the following are the prerequisites to testing Copilot:

- VS Code
- GitHub account
- GitHub Copilot license
- GitHub Copilot extension
- Node.js

## Explore Copilot

Let's make sure that Copilot is working by writing a quick example function. In this section, you will create a palindrome checker to showcase some of the basic interactions you will have with Copilot within your editor.

Start by opening a folder in VS Code. You can do this via the Explorer menu (see Figure 1.6) or the keyboard shortcut (Cmd+O/Ctrl+O).

> **NOTE**    Throughout this book, keyboard shortcuts will be displayed for both macOS and Windows OS.

Create a new folder called **copilot-test** and click Open within your Finder/Explorer window.

Add a new file to your open folder called `palindrome-checker.js` (see Figure 1.7).

Now you are ready to start writing the Node.js script. Let's start by typing a top-level comment in the `palindrome-checker.js` file, as shown here:

```
// node.js application that checks if a string is a palindrome
```

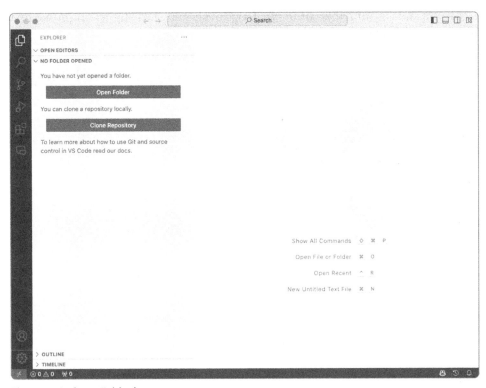

**Figure 1.6:** Open Folder button

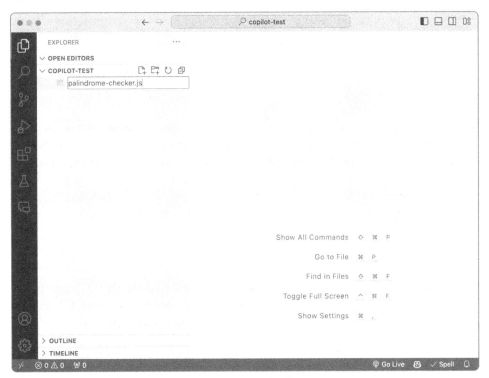

**Figure 1.7:** Creating the `palindrome-checker.js` file

As you start writing this comment, Copilot should start suggesting some text to complete it (see Figure 1.8).

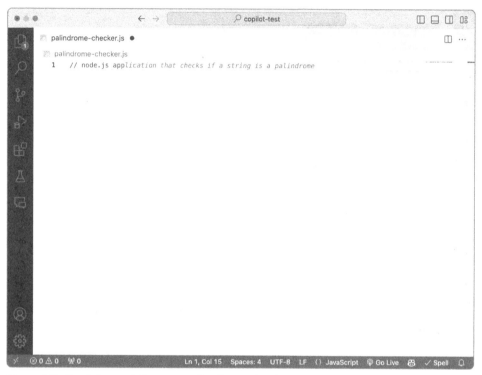

**Figure 1.8:** Copilot completion suggestion for top-level comment

You can accept the Copilot text completion by hitting the Tab key.

**NOTE** You can provide context to Copilot in several ways, such as descriptive file comments, inline comments, examples, filenames, imports, method names, variables, and open file tabs. You will see all these context types in action throughout this book.

With the comment at the top of the file, continue to the next line. You can provide additional context by adding some examples of palindromes you would like the checker to expect to receive.

```
// examples: racecar, taco cat
```

Without this example comment, there is a chance that the palindrome function will not account for phrase inputs. Adding this context is a way for you to continue to refine the context given to Copilot to get better output.

Now that you have a short, clear, and targeted comment for your file, you can add two line returns to the file to move on to the function implementation. If Copilot doesn't automatically give you the line you would like as a suggestion, you can start typing the statement you would prefer. Copilot will then use this additional context to drive a better completion suggestion for the current line you are working on.

In my case, I will accept a line comment describing a function to check if a string is a palindrome and implement the first line of the function name (see Figure 1.9).

**Figure 1.9:** Copilot completion suggestion for palindrome function

> **NOTE** GitHub Copilot is nondeterministic and may return different results for you even though you have the same comment structure within your file. We will cover the AI behind Copilot in depth in Chapter 2, "Decoding GitHub Copilot."

You can continue to accept and refine code completions provided by Copilot in the file. Accept suggestions with the Tab key or use the menu if available when hovering on the suggestion text.

After coding the `isPalindrome` function, you can continue to add some test cases. Copilot will most likely suggest continuing. But to ensure you get the output you want, add another line comment.

```
// test cases
```

After you add a new line, Copilot should start completing the test cases using the examples from the top-level file comment. Continue implementing these test cases (see Figure 1.10).

```
palindrome-checker.js  ×

palindrome-checker.js > ...
1    // node.js application that checks if a string is a palindrome
2    // examples: racecar, taco cat
3
4    // function to check if a string is a palindrome
5    function isPalindrome(str) {
6        // remove non-alphanumeric characters and convert to lowercase
7        str = str.replace(/[^0-9a-z]/gi, '').toLowerCase();
8        // reverse the string
9        let reversedStr = str.split('').reverse().join('');
10       // compare the original string to the reversed string
11       return str === reversedStr;
12   }
13
14   // test cases
15   console.log(isPalindrome('racecar')); // true
16   console.log(isPalindrome('taco cat')); // true
17   console.log(isPalindrome('hello')); // false
```

**Figure 1.10:** Palindrome function with tests

With the function and tests, you can now run this file to see if you get the expected output. If you are following along in VS Code, you can open the integrated terminal to run the function via the keyboard shortcut (Ctrl+`).

Within the integrated terminal that is open to the current location of your Node.js file, type the following to run the function:

```
node palindrome-checker.js
```

You should now see output indicating the expected results from your function (see Figure 1.11).

**Figure 1.11:** Palindrome function terminal run with results

## Conclusion

There are a multitude of ways in which GitHub Copilot will assist you in your developer workflow. So far, we have only scratched the surface of the capabilities Copilot provides. Up next, you will learn more about GitHub Copilot code suggestions, what data sources and training it uses, and privacy and security considerations that are important to know.

## Reference

[1] E. Kalliamvakou, 2022. "Research: quantifying GitHub Copilot's impact on developer productivity and happiness," https://github.blog/2022-09-07-research-quantifying-github-copilots-impact-on-developer-productivity-and-happiness

# Decoding GitHub Copilot

In this chapter, we will look at the AI behind GitHub. We will explore the genesis, advancement, and capabilities of GitHub Copilot. We'll delve into the security and privacy measures that safeguard our work, highlighting the importance of secure data handling and the mechanisms in place to protect our code. We will also explore the critical topic of copyright protections, ensuring that our use of GitHub Copilot aligns with legal standards. Lastly, we will review the GitHub Copilot Trust Center to equip ourselves with the necessary knowledge to navigate the complexities of using this powerful tool confidently.

- Uncover the AI Behind GitHub Copilot
- Understand Security, Privacy, and Data Handling
- Understand Copyright Protections
- Explore the GitHub Copilot Trust Center

## Uncover the AI Behind GitHub Copilot

The genesis of GitHub Copilot was enabled by rapid advancements in generative AI models like OpenAI's GPT-3. GPT-3, which stands for Generative Pre-trained Transformer 3, was the third iteration of OpenAI's GPT-n series of large language models (LLMs).

GitHub Copilot was first conceptualized in 2020 after GPT-3 was released. The GitHub team had routinely asked, "Should we think about general-purpose coding generation?" But the answer was always no. Until GPT-3, the ability to produce high-quality code suggestions in the required development scenarios was nonexistent [1]. Once the team got their hands on the GPT-3 model, they rapidly discovered that GPT-3 could perform at a very high level for code generation tasks.

Building on top of the already powerful GPT-3 model, in 2021, GitHub and OpenAI worked closely together on a new OpenAI model that was a descendant of GPT-3. The model was called OpenAI Codex. The Codex model was trained on billions of lines of code from publicly available sources as well as public GitHub repositories. The combination of the impressive general-purpose language model (GPT-3) and the massive code training dataset allowed the team to improve the capabilities of GPT-3 even further to interpret natural languages, like English and Spanish, into programming languages, such as JavaScript, Python Go, Perl, PHP, and more. This newfound ability to bridge the gap between natural languages and programming languages resulted in the Codex model having the capability to perform transpilation, explain the purpose of code files, and even refactor existing code based on the request of the prompt statement [2]. This technology is the bedrock of the GitHub Copilot code suggestion engine.

Since the advancements of the OpenAI Codex model, GitHub has been iterating consistently on innovative ways to integrate Copilot into the software development lifecycle. On December 29, 2023, GitHub Copilot Chat, powered by GPT-4, was released to all GitHub Copilot users. Copilot Chat is built on a mosaic of technologies working in concert to provide end users with bespoke expert advice when navigating the complexities of their codebases. With the combination of the OpenAI GPT-4 LLM, GitHub knowledge graph, local codebase indexing, language intelligence, and a processing pipeline, Copilot Chat can converse with you about your codebase and give verifiable and actionable responses empowering you to navigate your way to solutions with less friction and more fun.

Looking to the future, GitHub will continue to improve the AI behind Copilot. With the constant advancement in AI models, the team at GitHub will ensure you are receiving the most recent powerful model updates to keep you competitive in an ever-changing development landscape.

## Understand Security, Privacy, and Data Handling

Adhering to strict security measures is a critical aspect of GitHub Copilot. The team at GitHub utilizes a plethora of security strategies. In this section, we will cover secure transmission and encryption of your data, as well as runtime security measures to enhance protection.

## Message Transmission

When interacting with GitHub Copilot, all the required context to resolve your questions or completion suggestions must be transmitted to GitHub's services running on Azure. This data is passed via Hypertext Transfer Protocol Secure (HTTPS) over Transport Layer Security (TLS). This end-to-end encryption process ensures your data, code, and queries are all secure and processed only by the GitHub Copilot back-end services. HTTP over TLS is the global standard for safe and secure message passing.

## Data Storage

In this section, we will detail what GitHub Copilot data is stored at rest.

### Prompt and Suggestion Data

For business and enterprise users, data used for GitHub Copilot code suggestions and chat responses is not stored in persisted storage. This data is kept in-memory only for the duration of the API request. Once that is completed, the request data is cleared. Also, GitHub does not log user request data to further ensure your session data is protected.

For individual plan users, prompts and suggestions are retained by default unless you disable code snippet collection in your settings.

### User Engagement Data

GitHub stores user engagement metrics such as usage data and acceptance rates. This data may include pseudonymous identifiers to differentiate user activity. This is used to ensure the health and operation of the Copilot system. This user engagement is stored using Microsoft Azure's data encryption. Azure data encryption services meet the highest standards of security compliance. This data encryption adheres to the National Institute of Standards and Technology (NIST) Federal Information Processing Standard (FIPS) Publication 140-2 standards.

## Additional Security

In this section, we will cover the vulnerability prevention system and GitHub Advanced Security. It is important to note that you should always rely on additional security tooling like GitHub Advanced Security to ensure you are not injecting vulnerabilities for production codebases.

### Vulnerability Prevention System

GitHub Copilot employs a vulnerability prevention system that inspects generated code suggestions for security vulnerabilities before returning the suggestion to you. This prevention mechanism checks common security vulnerabilities in the suggestions such as hard-coded credentials, SQL injections, and path injections.

### GitHub Advanced Security

While GitHub Copilot and its dynamic security protection layers are important, it is critical that you always verify the Copilot suggestions for correctness and security integrity. Copilot's generated responses are not intended to fully automate the process of code creation. You need to use sound judgment and critical reasoning when reviewing code suggestions.

To ensure the code you commit to your repository is sound and secure, GitHub suggests using a static code analysis tool such as GitHub Advanced Security. This tooling scans your code for security issues, checks for secret keys being injected into source control, and audits your dependencies to ensure that you are not injecting security issues via third-party libraries.

## Understand Copyright Protections

GitHub Copilot has been trained on billions of lines of publicly accessible code. Some of this code is under copyright protection. It is important to note that copyright law permits the use of copyrighted works to train AI models [3]. When Copilot is trained on these repositories, the code is not saved to the model. The code is used only to train the model so it can make reasoned responses as to which token or word should appear next.

A simplistic example of how this works is if we have a text file with a series of numbers such as "1,2,3,4," and we send a request to Copilot for a code suggestion, Copilot will split our context into a series of tokens like this:

```
['1', ',', '2', ',', '3', ',', '4', ',']
```

The LLM will then process these token inputs and identify the pattern that is occurring. This will result in a predicted token that should occur next, which, in this case, is 5.

Building on the numeric list example, let's see how this works when we are coding a new method. If we have a Python function declaration such as this:

```
def greet(name):
```

then Copilot will split out our function declaration into a series of tokens:

```
['def', 'greet', '(', 'name', ')', ':']
```

The LLM will then process these token inputs and identify the pattern that is occurring. This will result in a predicted token that should occur next. In this case, the token most likely would be `print`.

The model then continues to predict the next tokens, resulting in a completed line of code.

```
def greet(name):
    print(f"Hello, {name}!")
```

While the code is not saved to the model, due to the way in which the training operations are conducted, there is a chance (less than 1%) that Copilot will produce results that match the code used to train the model [3]. It is important to understand that this is not copy-and-pasting. It is determining the best chain of code that matches the prompt and context it is operating within.

GitHub, with the support of its parent company Microsoft, has always provided copyright indemnification protections ensuring that you will be protected if any legal action is brought against you because of the use of GitHub Copilot.

At the Ignite conference in November 2023, Microsoft expanded its copyright support to all of its generative AI solutions and tools, further entrenching Microsoft's support to customers in this area. This commitment is called the "Customer Copyright Commitment (CCC)," and it ensures that all customers using Microsoft generative AI solutions are backed by the legal support of Microsoft if faced with legal issues.

**NOTE**    You must have the GitHub Copilot Policy setting called Suggestions Matching Public Code set to Blocked to be eligible for this legal protection. For more information, please see this page:

```
https://learn.microsoft.com/en-us/legal/cognitive-services/
openai/customer-copyright-commitment
```

## Explore the GitHub Copilot Trust Center

The GitHub Copilot Trust Center is a great place to go if you have any questions or concerns about using Copilot. There are videos, FAQs, resource links, and contact information to give you the confidence you or your organization need before adopting GitHub Copilot into your development workflow.

For more information, please visit the GitHub Copilot Trust Center at this location:

```
https://resources.github.com/copilot-trust-center
```

## Conclusion

In this chapter, our exploration of GitHub Copilot has unveiled the remarkable AI driving this innovative tool, emphasizing its development, security measures, and commitment to copyright compliance. Through understanding the intricate layers of protection and legal foresight integrated into GitHub Copilot, alongside the resources available in the Trust Center, we are now better positioned to leverage this technology. As we move forward, equipped with this knowledge, we can confidently incorporate GitHub Copilot into our development workflows, harnessing its potential to streamline our coding processes and enhance our productivity.

## References

[1] S. Verdi, 2023. "Inside GitHub: Working with the LLMs behind GitHub Copilot," `https://github.blog/2023-05-17-inside-github-working-with-the-llms-behind-github-copilot`

[2] OpenAI, 2021. "OpenAI Codex," `https://openai.com/blog/openai-codex`

[3] GitHub, 2023. "GitHub Copilot Trust Center," `https://resources.github.com/copilot-trust-center`

# Part

## II

# GitHub Copilot Features in Action

## In This Part

# Exploring Code Completions

In this chapter, we will do a deep dive into the code completion capabilities of GitHub Copilot. We will cover all the details you need to get the most out of Copilot code completions. While code completions are incredibly intuitive, we will explore various features that will enable you to create more refined solutions that meet the needs of your development plan.

- Introducing Code Completions
- Working with Copilot Code Completions
- Discovering the Toolbar and Panel
- Updating Copilot Settings
- Leveraging Keyboard Shortcuts

## Introducing Code Completions

The developer experience within integrated development environments (IDEs) has been getting progressively better for decades with features such as spell-check, IntelliSense, and code snippets. All these features, and more, have culminated in a rich developer experience enabling millions of developers to create high-quality software that drives today's industry.

With the release of GitHub Copilot, code completions within IDEs have been a game-changer for developer productivity. Copilot code completions can assist you in writing code faster, refactoring code, writing code you are unfamiliar with, creating documentation, and even writing unit tests!

Code completions are accessible right within your IDE editor window. These code suggestions can be accepted as a whole, by line, or by word. The length of the code completions can vary based on the location you are currently typing. Let's dive into the details and understand how to best utilize Copilot code completions.

# Working with Copilot Code Completions

Copilot context is the information necessary to produce responses bespoke to your current IDE editor state. The better the context, the better the responses you will get. You can provide context via open file tabs adjacent to your current document, top-level comments, line-level comments, and well-named variables and methods.

In this section, we will explore each of these context options to enable you to work faster and better with your AI-powered pair programmer, GitHub Copilot!

## Prerequisites

To follow along with this example, you will need the following prerequisites installed:

- Visual Studio Code:
  `https://code.visualstudio.com/download`
- GitHub Copilot Extension:
  `https://marketplace.visualstudio.com/items?itemName=GitHub.copilot`
- Node.js:
  `https://nodejs.org/en/download`

## Naming Your File

A simple way to get Copilot to create better results is to use a descriptive filename. Copilot will be able to use the words within your filename and the file type to guide its responses. Let's start by adding a new file called `roman-to-integer.js`.

## Top-Level Comment

Building on the filename and type, you can add a filename comment to your code file to add more context to Copilot's decision engine.

Within the `roman-to-integer.js` file, type the following comment:

```
/**
 * create a node.js app that gets a roman numeral via user input
 * and outputs the correct integer value
 */
```

After typing this comment, hit the Enter key and wait for Copilot to respond with a code completion suggestion. If you don't see one, you can initiate a response with the keyboard shortcut (Option+\ or Alt+\), as shown in Figure 3.1.

**Figure 3.1:** Copilot code completion result

Accept the response from Copilot with the Tab key. Continue to hit the Enter key to progress down your file and allow for Copilot to respond with additional code that meets the needs of your top-level comment (see Figure 3.2).

> **NOTE** Always verify the output provided by Copilot for accuracy and secure coding practices.

**Figure 3.2:** Additional code completion result

Continue to accept the responses and write the remainder of the `roman-to-integer.js` code that is required for the file to run successfully. After you have completed the code completions and writing, the file should contain a `readline` import, `readline` variable, `readline` question and answer, and `romanToInt` function.

Now you should be able to run the `js` file via Node. Open your terminal via the keyboard shortcut (Ctrl+`) or with the command menu (see Figure 3.3).

Now, within the terminal window, type the following:

```
node roman-to-integer.js
```

Hit the Enter key, and you should see the prompt from the Node.js app, allowing you to provide a Roman numeral.

This should have provided you with a working example of an application that can convert Roman numerals to integers. In the next section, we will explore how you can expand upon this example using other methods of the code completion feature set.

**Figure 3.3:** Panel visibility menu item

## Using Meaningful Names

To help Copilot understand your intent, it is critical to use descriptive names for things such as classes, methods, and variables. Avoid abbreviations, redundant names, and ambiguous terminology.

One powerful way to use Copilot is to write the method of the operation that you would like to produce in the method you would like to use. Let's explore this use case in our Roman numeral converter application.

Let's add some validation to the user input. Within the question function, it would be great if we could validate the user input. You can add a descriptive name of a validation method you have not yet created to guide Copilot to assist you in completing this task (see Figure 3.4).

With this new code added to the application, let's continue to add the `isRomanNumeral()` method. Before the question method, add a new line, and Copilot will most likely already be thinking of what you want to accomplish by the method that you have just "stubbed" out in the question response section (see Figure 3.5).

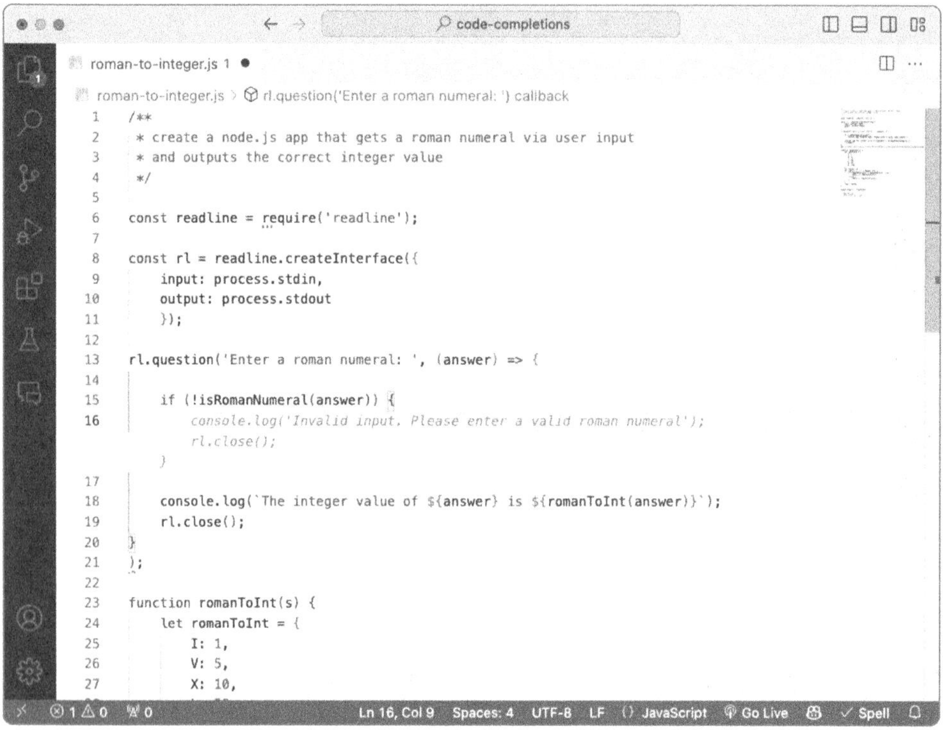

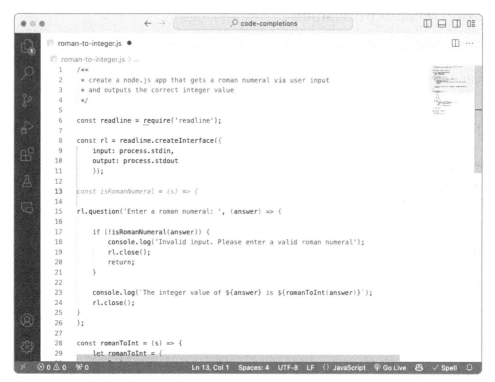

**Figure 3.4:** Method name driving code completion

**Figure 3.5:** Method code completion

Accept the Copilot suggestions and press Enter and Tab until you have completed the `isRomanNumeral()` function. After you have the completed function, proceed to the terminal again and run the application with the following command:

```
node roman-to-integer.js
```

You should now be able to see your validation method in action, with output shown to the user if they were to input an incorrect Roman numeral (see Figure 3.6).

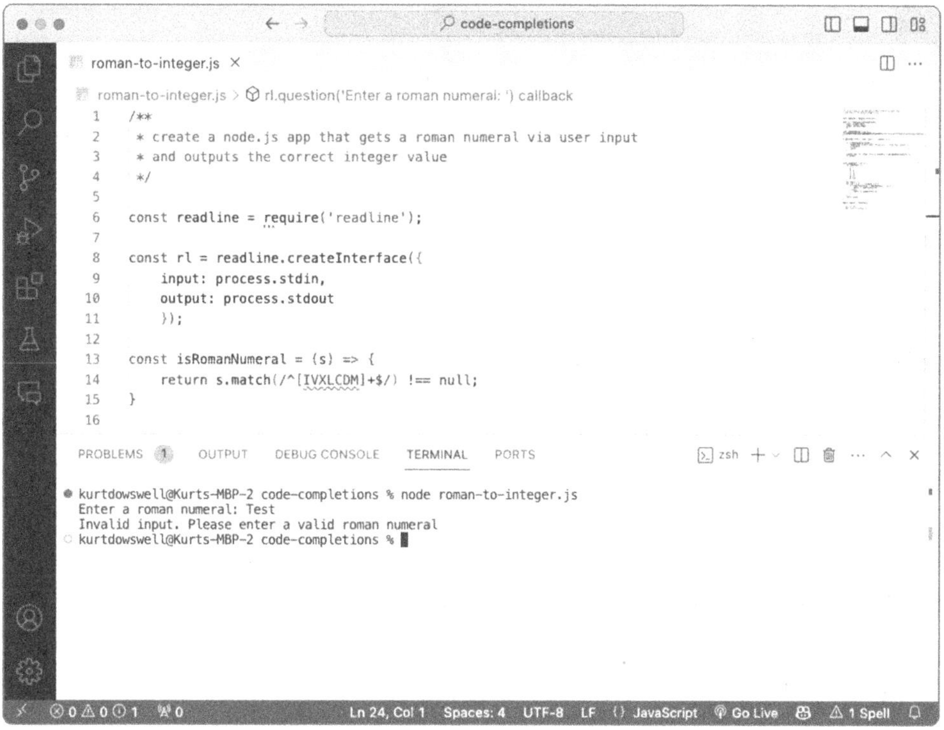

**Figure 3.6:** Validation method output test

## Writing Specific Comments

As you have seen, inline chat is a great option to get code suggestions right where you want them. Another fantastic approach is to use inline comments with short, specific, and targeted language.

Here we will explore how to add a help message for users of your application using a comment to drive the development of this feature. Within the question function, let's add an inline comment before the validation method.

```
// If user types 'help', definition of roman numerals will be displayed
```

Hit the Enter key after this comment and wait for Copilot to respond with a suggestion. If Copilot does not initiate a code completion suggestion, you can manually trigger this by using the keyboard shortcut (Option+\ or Start+\). You should get something like Figure 3.7.

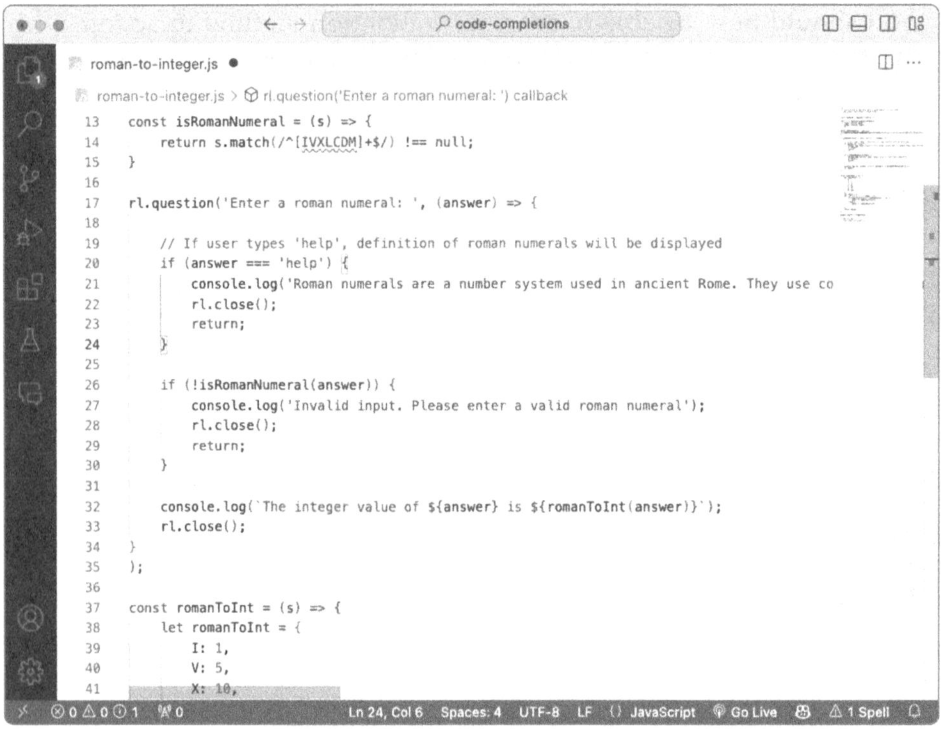

**Figure 3.7:** Inline comment with Copilot suggestion

## Referencing Open Tabs

When working on an existing codebase, it is important to follow coding standards that exist within the application. When coding with a single file, Copilot does not automatically traverse your application code to find relevant files that it can use for code completions. It is up to you to provide additional context to Copilot.

One great way to add context to support bespoke code completions is to have relevant code files open along with the code you are actively working on. Copilot will retrieve relevant code blocks from open tabs to assist in providing you with a better answer.

You can see this in action by creating a new file in VS Code. Let's call the new file `integer-to-roman.js`. In this file, we will start with a top-level comment to provide context to Copilot about our intent within this file (see Figure 3.8). Add the following comment to the top of this file:

```
// Integer to roman numeral app
```

After entering the top-level comment, hit the Enter key and begin to review and accept the code completions that Copilot is providing. You will see Copilot adapting the code to meet the need of this new file while following the coding design of the open `roman-to-integer.js` tab.

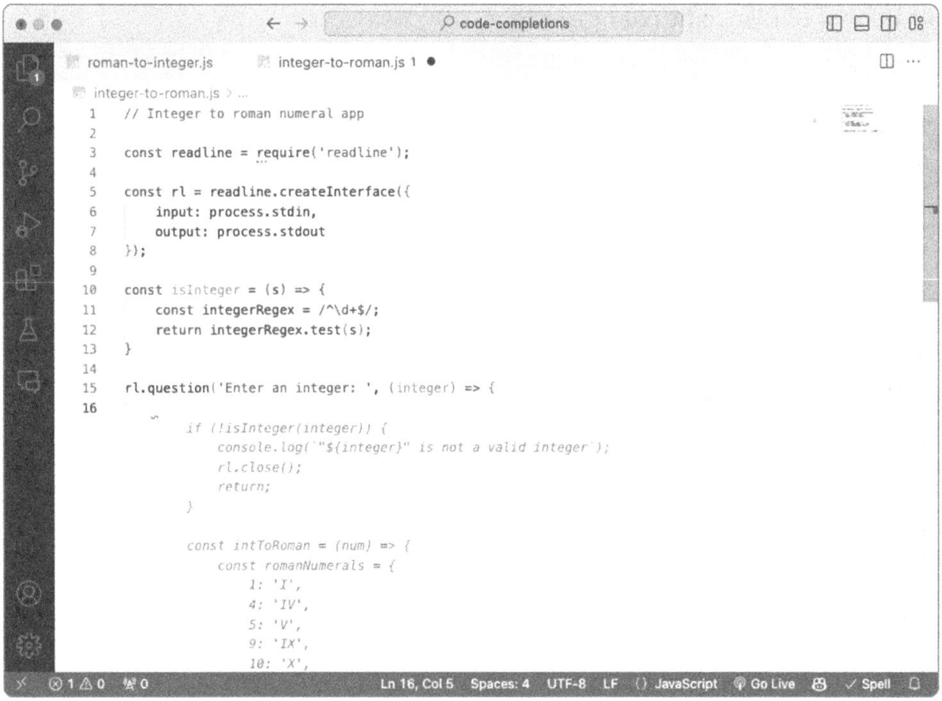

**Figure 3.8:** Top-level comment and open tab adding context

After you have accepted and refined the code completions, you can now execute this Node application. Here you will find that Copilot has conformed to your coding style from the referenced document, understood your intent with your new file based on the filename and top-level comment, and produced a well-crafted output for you to refine further and iterate on as you see fit.

## Discovering the Toolbar and Panel

This section introduces the functionalities of the Copilot Toolbar and Panel, essential tools in VS Code for navigating and selecting from multiple code completion suggestions efficiently.

### Detailing the Completions Toolbar

Within VS Code, there is a toolbar that is visible by default when you hover over the suggestion text (see Figure 3.9). This code completion menu experience will vary depending on your IDE, so please refer to the later chapters detailing additional IDE-specific configurations.

**Figure 3.9:** Code completion toolbar

Whenever Copilot has multiple potential solutions to the next code, this toolbar is useful if you'd like to iterate quickly over potential options via the arrow buttons on the left side of the toolbar. The toolbar also allows you to accept the entire suggestion (Cmd+Tab/Ctrl+Tab) or accept a single word at a time (Cmd+Right Arrow/Ctrl+Right Arrow).

If you'd like to accept an entire line or adjust the toolbar's default visibility, you can find these options within the ellipsis menu on the right.

## Discover the Completions Panel

To see what variations of code solutions Copilot is curating for you, you can leverage the Completions panel. You can find this by using the Command menu (Cmd+Shift+P/Ctrl+Shift+P), searching for "Open Completions Panel," and selecting the result. You can go directly to the Completions panel via the keyboard shortcut (Ctrl+Enter) as well (see Figure 3.10).

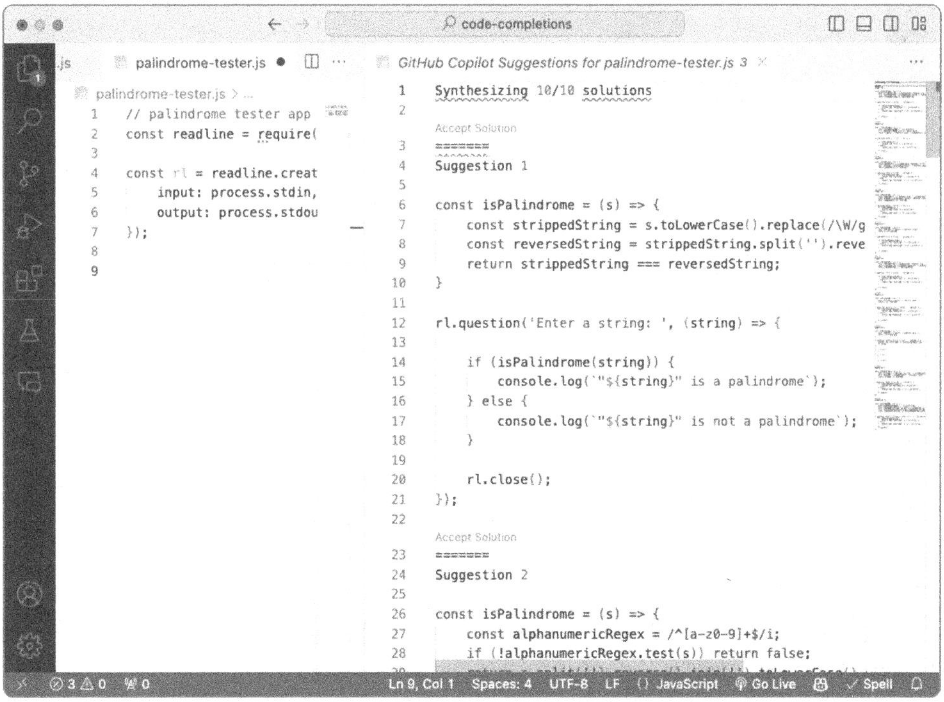

**Figure 3.10:** Completions panel

This panel gives up to 10 different code completion suggestions to review and accept. When you are not satisfied with the initial result provided by the code completions, this can be a helpful tool because it allows you to see various other completion options.

## Updating Copilot Settings

If you would like to adjust the default settings for Copilot, you can do so. To view the Copilot settings, open the Settings menu using the gear icon in the left sidebar menu of VS Code, using the keyboard shortcut (Cmd+,/Ctrl+,), or using the Copilot Status menu accessible from the extension icon.

With the Settings page open, filter down to the GitHub Copilot settings if you have not already (see Figure 3.11).

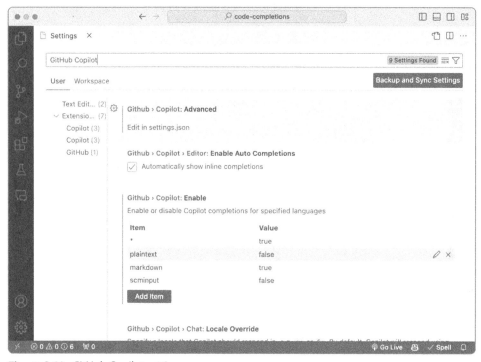

**Figure 3.11:**  GitHub Copilot settings

Here you can adjust settings such as file type enable settings, locale overrides, chat preferences, and more.

Within the VS Code advanced settings (see Figure 3.12), you can update a variety of settings to customize your Copilot responses. I will detail a few of the settings available for you to alter. Please note that these settings are valid only for VS Code.

> **NOTE**   Edit these settings only if necessary. The default behaviors of Copilot have been tuned for the best user experience, and altering them may diminish the quality of the Copilot responses.

**Figure 3.12:** GitHub Copilot advanced settings

## inlineSuggestCount

Update this value if you would like to control the maximum number of inline suggestions that are produced.

## length

The length setting allows you to specify a maximum length for code suggestion responses.

## listCount

The listCount setting (Ctrl+Enter) controls the limit of code suggestions that you will be shown.

## Leveraging Keyboard Shortcuts

Keyboard shortcuts help keep us in the flow of coding by allowing us to keep our hands on the keyboard while typing commands and code. Let's look at ways we can leverage Copilot's keyboard shortcuts to help us work even faster while interacting with our pair programming assistant.

You can access the Copilot keyboard shortcuts from the Copilot Status menu viewable after clicking the Copilot extension icon on the bottom toolbar. You can also quickly access them via a keyboard shortcut (Cmd+K Cmd+S/Ctrl+K Ctrl+S). After opening the Keyboard Shortcuts panel, you can filter down to the Copilot shortcuts to view all that are available (see Figure 3.13).

There are bindable keyboard shortcut commands for nearly all of the Copilot actions that you can take. There is also a subset that have predefined keybindings. As you use Copilot more, make sure to take note of repetitive tasks that you are performing and consider making a keybinding for that action. The following are my suggestions.

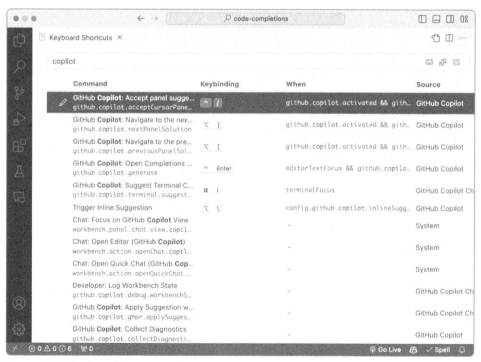

**Figure 3.13:** Keyboard shortcut settings

## Focus on GitHub Copilot View

The Focus on GitHub Copilot View keybinding is not set by default. This is an example of a command that I want to be a keyboard shortcut because it suits my workflow. To align it with other left menu bar view shortcuts, I assigned this command as follows:

- **Mac:** Shift+Cmd+C
- **Windows:** Shift+Alt+C

Doing this enables you to quickly view the menu view for Copilot Chat. This can speed up your workflow for ongoing conversations you are having with Copilot about your code.

## Suggest Terminal Command

The Suggest Terminal Command action will open the Inline Chat dialog when you are within the editor window. This command will also open the quick chat view with the `@terminal` command when you are in the integrated terminal window.

- **Mac:** Cmd+I
- **Windows:** Control+I

## Triggering Inline Suggestion

You can get Copilot to trigger a response by deleting spaces or tabs and then returning to the location where you were previously. But instead of adding the additional keystrokes, try using the Trigger Inline Suggestion keyboard shortcut. This shortcut will show you a preview of the code completion for the remainder of the line or function you are currently using.

- **Mac:** Option+\
- **Windows:** Alt+\

## Navigate to the Next Panel Suggestion

After a code suggestion is visible in the editor at your current location, you can cycle through potential completions that have been synthesized if there are more than one. This will allow you to quickly iterate over the options to accept instead of clicking through menus or customizing the prompt when the suggestion you prefer might be the second or third option in the list of generated results.

- **Mac:** Option+]
- **Windows:** Alt+]

### Navigate to the Previous Panel Suggestion

This keyboard shortcut allows you to navigate backward through the code completion suggestions.

- **Mac:** Option+[
- **Windows:** Alt+[

### Open Completions Panel

With this shortcut, you can open the completions panel to see all the potential completions that Copilot has generated for the location you are currently on in the editor window.

- **Mac:** Ctrl+Enter
- **Windows:** Ctrl+Enter

## Conclusion

In this chapter, we have covered in detail GitHub Copilot's code completion capabilities, which are crucial for enhancing your coding efficiency and creativity. By introducing code completions, demonstrating how to work with Copilot, discovering its toolbar and panel, reviewing settings, and leveraging keyboard shortcuts; this chapter empowers you with the knowledge to harness Copilot's potential. As we've seen, Copilot is more than just a tool for generating code; it's a partner in your development process, enabling the creation of refined solutions that align with your unique development goals.

# Chatting with GitHub Copilot

While code completions allow for tightly integrated responses to keep you in the flow of coding, Copilot Chat enables you to have robust conversations about your code in an intuitive way. Copilot Chat can help you understand code, learn new topics of interest, refine code files, write tests, create documentation, and learn the features of Copilot.

Let's dive in to the things that you need to know to get working with Copilot Chat!

- Discovering Copilot Chat
- Defining Prompt Engineering with Copilot Chat
- Commanding Your Conversation with Precision

## Discovering Copilot Chat

This section introduces Copilot Chat, an AI-powered companion designed to streamline your coding process. We will outline how to effectively utilize chat features to enhance code understanding, problem-solving, and productivity within your development environment.

## Chatting in the Sidebar

The sidebar chat window is a great place to converse with your pair programmer, GitHub Copilot. Whether you have a question about the code you are working on in the current file, a question about the workspace, or a question about the integrated development environment (IDE), Copilot Chat in the sidebar is a great place to start (see Figure 4.1).

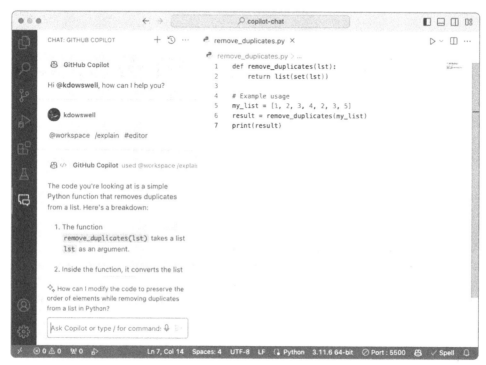

**Figure 4.1:** Copilot Chat sidebar

In this example, you will see that you can ask Copilot questions about the current editor tab that is visible to the right using the following statement:

```
/explain #editor
```

The `@workspace` agent keyword will be automatically injected into the prompt when you type the `/explain` command.

## Maximizing Conversations with the Editor View

If you would prefer to have a full-screen view when chatting with Copilot, you can open an editor window for a Copilot chat session (see Figure 4.2). This editor-based chat can be accessed via the command menu by searching for Open

Chat In Editor. Also, within the Copilot sidebar chat window, you can move your conversation to the editor view using the ellipsis menu at the top right and selecting Open Chat In Editor.

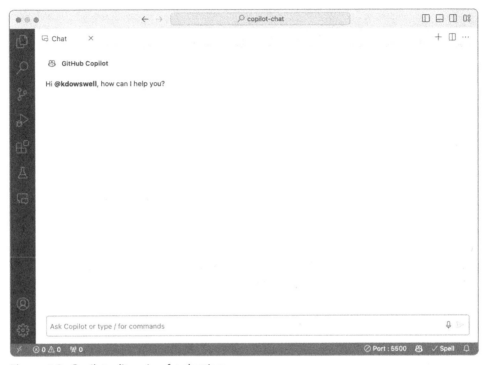

**Figure 4.2:** Copilot editor view for chatting

## Expanding Your Conversation to a New Window

If you'd like to break out of the IDE and continue the conversation with Copilot in a dedicated window, you can also do this via the ellipsis menu at the top right of the Copilot sidebar chat window (see Figure 4.3).

This ability to split out conversations to multiple editor tabs and windows allows for a lot of flexibility. If you have a multimonitor setup or a larger display, expanding your conversation with Copilot to a new window works great.

In addition to this ability to expand your conversation canvas, you are also able to run several concurrent conversations with Copilot in multiple tabs or windows so you can customize your workflow with Copilot even further (see Figure 4.4).

The chat experience in a new window works great to allow you to have more real estate and highlight code for context within your editor and not disrupt the flow of navigating your workspace and editing.

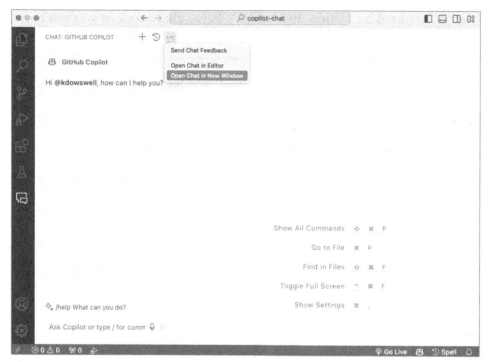

**Figure 4.3:** Opening the chat in a new window

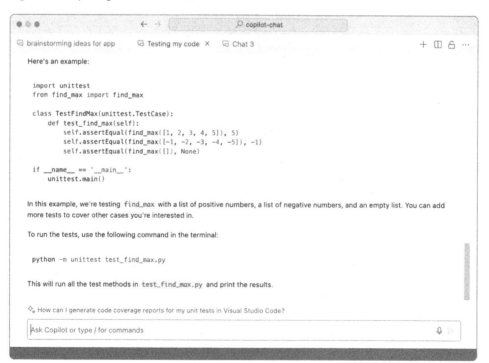

**Figure 4.4:** New window chat with multiple conversation tabs

**NOTE** Each conversation tab or window with Copilot is separate from one another. This means the chat prompts and responses are not used by other chat instances.

## Shifting the Conversation to the Right

If you'd prefer to keep your conversation within the IDE but allow for easier navigation of your workspace, you can pin your conversation to the right menu as well.

Within VS Code, this can be accomplished by toggling the visibility of the secondary sidebar. After that sidebar is visible, you can drag the Copilot chat window from the primary sidebar to the secondary sidebar (see Figure 4.5).

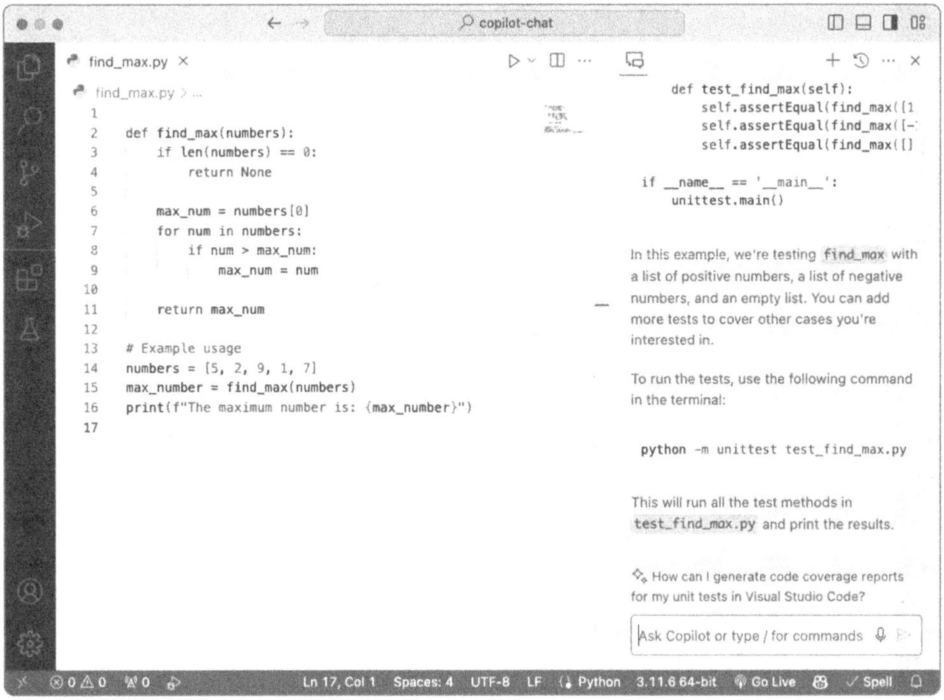

**Figure 4.5:** Right sidebar Copilot conversation

## Utilizing Inline Chat

If you need a more targeted and quicker chat with Copilot, inline chat is a great way to iterate on your code designs, get questions answered, document, and even generate unit tests. When using inline chat, your chat context will be focused on the current location of your cursor or the selected code you have highlighted (see Figure 4.6).

To activate inline chat, you can use the keyboard shortcut (Cmd+I/Alt+I) or right-click in the editor and use the Copilot menu (see Figure 4.7).

**Figure 4.6:** Inline chat

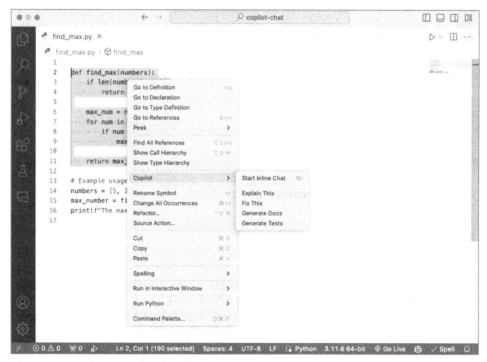

**Figure 4.7:** Copilot menu for inline chat

## Discovering Quick Chat

Quick chat is most frequently activated when interacting with the embedded terminal window within VS Code. This will be useful if you get an error message, have questions about the last terminal command, and more.

Let's look at an example terminal statement that we incorrectly type and execute (see Figure 4.8).

**Figure 4.8:** Copilot sparkle icon and quick-fix menu

After getting an error, a common workflow for developers is to copy the error that they received and search for a solution from a developer site, blog, or official documentation. With Copilot, you can stay in your flow and find a solution to your issue right within your IDE (see Figure 4.9).

As shown in this figure, you are able to see a justification of the error from our last terminal command, which Copilot automatically knows is our desired request based on our terminal menu selection made previously.

This justification goes one step further, providing us a viable solution to our error with an executable command that we can inject into our terminal and attempt to run.

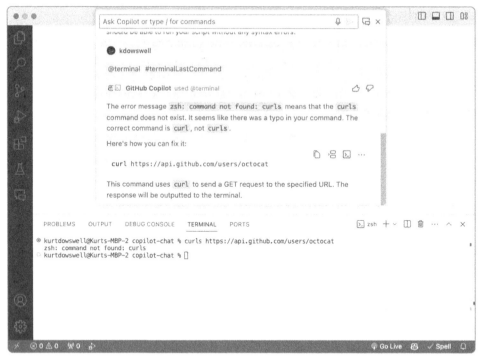

**Figure 4.9:** Copilot quick chat with suggested fix

In addition to this quick chat experience, GitHub Copilot is also available via an extension for the GitHub command-line interface (CLI). We will cover this in depth later in the book.

## Defining Prompt Engineering with Copilot Chat

Prompt engineering is the process of tailoring your instructions to AI systems to get your desired results. When working with Copilot, it is important to understand the fundamentals of a good prompt.

When working from a blank slate, prompt engineering is most important. As you define your problem with context more via commands, file references, documentation, or conversation history, you can reduce the amount you must specify with Copilot because it will understand your needs as you have specific context to a greater extent.

### Understanding the Basics

Figure 4.10 shows the basic prompt structure of Copilot.

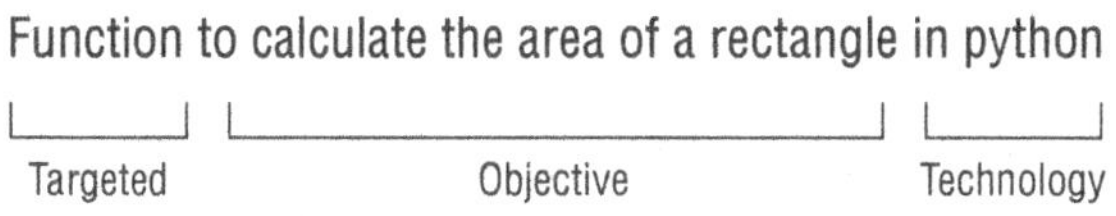

Function to calculate the area of a rectangle in python

| |  | |  | |
| Targeted | Objective | Technology |

**Figure 4.10:** Basic prompt structure

## Prompting for Code

Here are some examples of prompts to Copilot that are short, clear, and focused:

```
Write a program to print "Hello, World!" in C#

Define a class for a vehicle that has properties such as make, model,
and year in Python

Create a function to calculate the area of a rectangle in JavaScript

@workspace create a GitHub Actions workflow for my API
```

## Prompting for Solutions

When you are unsure of the solution you want from Copilot, you can utilize discovery-focused prompts like the following:

```
Can you suggest a more efficient way to implement this function?

What are some best practices for optimizing SQL queries in Python?

Do you have any recommendations for libraries that can simplify parsing
JSON in Java?

What possible methods could we use to reduce the time complexity of
this algorithm?

Can we brainstorm some approaches to handle concurrent transactions in
a database?

What tools or frameworks could we leverage for automated testing of this
web application?

What are the best practices for managing state in a React application?
```

## Having a Single Clear Objective

Having a clear singular objective per request to Copilot is a defined best practice. If you are stuck thinking how you can break down a problem, simply ask Copilot to assist you in defining your problem in more detail before you make code requests.

### Specifying a Specific Technology

When you need your output to be in a specific programming language or to work with a library you know you would like to use, try including increased specificity to the prompt you are creating to fine-tune the results from Copilot.

If you are already within the context of a `.js` file, as an example, you will most likely not need to specify the language in your prompt because Copilot will be able to decern you want a JavaScript-oriented response.

### Keeping Prompts Short

Writing extensive descriptions with exhaustive details can reduce the quality of your results. Instead, keep your prompts as concise and targeted as you possibly can.

After you get your initial results from Copilot, keep iterating on the result using targeted refactors to the code. This will allow you to reach your overall goal while maintaining high-quality results from Copilot.

## Gaining Context in Chat

This section delves into the importance of providing context during your interactions with Copilot Chat. By incorporating open tabs, editor specifics, and file or selection details, you can significantly enhance Copilot's ability to understand your coding style, preferences, and requirements. Whether you're starting from scratch or building upon existing work, learning how to effectively communicate context can lead to more accurate and style-consistent code generation.

### Open Tabs Context

In addition to file you are currently working in, Copilot will look for relevant information in adjacent tabs you currently have open. This helps keep style consistency from other files you have already completed. Try to keep a file open that is of a similar type to the one you are working on to help guide Copilot adhere to your style and preferences.

If you are working from a blank slate, adding context to your conversation with Copilot can be a helpful way to set the stage for better results when you want to produce code.

### Editor Context

In VS Code, to give Copilot context to the file you are currently editing, use the `#editor` tag in your prompt (see Figure 4.11). This will give Copilot the code you are currently viewing in your editor as context.

**Figure 4.11:** Copilot prompt with the #editor tag

In other IDEs, the #editor tag may not be available, even though the Copilot team attempts to align features and user experiences whenever possible.

In this example, we used the following prompt:

```
@workspace /explain #editor
```

This allows us to get a full definition of the code within the editor window.

### File Context

If you don't have the file open that you know you want an answer about, you can use the #file tag to specify the file you would like to have considered. You can also use the #file tag for multiple files within a single prompt if necessary (see Figure 4.12).

In the previous example, when we enter #file, we will see a menu appear. Select that option, and you will then see a search box to find the appropriate file. After selecting your file, you will see the #file tag with the associated file in your prompt.

Adding context via the #file tag may differ from one IDE to the next. The Copilot team attempts to align features whenever possible.

**Figure 4.12:** Copilot prompt with a `#file` tag

### Selection Context

When interacting with Copilot via a chat window, if you have text selected in your editor, Copilot will automatically use that code as context for the prompt that you send.

You can also specify declaratively to Copilot that you would like it to consider the selected text by using the `#selection` tag.

Currently, this tag is implemented only in VS Code. In the future, this may change.

## Commanding Your Conversation with Precision

Copilot Chat provides powerful commands that help jump-start your conversation with Copilot. This allows you to keep your prompts short and targeted without having to repeat the context of the desired output you are looking to have.

## Querying with @workspace

The @workspace agent within Copilot is designed to help you with various tasks within your current workspace. We will explore the commands that you can use to direct the @workspace agent on what you want it to do.

The @workspace agent is also capable of answering questions directly about files in your project without attached commands. A workspace includes all the files in your project, not just the tabs that are open. Using this agent keyword will indicate to Copilot that it should look for context in files within your workspace and then use those files to generate a response that best fits your needs. When using this feature, responses will be slower than something like a code completion due to the complexity and context size.

### Learning with /explain

The /explain command allows you to quickly guide your conversation with Copilot to code you are working on or concepts you would like to discuss in your chat window. Let's explore some ways that you can use the /explain command.

If you are working in an editor, you can use the Copilot menu to initiate quick commands. In this case, let's use the Explain This menu item (see Figure 4.13).

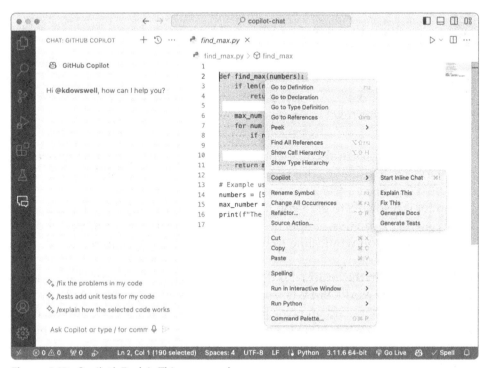

**Figure 4.13:** Copilot's Explain This command

Now within the file editor, you can activate inline chat (Cmd+I/Alt+I) and type / to get a list of the available commands within the inline chat dialog. You can now select the /explain command. If you have a question about code you are working on, make sure to select the code in question before sending your question to Copilot (see Figure 4.14).

**Figure 4.14:** Inline chat /explain command

If you prefer, you can also Copilot questions about your code from the sidebar chat window. Just make sure to highlight the code you would like to have explained (see Figure 4.15).

Copilot is also able to give you a full explanation about the current file you are reviewing. To do this, simply use the #editor tag in your prompt to indicate to Copilot that you would like to have it consider the visible section of your working document.

Working within the terminal is deeply engrained in the workflows of developers all over the world. But when something goes wrong within your terminal, or you don't understand an error that has occurred, lean on Copilot to assist you in getting an answer quickly and bespoke to your pressing needs. When an error occurs, you can use the sparkle icon as your quick path to an explanation by Copilot (see Figure 4.16).

**Figure 4.15:** Chat window /explain command

**Figure 4.16:** Sparkle menu's Explain using Copilot command

If you don't have the quick fix menu available, you can highlight the terminal lines in question and use the Copilot menu to initialize a quick chat with Copilot to get an answer in a snap (see Figure 4.17).

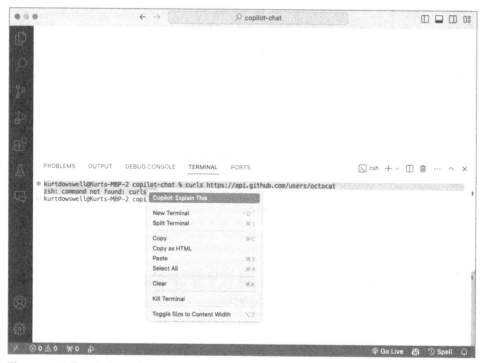

**Figure 4.17:** Terminal window's Copilot: Explain This command

### Generating Tests with /tests

Unit testing allows you to iterate on your programs while having confidence in your work. You can uncover bugs, increase your code quality, get greater refactoring confidence, and amplify your long-term development speed.

All these benefits are great, but when you are in the flow of coding a new feature, it can be hard to find the mental effort to establish all the additional code that is required to test your functions.

Our pair programming assistant, GitHub Copilot, is great at helping us write unit tests. Copilot helps generate boilerplate test code and generates a great starting point for our assertions on our method under test.

Let's look at some examples. Like with the /explain command, you can ask Copilot to generate tests using the /tests command. One option is to highlight the method that you would like to have tests created for, right-click, and use the Copilot menu to select Generate Tests (see Figure 4.18).

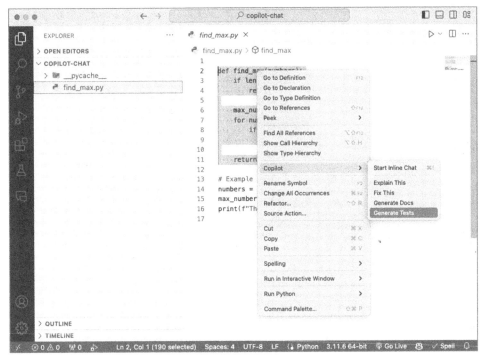

**Figure 4.18:** Generate Tests command

Another option to generate tests is to use the inline chat dialog with your method selected that you would like tests created for (see Figure 4.19).

Using this inline chat /tests command will result in an inline preview of assertion methods that you can review and accept.

**NOTE**   You can guide Copilot into creating better unit tests by having an example file open with existing unit tests that match the structure you would like. Also, you can include prompt details like the type of tests you would like or the testing libraries that should be used.

Within the chat window with Copilot, you can use the /tests command as well. You still need to provide Copilot with the context of your preferred test method by selecting it, or you can reference the visible section of the editor via the #editor tag (see Figure 4.20).

After you have executed the /tests command with one of the methods shown previously, you should end up with output that allows you to start testing your method to ensure it is functioning properly (see Figure 4.21).

**Figure 4.19:** Inline chat /tests command

**Figure 4.20:** Window chat /tests command

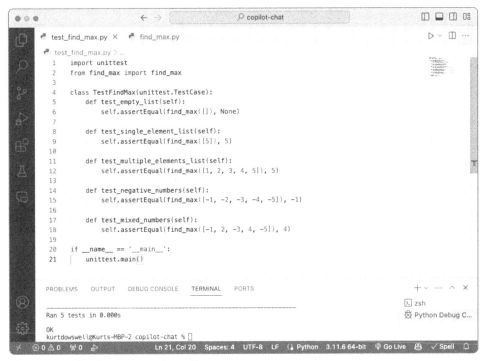

**Figure 4.21:** Copilot-generated test file

With this test file, you can see that Copilot has created a good list of assertions that will ensure you have a well-functioning method. From this starting point, you can add assertions for floating-point numbers, strings, and nonarray input values. You can use code completions or chat to brainstorm additional test cases that you would like to add.

### Finding a Fix with /fix

Whenever you are confronted with compilation errors in your code, you can go down a long path of solutioning via searching developer forums, documentation sites, and more. Let's see how easy it is to use Copilot to find a fix to a compilation error in code.

In the following example, we have a compilation error in our code. A great way to get a code suggestion from Copilot is to use the inline chat dialog. Simply select the part of the code you are working on that has the error and open the inline chat (see Figure 4.22).

Here you will see that we have an autopopulated prompt for Copilot based on the error in the code that was currently selected. Here you can add detail or modify the prompt. Once you are happy with the prompt, you can send that /fix request to Copilot and review the inline modification to the file (see Figure 4.23).

**Figure 4.22:** Compilation error with the /fix command

**Figure 4.23:** Compilation error solution using the /fix command

You can see that Copilot has provided a code modification for you, along with a justification of the fix action taken.

If the response provided is not up to par with what you expect, you can discard the change, iterate on another alternative, or respond with feedback to help train Copilot in the future with the Helpful and Unhelpful response buttons.

## Scaffolding with /new

If you are starting from scratch on a new idea, you can scaffold a new codebase bespoke to your application needs. Let's look at this in action with a request to Copilot using the @workspace directive with the /new command.

You can prompt Copilot with a request like this:

```
/new python rock paper scissors game
```

With this request submitted, you will see a response from Copilot with a suggested workspace structure (see Figure 4.24). This structure will align with your initial request and combine it with the project standards for the language and any additional details you provided in the request.

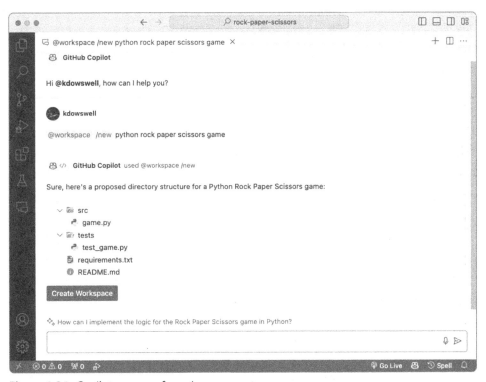

**Figure 4.24:** Copilot response from /new request

After reviewing the proposed workspace scaffolding, you can click Create Workspace, find your parent folder for the project, and then allow Copilot to generate the contents of each file in the project. This will result in a solid starting point to work from. In this case, we've created a functional game of Rock Paper Scissors with unit tests covering our game.

### Crafting with /newNotebook

You can use the `/newNotebook` command to initialize a Jupyter Notebook. The powerful part to reiterate here is that with Copilot you can get a jump-start on a structure, libraries, and code files that are bespoke to your needs.

In this example, you will see how a common Jupyter Notebook for exploratory data analysis (EDA) can be quickly created with a scaffolding that enables you to start to iterate on a solution instead of building everything from scratch.

First, we will start with a `@workspace` agent command `/newNotebook`. Our prompt is following our prompting strategy of having specific and targeted language specifying our needs.

Copilot will respond with a suggested outline for our notebook (see Figure 4.25). If this looks good, you can proceed to the next step and click Create Notebook.

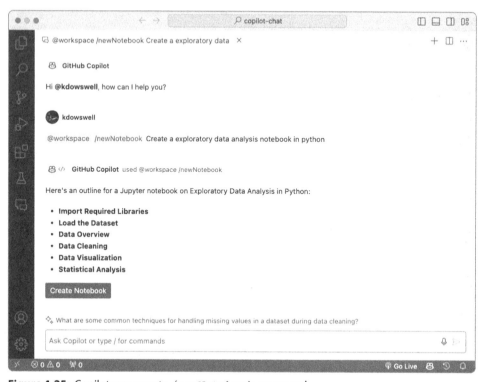

**Figure 4.25:** Copilot response to `/newNotebook` command

Copilot now generates all the sections and inserts starter code for our tasks of data analysis (see Figure 4.26).

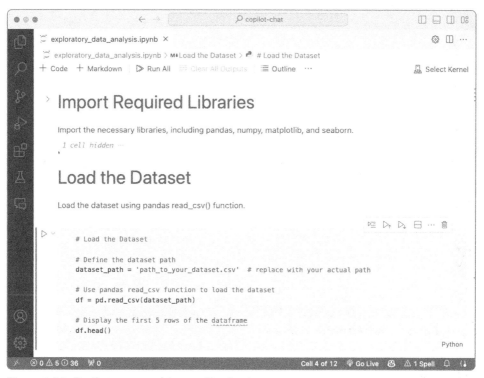

**Figure 4.26:** Copilot-generated Jupyter Notebook

You are now empowered to iterate on this initial design and start working on solutions!

## Engaging with @vscode

If you have a question about a feature of VS Code, you can use the `@vscode` agent for any questions you might have. If you are just starting out in VS Code, you might be curious how to install an extension to support your programming language of choice. Instead of searching the Web for an answer, you can stay in the flow and search for an answer using Copilot (see Figure 4.27).

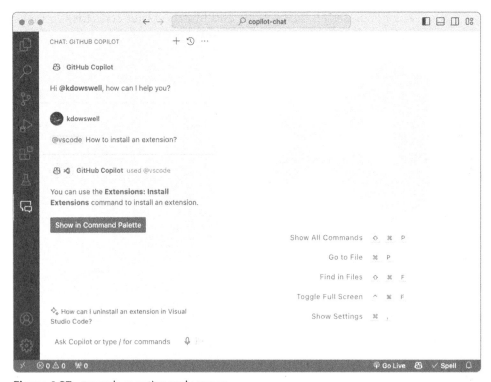

**Figure 4.27:** @vscode question and answer

### Inquiring with /api

If you are working on VS Code extension development, you can use the /api command to discover ways to interact with elements of VS Code programmatically.

## Learning with @terminal

Working with the terminal is such a powerful workflow for developers. While there is great power in the speed in which you can perform tasks, the learning curve for how to best perform tasks within the terminal can be high.

The @terminal agent is here to help with questions and tasks that you would like to perform using the terminal (see Figure 4.28).

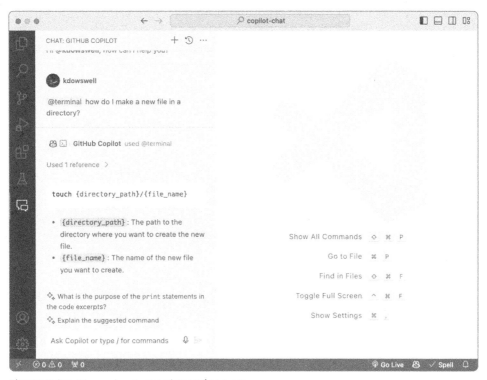

**Figure 4.28:** `@terminal` question and answer

## Conclusion

In this chapter, we have meticulously explored the diverse interaction mechanisms available with Copilot via Chat, offering a comprehensive guide to harnessing this powerful tool within the development workflow. By navigating through sidebar conversations, editor views, inline queries, and the strategic use of context-specific tags, we have uncovered the depth of Copilot Chat's capabilities in understanding and assisting with coding tasks. This detailed examination not only sheds light on the versatility and adaptability of Copilot Chat but also underscores its significance as an intelligent assistant that can enhance coding efficiency, facilitate problem-solving, and foster a more intuitive coding environment.

Leveraging the insights from this chapter, you can capitalize on the full spectrum of functionalities offered by Copilot Chat. Whether it's refining code, debugging, writing tests, or generating documentation, Copilot Chat stands ready as a collaborative partner, equipped to navigate the complexities of software development alongside you.

# Part

# III

# Practical Applications of GitHub Copilot

## In This Part

# Learning a New Programming Language

In this chapter, we will explore how you can interact with Copilot to learn a new programming language. With Copilot, you can quickly get answers to questions about languages, gain bespoke insights based on your previous knowledge, get examples, run tests, and ask questions as you learn, all within the integrated development environment (IDE)!

The chapter will be using VS Code to showcase how to learn with GitHub Copilot and will be using Copilot Chat extensively. It is important to note that Copilot Chat is not available in all IDEs. In addition, the Chat experience is slightly different from one IDE to another. Although there are differences, most of the information shared will be transferrable to other IDEs.

- Introducing Language Education with Copilot
- Setting Up Your Development Environment
- Learning the Basics
- Creating a Console Application
- Explaining Code with Copilot
- Adding New Code
- Learning to Test

## Introducing Language Education with Copilot

According to the TIOBE Index, an indicator of the popularity of programming languages, there are 50 programming languages that have a popularity index greater than 2% [1]. The TIOBE Index has been around for decades. It uses references from Google, Wikipedia, and more to review the trends in our industry.

In recent years, C# (pronounced "C Sharp") has gained popularity. In 2023, TIOBE awarded C# with its "Programming Language Hall of Fame" award. This award is given to the programming language with the highest rise in ratings in a year.

C# is a powerful object-oriented programming language developed by Microsoft in the early 2000s. It was designed to be simple, powerful, type-safe, and developer-friendly.

You may not have used this language before, but we will use this as a good example of how you can use Copilot to help you learn a new language that you might not have thought to try previously.

## Setting Up Your Development Environment

In this section, you will be setting up your development environment for our example project. This environment setup is only required if you choose to follow along with the coding exercise.

### Prerequisites

To follow along with this example, you will need the following prerequisites installed:

- Visual Studio Code
- GitHub account with Copilot plan
- VS Code GitHub Copilot extension

### Setup Guide

The first thing you need to do when learning a new language is ensure that your development environment is configured properly. In the example you will see in this chapter, you will be learning the C# programming language.

Let's leverage Copilot Chat to help set up the environment. The following will get Copilot to guide us to the necessary resources and steps to get started (see Figure 5.1):

```
help me setup my computer to run c#
```

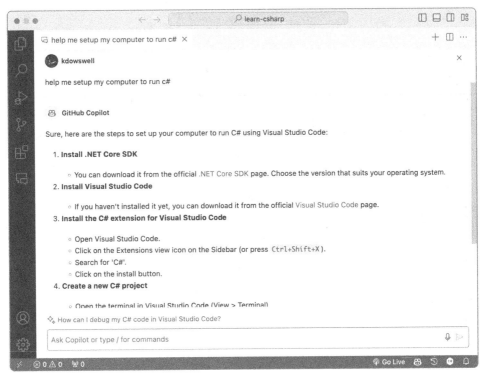

**Figure 5.1:** Copilot chat instructions

The prerequisites that Copilot correctly identified before we can run a C# application is the .NET Core SDK. It is also useful to have an IDE, so Copilot has suggested Visual Studio Code. Head to the following URL to download the .NET Core SDK:

```
https://aka.ms/dotnet-core-download
```

After you have installed the .NET Core SDK to enhance your developer experience within VS Code, it is helpful to have the C# extension as Copilot has indicated in the setup instructions. If you are not in VS Code, you will still be able to run the C# application using the dotnet command-line interface (CLI).

Let's navigate to the Extensions panel on the Action Bar. You will find the Extensions panel identified by the "squares" icon (see Figure 5.2).

1. Open the Extensions panel.

2. Search for "C#."

3. Within the "C#" extension result, click Install.

Microsoft encourages you to install the C# Dev Kit, which contains the C# extension. For the purposes of this demo, you will just need the C# extension. But if you are interested, exploring the features of a rich developer experience via the C# Dev Kit might interest you.

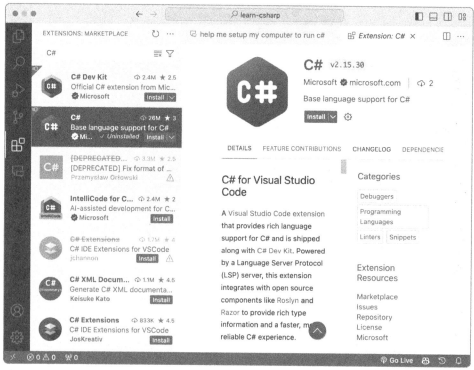

**Figure 5.2:** VS Code Extensions panel

# Learning the Basics

With your environment setup, I will now guide you through using Copilot to assist you in learning the basics of a new programming language.

## Prerequisites

To follow along with this example, you will need the following prerequisites installed:

- Visual Studio Code:
  `https://code.visualstudio.com/download`
- GitHub Copilot extension:
  `https://marketplace.visualstudio.com/items?itemName=GitHub.copilot`
- GitHub account:
  `https://github.com/signup`
- GitHub Copilot license:
  `https://github.com/features/copilot/plans`

## Learning C# with Copilot

Now that you have used Copilot to gain an understanding of the setup and that you need to learn a new programming language, let's start a new chat with Copilot. You'll ask Copilot to give you a basic understanding of C#. Working with Copilot allows you to be creative in how you prompt. So, if you work in a certain industry, have a hobby you would like to incorporate into your learning, or are interested in a specific topic, you can prompt Copilot to use that as a basis for its responses. In this case, we will use pirates as our theme for learning C#. Let's start with a prompt like this (see Figure 5.3):

```
teach me c# language basics. use pirates
```

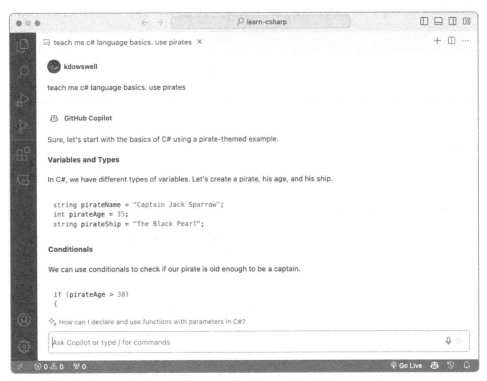

**Figure 5.3:** Copilot response to C# language basics prompt

> **NOTE**  GitHub Copilot is nondeterministic and may return different results for you even though you have the same prompt text.

Copilot should generate a series of sections describing variables, types, conditionals, loops, arrays, functions, and classes. If there are language topics that you care to learn more about, you can continue your conversation with Copilot to learn more about your topic of choice. You will notice Copilot suggesting follow-up questions at the bottom of the chat response based on the previous context of the conversation.

# Creating a Console Application

Now that you have gained some insights into how the C# programming language works, I will detail how you can expand this knowledge with a console application showcasing some of the basic features of C#.

## Prerequisites

To follow along with this example, you will need the following prerequisites installed:

- Visual Studio Code (VS Code)
- GitHub account
- GitHub Copilot license
- GitHub Copilot extension
- .NET Core SDK
- VS Code C# extension

## Creating a C# Console Application with Copilot

There are multiple ways you can leverage Copilot to create your console application. We will be using chat to discover the best way to create your console application manually via the dotnet CLI. It is important to note that Copilot does support creating new workspaces via the /new command. For example, you could use the following command:

```
@workspace /new net8 c# console app called PiratesExample with test
project using NUnit
```

When giving instructions to Copilot, context and clarity are critical for you to receive the output you would like. In this case, specifying the dotnet version, language, project name, and test framework gave Copilot the context needed to give you a great result.

Now let's explore how you can converse with Copilot to discover how to create a C# console application and run it manually. Remember, you can create a prompt specific to your topic of choice so that Copilot gives you instructions that are targeted to you. Try prompting Copilot with something like the following:

```
How do I create a c# console app and run it?
```

With this prompt to Copilot Chat, you should get a result indicating the steps required to run a C# program in VS Code. This will include things like the following (see Figure 5.4):

1. Install the .NET Core SDK.

2. Open VS Code.

3. Open the terminal in VS Code.

4. Navigate to the directory you want to create your project in.

5. Create a new console application with the `dotnet` CLI with a command such as `dotnet new console -n PiratesExample`.

6. Navigate to your new project in the terminal with the `cd PiratesExample` command.

7. Open your project in VS Code with the `code .` command within the terminal window.

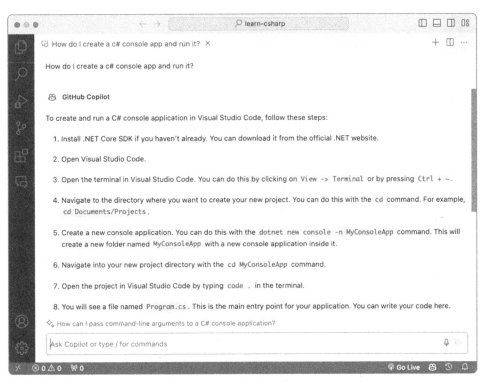

**Figure 5.4:** Copilot response for how to create C# console app

After following these steps, you should have a VS Code window with the pirate example project created (see Figure 5.5).

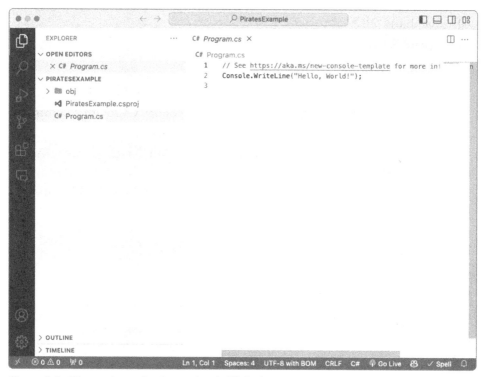

**Figure 5.5:** C# console application project in VS Code

With the example C# application, you can now continue to add code to explore the language features of C#. Let's open Copilot Chat to get a `Pirate` class started so that you can learn more.

After opening Copilot Chat, you can enter a prompt like the following:

```
Create a C# Pirate class with name, age, and ship properties
```

This prompt adds enough context about your technology and language of choice to produce a consistent result. The less context you provide Copilot, the more freedom it will have in giving you responses. In this case, you should see something like Figure 5.6). With this response code, you should be able to create a `Pirate.cs` class from the code generated by Copilot.

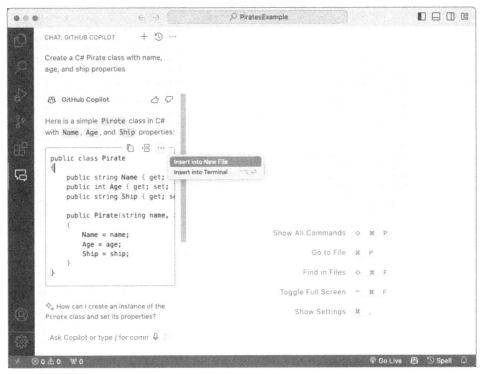

**Figure 5.6:** Copilot chat response to request to create a `Pirate` class

# Explaining Code with Copilot

After you have created a `Pirate.cs` class, let's explore how you can learn more about this generated code. If you are unsure of what some of the syntax means, you can leverage the `/explain` command in Copilot Chat. This will help set the context for Copilot to give you a response that will focus on explaining the code you are looking at versus creating new code or tests (see Figure 5.7).

You can use the `/explain` command on a selected code or entire files. There are some differences in how commands work between IDEs. For VS Code, Copilot will automatically inject the `@workspace` agent keyword when using commands. In addition, in VS Code Copilot requires that you specify the target of your request in the window chat view if you want to include code in context for Copilot. Here we used the `#editor` tag to specify the scope of the code visible within the editor window.

**Figure 5.7:** Copilot `/explain` chat command for `Pirate` class file

## Adding New Code

A great way to learn with Copilot is to use Copilot code completions. Keeping you right within the flow of your working document, you can use inline comments to tell Copilot to provide you with code segments that you would otherwise struggle to implement when using a new language. Let's use this strategy to create a new method in the `Pirate.cs` class file.

Under the constructor, add the inline comment `// greeting method` and add a new line. You should then see a code suggestion from Copilot to complete this method (see Figure 5.8):

This is a powerful way to interact with Copilot while you are coding. You can ask for logical expressions, methods, properties, and more!

An example of this would be to add additional methods to your `Pirate` class. In my case, I'll add a new inline comment after the `Greeting()` method as follows:

```
// attack pirate method
```

This will result in Copilot providing you with a new method Insert of code suggestion that enables you to quickly extend the functionality of the `Pirate.cs` class.

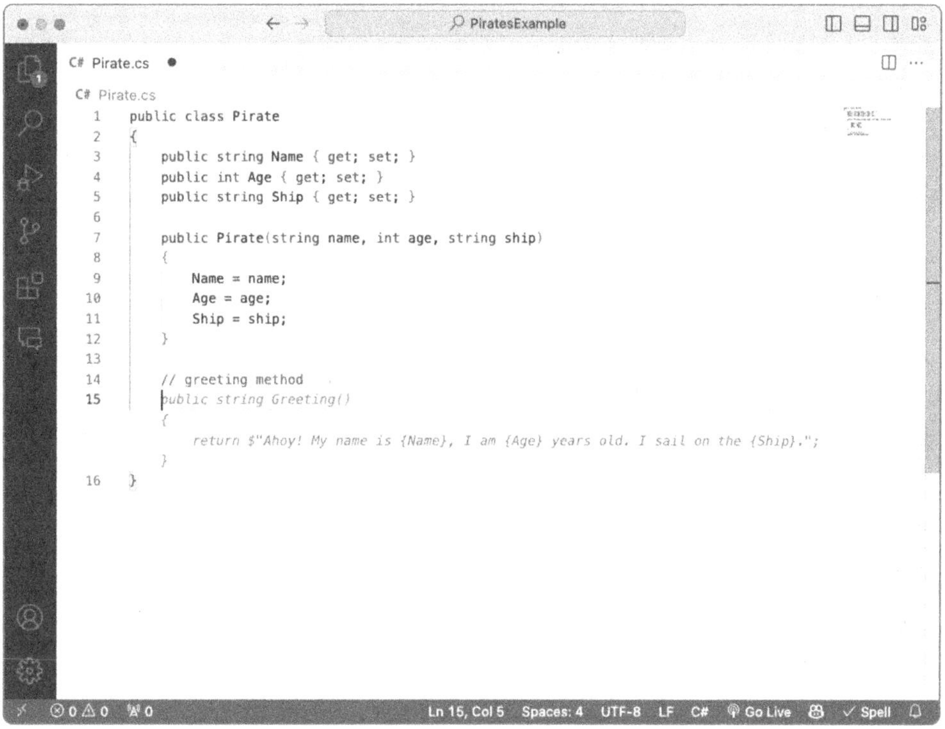

**Figure 5.8:** Copilot code completion for new method

## Learning to Test

With any programming language, it is critical for you to understand how you can effectively test your code. Each language and framework has different testing methodologies. In this section, you will explore how you can leverage Copilot to help guide you in learning C# testing methodologies.

Before getting started with adding your unit tests, you should move your existing project files into a new child folder. You can do this by creating a new folder in your workspace called `PiratesExample`. Then, simply cut and paste your `Pirate.cs`, `PiratesExample.csproj`, and `Program.cs` classes into the `PiratesExample` folder.

As we have done in previous sections, let's ask Copilot how we can learn a new aspect of the language we are learning. In this case, you will ask Copilot how you can create unit tests for the C# pirate example project (see Figure 5.9).

Here's the example prompt:

```
@workspace How can I create unit tests for my C# program using the
dotnet cli?
```

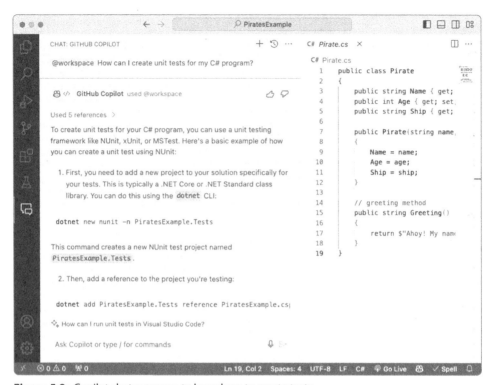

**Figure 5.9:** Copilot chat response to learn how to create tests

In this case, Copilot returned a result indicating that there are multiple types of testing frameworks. And the example CLI command that was given uses the NUnit testing framework. Instead of using the suggested command, you can aso explore the pros and cons of each of the testing frameworks available with Copilot to ensure that you are making the best choice for the project you are working on. In our example, we will continue with our suggested `dotnet` CLI command using `NUnit`.

When using the `@workspace` agent within VS Code, Copilot will index our codebase and scan for relevant files that will help generate a better response. Copilot chat agents do not exist in all IDEs. If you are working in another IDE, you will need to specify additional context in your prompt to get a similar output. Agents allow you to get quality results tailored to your needs without having to research and construct robust prompts.

Within the Copilot response for creating unit tests, it suggested that we create a new project for our tests. If you are new to C#, it might not be immediately obvious why this is the suggested pattern. Thankfully, you can ask Copilot why this was suggested. Use the following prompt:

```
Why is it important to have our unit tests in a separate project?
```

Copilot will respond with several valid reasons to this common practice, including separation of concerns, avoiding deployment of test code, dependency management, build performance, and organization considerations.

Copilot Chat within VS Code allows you to copy code snippets to your clipboard, insert code into your current file, create a new file, or insert code into the terminal. Here you can leverage the insert into terminal functionality (see Figure 5.10).

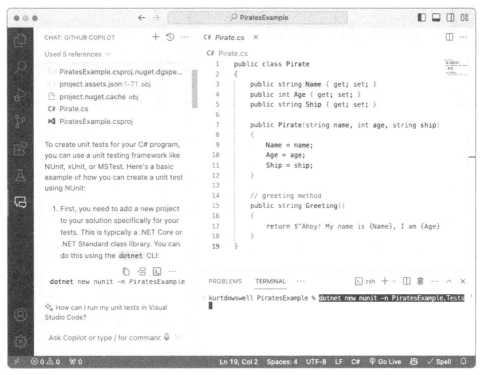

**Figure 5.10:** Copilot chat insert into terminal

After you run the command `dotnet new nunit -n PiratesExample.Tests`, the `PiratesExample.Tests` project should be created.

You can then follow Copilot's next suggestion to add a reference to the `PiratesExample` project. Enter the following command into the terminal:

```
dotnet add PiratesExample.Tests reference PiratesExample
```

Copilot should have suggested how to run our unit tests project. If it hasn't, you can ask for a dotnet CLI command to run unit tests, and you should be able to see the command for this is `dotnet test`. After running this, you will see an error indicating the working directory does not contain a project or solution due to us moving out of the `PiratesExample` project. You can use the quick-fix menu and have Copilot give you a justification and potential fix for the terminal issue we have encountered (see Figure 5.11).

**Figure 5.11:** Copilot explaining the last terminal command via a quick-fix menu

Now that you know how to properly run the `dotnet test` command, you can run it and get a successful build and run of the test project (see Figure 5.12).

With the unit test project now running, you can have Copilot create a starting point for exploring how to test the `Pirate.cs` class. Let's begin by opening the `Pirate.cs` file. To create a test for the `Greeting()` method, it is important to give Copilot the context it needs in order to create a quality starting point for the test file. You can do this in a couple of different ways.

## Creating Context with Selection

With the `Pirate.cs` file open, let's select all the text within the file. With the text selected, you can simply chat to Copilot.

```
/tests for Greeting method
```

This request to Copilot will use the selected code for the entire file as context and target the tests to the scope provided in the prompt (see Figure 5.13).

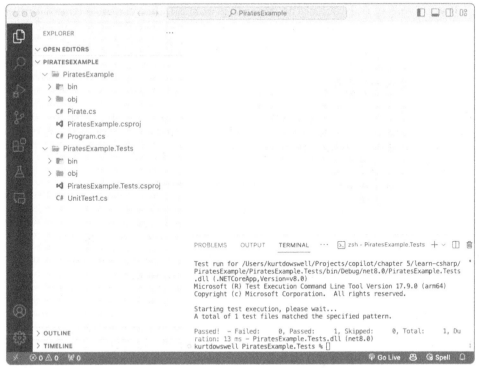

**Figure 5.12:** Successful run of unit tests via the `dotnet test` command

**Figure 5.13:** Copilot chat response for `Greeting method` tests

If you were to only select the `Greeting method`, the response from Copilot would only use that information to consider the response. This would result in a test that does not use the constructor that we implemented earlier.

## Creating Context with Tags

In addition to using the selected text as the context, you can use tags that allow Copilot to consider additional lines of code. This feature may not be the same for all IDEs. As of this writing, the concept of referencing a file via a tag is mostly shared between IDEs.

Using this technique, you can change the prompt to the following:

```
/tests for Greeting method #file:Pirate.cs
```

After typing the `#file` tag, you should see a menu to select the file that you want to reference. With this prompt, you should get a similar result to the previous example using the selected text for the entire file.

## Running Tests

Now that you have generated a baseline test for the `Pirate.cs Greeting()` method, you can add this generated code to the test project. After adding this file, you can run the `dotnet test` terminal command to initiate a new test (see Figure 5.14).

In my case, I needed to add namespace to the `Pirate.cs` class on the first line of the file for the generated unit tests to run.

```
namespace PiratesExample;

public class Pirate
{
    public string Name { get; set; }
    public int Age { get; set; }
    public string Ship { get; set; }

    public Pirate(string name, int age, string ship)
    {
        Name = name;
        Age = age;
        Ship = ship;
    }

    // greeting method
    public string Greeting()
```

```
    {
        return $"Ahoy! My name is {Name}, I am {Age} years old. I sail
on the {Ship}.";
    }

    // attack pirate method
    public string Attack(Pirate pirate)
    {
        return $"{Name} attacks {pirate.Name}";
    }
}
```

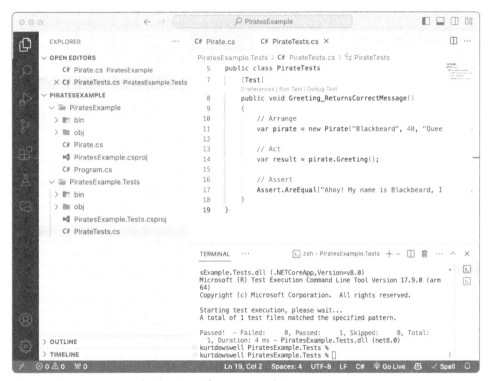

**Figure 5.14:** Greeting method unit test for `Pirate` class

## Conclusion

This chapter provided a comprehensive guide on how to utilize GitHub Copilot to learn a new programming language. Copilot's ability to provide bespoke insights and examples tailored to your interests and needs makes the process of learning a new programming language less daunting and more engaging.

This chapter highlighted the flexibility and power of using Copilot in an IDE like VS Code. Whether you're exploring basic concepts, adding new code, or learning through testing, Copilot serves as a valuable companion that accelerates the learning curve and enriches the educational experience.

This practical application has shown you how Copilot can act as a mentor that guides you through the intricacies of a new programming language, leveraging your previous knowledge and adapting to your learning style. As you've seen with the C# example, Copilot can provide personalized assistance every step of the way, regardless of the programming language you choose to learn, from setup to sophisticated coding practices.

# Reference

[1] TIOBE, "TIOBE Index for February 2024," 2024. [Online]. Available: `https://www.tiobe.com/tiobe-index`

# Writing Tests with Copilot

Testing is a cornerstone of software development, ensuring that code not only works as intended but also is robust and reliable. In this context, GitHub Copilot emerges as a transformative tool, offering developers an AI-powered assistant capable of streamlining the testing process. Through its ability to suggest, generate, and refine test cases, GitHub Copilot enhances both the efficiency and coverage of software tests.

This chapter aims to explore the practical benefits of leveraging GitHub Copilot for writing tests. From unit and integration tests to more specific scenarios like testing regular expressions and form input validators, we'll demonstrate how GitHub Copilot can accelerate the creation of comprehensive test suites.

- Establishing the Example Project
- Adding Unit Tests to Existing Code
- Exploring Behavior-Driven Development with Copilot

## Establishing the Example Project

If you would like to follow along with this coding example, you can download a copy of the starter project `todo-api-ch06-starter` in the Chapter 6 folder.

```
www.wiley.com/go/programminggithubcopilot
```

The project example you will be using is a simple to-do application. In this first section, you will be setting up the application programming interface (API) for the project so that you can see how GitHub Copilot can facilitate creating several different types of tests for a back-end API.

The API project used in this chapter is a NestJS API. This framework provides a robust testing suite and will enable us to cover several topics from unit tests to integration tests and show how to leverage Copilot to assist write tests along the way.

## Prerequisites

To follow along with this example, you will need to install the following prerequisites:

- Visual Studio Code:
  `https://code.visualstudio.com/download`
- GitHub Copilot extension:
  `https://marketplace.visualstudio.com/items?itemName=GitHub.copilot`
- Node.js:
  `https://nodejs.org/en/download`
- NestJS:
  `https://docs.nestjs.com/first-steps`
- Jest extension:
  `https://marketplace.visualstudio.com/items?itemName=Orta.vscode-jest`
- Coverage Gutters extension:
  `https://marketplace.visualstudio.com/items?itemName=ryanluker.vscode-coverage-gutters`

To get started with the `todo-api-ch06-starter` example project, download it from the link provided earlier. Once you have this project downloaded, open the root folder in VS Code. Once the project is open, you should see the `todo-api` source files.

Open the integrated terminal in VS Code. At the project root, run the following command:

```
npm install
```

After installing packages for the project, start the compilation mode watching for changes and compiling when updates occur.

```
npm run start:dev
```

With the start script running, open a second terminal and run the following command:

```
npm run test:watchAll
```

You will now have unit tests triggered on each change that will output coverage results.

Lastly, if you would like to see inline test coverage results, run the `coverage gutters: watch` process via the command palette or with the right-click menu from any open editor.

# Adding Unit Tests to Existing Code

In this section, you will explore how Copilot can assist you in writing unit tests for existing code. Traditionally, unit test creation tooling has gone only as far as stubbing out test methods that align with your methods under test. With Copilot, you can generate unit tests that match your methods under test as well as provide a great starting point for the core components of your test methods.

## Driving Unit Test Creation with Comments

As you have seen in previous examples, you can provide Copilot context to give quality code completions for you with top-level comments as well as inline comments. Let's open the `todo.controller.spec.ts` file and add a unit test with an inline comment. Under the "should be defined" test, add the following comment:

```
// Add test for the create method
```

After adding a new line under this comment, you will see a code completion suggestion from Copilot (see Figure 6.1).

Given the context that you have provided Copilot, you should get a quality starting point for the unit test that will cover the `create()` method in the `todo.controller.ts` tab that is open adjacent to the test file. After running this test, you will see that this does not match the expected result of the service layer (see Figure 6.2).

If you had opened the `todo.service.ts` file before typing the inline comment for the new test, Copilot would have created a test that aligns with the existing code in the service. This service code currently returns a placeholder string instead of an object type.

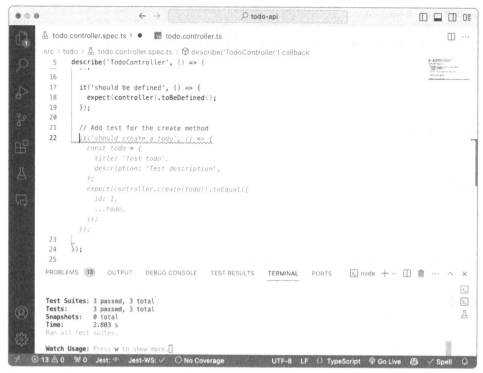

**Figure 6.1:** Test code completion from an inline comment

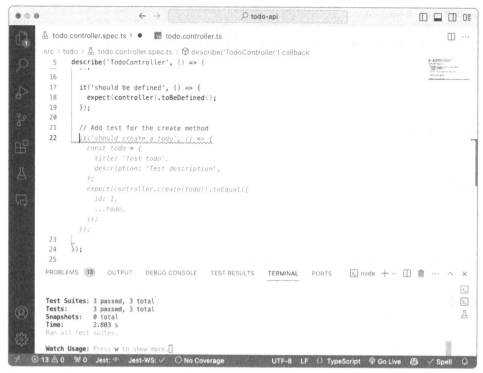

**Figure 6.2:** Test failure from the new test

Later you will find that it will be necessary to modify this code to mock the results from the service layer to remove the dependency on an external database call.

Let's add an `isCompleted` property to the service result object that you are expecting in the unit test to round out what you would like to have returned from the service function when creating a new to-do item (see Figure 6.3).

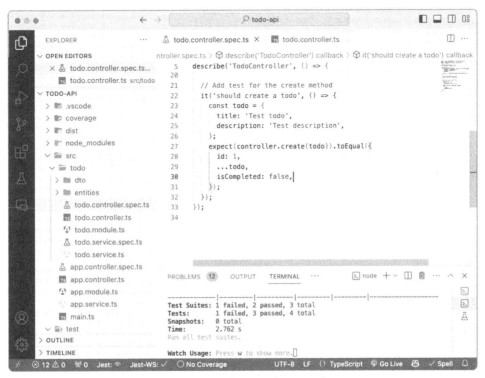

**Figure 6.3:** Is Completed Property added to the test object result

Let's update the `create-todo.dto.ts` DTO and `todo.entity.ts` entity files with the following properties:

```
export class CreateTodoDto {
  title: string;
  description: string;
}
export class Todo {
  id: number;
  title: string;
  description: string;
  isCompleted: boolean;
}
```

Now that you have a test case and object types that represent the desired result from the service layer, let's refactor the `todo.service.ts` file to align with this unit test and get a passing test.

With the new properties added to the DTO and entity classes, let's update the create method to align with the expected result from the unit test. For this update, you can utilize Copilot code completions to help guide you in typing out the return object.

```
create(createTodoDto: CreateTodoDto): Todo {
  return {
    id: 1,
    ...createTodoDto,
    isCompleted: false,
  };
}
```

After you update the `create()` service function to align with the object type properties specified earlier, you can then run the tests and you should see a passing result (see Figure 6.4).

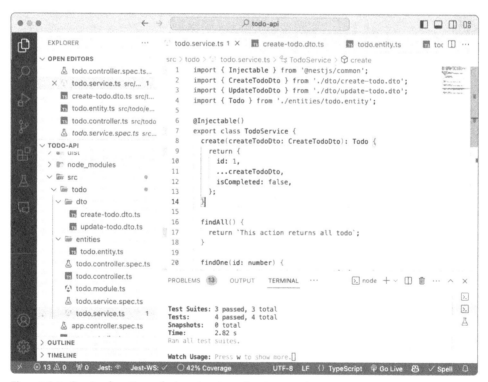

**Figure 6.4:** Service function refactored and passing test result

## Using Inline Chat to Generate Tests

Let's continue adding some tests for the project. In this section, you will explore using inline chat to drive the generation of some default test cases for an entire class file.

First open the `todo.service.spec.ts` file. This file has a default test. Instead of using this, you will delete the contents of this file and click Save.

After you have no code in the `todo.service.spec.ts` file, open the `todo.service.ts` class. With this service open, you will select all the content in the file to give Copilot the context it needs to generate the tests.

With all the content selected, open the inline chat via the keyboard shortcut or the menu (see Figure 6.5).

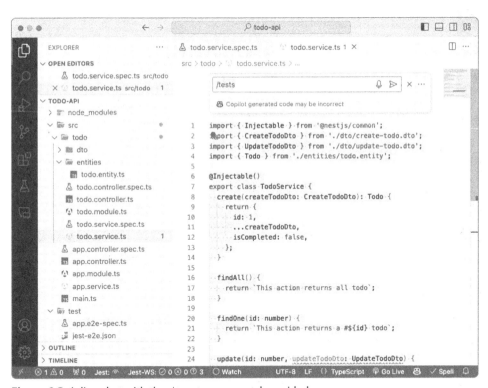

**Figure 6.5:** Inline chat with the `/tests` command provided

After you have the inline chat dialog open, you can use the `/tests` command to indicate to Copilot that you would like tests created for the methods that are selected in your file. Copilot will search for existing test class files that match the naming convention of your file under test.

Copilot will allow you to review the changes that have been generated and apply them if you choose to accept them. If you don't like the tests Copilot created, you can further guide the inline chat prompt to produce better results.

With the tests generated to your liking, you can head over to the `todo .service.spec.ts` file. Here you will find the generated tests from your inline chat request to Copilot. Remember, GitHub Copilot is nondeterministic and may produce different results than the ones that I have. You should find a test that covers each of your service file functions and validates the methods according to their current parameters and response types (see Figure 6.6).

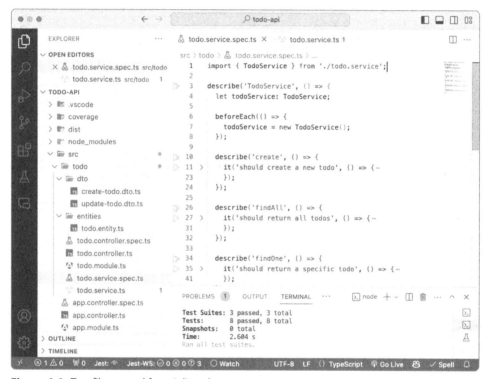

**Figure 6.6:** Test file created from inline chat request

## Exploring Behavior-Driven Development with Copilot

A common scenario in software development is getting a specification or requirement from your product team indicating a need for your customers. Copilot can help you create tests from specifications, leading to better and more stable software solutions.

The practice of testing from a requirement is called *behavior-driven development* (BDD). BDD is an evolution of *test-driven development* (TDD). It emphasizes collaboration between the development team and product team members. BDD testing is enabled by a requirements-writing language such as Gherkin. This allows product team members to communicate clear expectations of a requirement to the development team and, as you will see in this section, help drive the creation of tests that validate functionality. In our requirements examples, you will be using the Gherkin syntax.

## Adding User Accounts

In this scenario, you have received a feature request with a user role, need, and value. You also have two scenarios, written in Gherkin syntax, that you will be creating test cases against to ensure you meet the needs of the requirement.

The following is the example requirement:

```
Feature: User Account Creation
  As a user,
  I want to be able to add an account,
  So that I can work on my to-do list

  Scenario: Successful Account Creation
    Given I am on the registration page
    And I enter valid username and password
    When I click on the register button
    Then I should be redirected to my personal to-do list page
    And I should see a confirmation message that my account has
been created

  Scenario: Failed Account Creation - User Already Exists
    Given I am on the registration page
    And I enter a username that is already taken
    When I click on the register button
    Then I should see an error message that the username is
already taken
```

### *Setup*

To begin, let's first use the NestJS command-line interface (CLI) to add a new resource to the codebase for your users. In a terminal window at the project root, execute the following command:

```
nest g resource user
```

After choosing the REST API and clicking Yes to the CRUD entry points, you should have a new resource added to the todo-api codebase (see Figure 6.7).

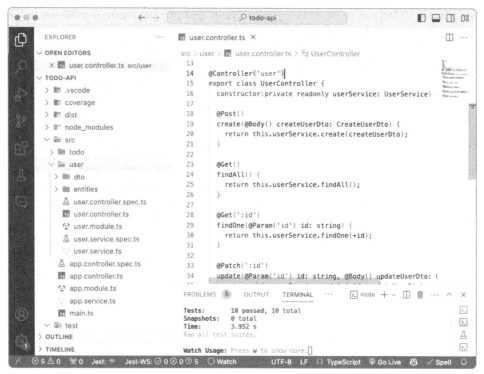

**Figure 6.7:** User resource created

### End-to-End Tests

Now that you have established a resource for your user feature, let's look at how you can use Copilot to assist you in writing your BDD tests.

End-to-end (E2E) tests are a great fit for BDD-style tests because they are generally written from the perspective of user interaction with your system. Thankfully, the NestJS framework assists you in generating these tests.

Scrolling down in the codebase, you will find a test folder at the root level of your project. This has, by default, a test class for the main application entry point.

Let's open the app.e2e-spec.ts class for context so that Copilot will know how to assist you in writing the new tests (see Figure 6.8).

As specified in the package.json file, you can run these E2E tests with the npm run test:e2e command in the terminal.

With the user.controller.ts and app.e2e-spec.ts files open, let's add a new class for our BDD tests. you can add this E2E test in the test folder and call it user-creation.e2e-spec.ts. Within this file, you can then add the requirement as a top-level comment to drive your test creation (see Figure 6.9).

**Figure 6.8:** App end-to-end test

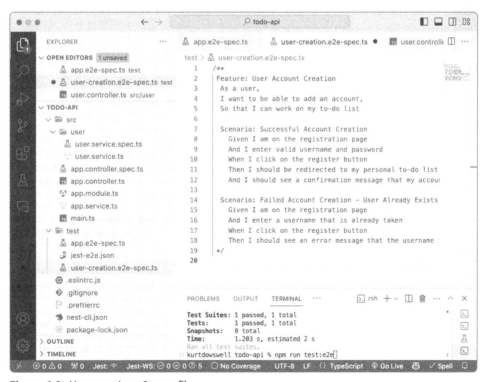

**Figure 6.9:** User creation e2e test file

With this top-level comment in place and our `user.controller.ts` and `app.e2e-spec.ts` tabs open, you have a great context for Copilot to assist you in completing your testing class.

Let's add the same import statements as in the `app.e2e-spec.ts` file after the comment to initialize Copilot's code completion suggestion (see Figure 6.10).

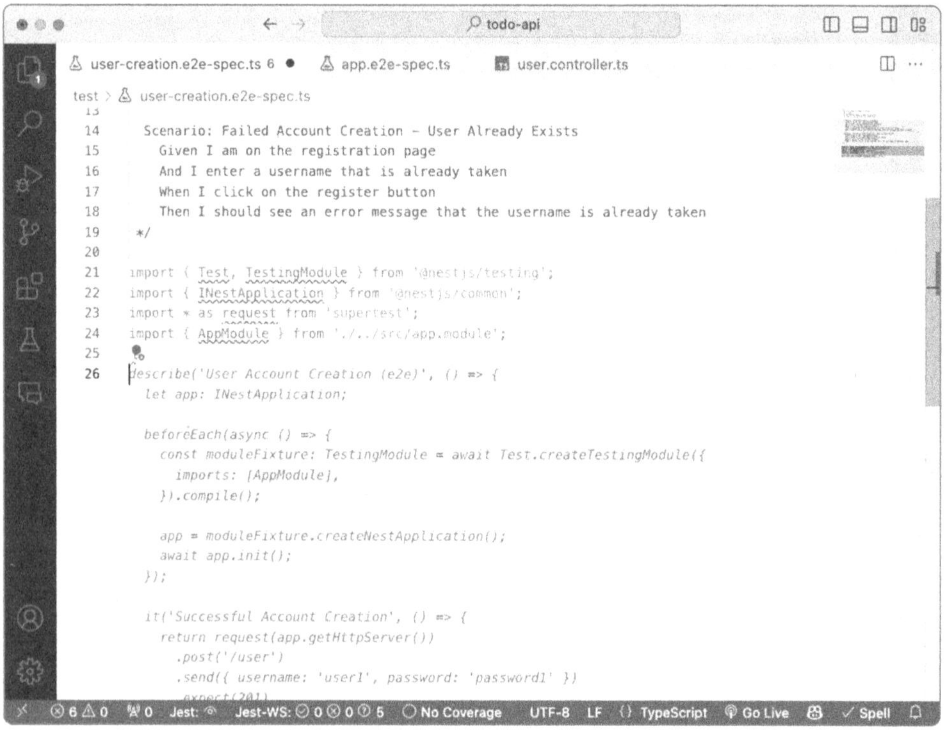

**Figure 6.10:** User creation E2E test file with Copilot code Suggestion

After accepting the code from Copilot, ensure that it matches the desired testing constraints and modify as needed. You can iterate on this process either to refine the top-level comment or to add guiding code to steer Copilot into providing you with the best possible code suggestions.

When you run these tests, you will find that your new tests fail due to the specification you are coding not matching the existing API functionality (see Figure 6.11).

With these tests, you can implement your new code with confidence. For this example, you will stop short of doing the code refactors necessary for this feature.

**Figure 6.11:** User creation E2E test file failing test run results

## Conclusion

As you have seen in this chapter, GitHub Copilot can greatly enhance your ability to write quality tests in a variety of situations. Whether you are writing unit tests for existing code, integration testing a new system component, or doing end-to-end testing on a vertical slice of your system functionality, Copilot is there to help you create test suites that are more robust while allowing you to stay in the flow of coding new features.

# Diagnosing and Resolving Bugs

In this chapter, you will take a closer look at how Copilot can help you diagnose and resolve bugs. In these chapter examples, you will see a variety of circumstances that Copilot enables you to resolve coding issues without leaving your development flow.

- Establishing the Example Project
- Fixing Syntax Errors
- Resolving Runtime Exceptions
- Resolving Terminal Errors

## Establishing the Example Project

If you would like to follow along with this coding example, you can download a copy of the starter project `todo-api-ch07-starter` in the Chapter 7 folder.

```
www.wiley.com/go/programminggithubcopilot
```

The application programming interface (API) project you will be using is a NestJS API. This example project will enable you to see common scenarios of application development bugs that might occur and how you can use Copilot to assist in fixing them.

## Prerequisites

To follow along with this example, you will need to install the following prerequisites:

- Visual Studio Code:
  ```
  https://code.visualstudio.com/download
  ```
- GitHub Copilot extension:
  ```
  https://marketplace.visualstudio.com/items?itemName=
  GitHub.copilot
  ```
- Node.js:
  ```
  https://nodejs.org/en/download
  ```
- NestJS:
  ```
  https://docs.nestjs.com/first-steps
  ```
- Jest extension:
  ```
  https://marketplace.visualstudio.com/items?itemName=Orta
  .vscode-jest
  ```
- Coverage Gutters extension:
  ```
  https://marketplace.visualstudio.com/items?itemName=ryanluker
  .vscode-coverage-gutters
  ```
- ESLint:
  ```
  https://marketplace.visualstudio.com/items?itemName=dbaeumer
  .vscode-eslint
  ```

To get started with the `todo-api-ch06-starter` example project, download it from the link provided. Once you have this project downloaded, open the root folder in VS Code. Once the project is open, you should see the `todo-api` source files.

Open the integrated terminal in VS Code. At the project root, run the following command:

```
npm install
```

After installing packages for the project, start the compilation mode watching for changes and compiling when updates occur:

```
npm run start:dev
```

With the start script running, open a second terminal and run the following command:

```
npm run test:watchAll
```

You will now have unit tests triggered on each change that will output coverage results.

Lastly, if you would like to see the inline test coverage results, run the `coverage gutters: watch` process via the command palette or with the right-click menu from any open editor.

## Fixing Syntax Errors

In this section, you will be leveraging the ESLint VS Code extension to highlight issues with your code, enabling Copilot to quickly provide corrective suggestions for you to review. ESLint is a static code analysis tool that finds problems with your code and highlights the issues directly in the editor for you to review.

In this example, you will look at a simple example of how Copilot can assist you in resolving a language syntax error that your ESLint extension has indicated.

Building on the example project from Chapter 6, let's head to the `user.service .ts` class. Here if you were to remove the ending characters of the `create()` method return line, you would get a TypeScript syntax error (see Figure 7.1).

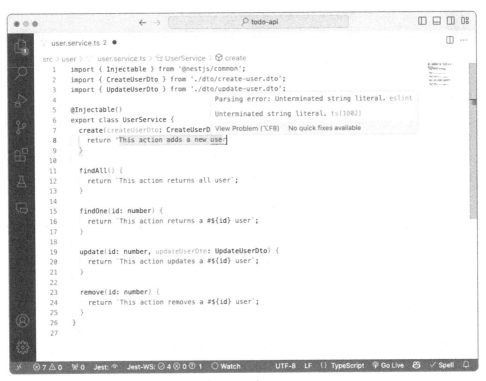

**Figure 7.1:** Syntax error with highlighted code and error message

In this situation, inline chat is a powerful way to access Copilot to enabling you to get a targeted answer for your syntax issue. With your cursor position on the syntax error, in this case the "user" string, you can activate inline chat via the keyboard shortcut or via the menu. After activating inline chat from with your current position on the syntax error, Copilot will automatically input a suggested prompt (see Figure 7.2).

**Figure 7.2:** Inline chat response from Copilot

In addition to pre-filling the prompt, after you submit your request to Copilot, you will also see that Copilot provides an instruction of how to properly fix this syntax issue.

If you are happy with the modified code that is previewed under the dialog, you can accept the change and see the updated code according to Copilot's suggestion.

In this case, Copilot's code suggestion would have been a reasonable way to solve the compilation issue because it was an obvious fix. But in the case that the error is not as obvious, it is nice to use inline chat to have a prepopulated prompt and suggested fix directly in the editor to keep you moving.

As you will see, you still have some syntax errors that do not align to the TypeScript rules. These are the data transfer objects (DTOs) you have defined but never used. If you were to blindly accept Copilot's suggestion here, you would be taking a step backward away from the designed goal of creating and updating new users (see Figure 7.3).

**Figure 7.3:** Bad inline chat response from Copilot

**NOTE**    Always carefully review Copilot suggestions as they may not always align with your desired outcome.

## Resolving Runtime Exceptions

When programming, syntax and compilation errors are catch issues with the organization and code adherence to the guidelines of the language you are programming with.

A common type of exception that occurs in development is a null reference exception. Let's explore how Copilot can assist you in adjusting your code based on an exception that occurs while executing your application processes.

In this example, you will build some of the functionality of the `create()` method in the `user.service.ts` class.

### Setup

First let's add username and password properties to the `create-user.dto.ts` DTO class.

```
export class CreateUserDto {
  username: string;
  password: string;
}
```

With those properties in place, you can add some basic functionality to the user.service.ts class.

```
// Import Statements
@Injectable()
export class UserService {
  users: User[] = [];

  create(createUserDto: CreateUserDto) {
    const { username, password } = createUserDto;

    const hashedPassword = password;

    const newUser: User = {
      username,
      password: hashedPassword,
    };

    this.users.push(newUser);
    return 'Account created';
  }

  // Remainder of Code
}
```

With this code established, let's continue to add a unit test of this method with a null DTO object. Open the user.service.spec.ts file and add a comment to drive a test that will validate that the null reference scenario is handled properly (see Figure 7.4).

```
// create null parameter throw BadRequestException
```

After generating this test, you will need to import the BadRequestExcpetion class. Also, you will see that Copilot, in this case, suggests a deprecated function called toThrowError versus the preferred toThrow. Because Copilot does not receive real-time updates of packages and libraries, you may receive responses that need to be adjusted like this example has highlighted.

With those adjustments in place, you can now run this test and observe the function's behavior when receiving a null parameter. You will see that the test has failed with a TypeError thrown instead of the expected BadRequest Exception (see Figure 7.5).

**Figure 7.4:** Inline comment for null parameter create method test

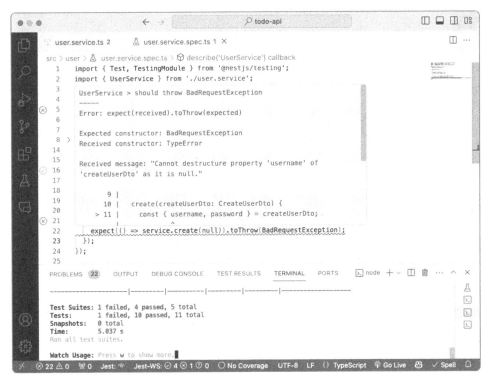

**Figure 7.5:** Create method test failure

To initialize your unit test session, if you haven't already, you can run the following command:

```
npm run test:watchAll
```

You can now open the `user.service.ts` file and add the necessary code to throw `BadRequestException` when you receive a null parameter in the user service function.

When you add a new line after the create method signature, you will likely get a code suggestion from Copilot to add a guard statement against the null parameter (see Figure 7.6). This is due to the context that Copilot has with the adjacent test file tab open.

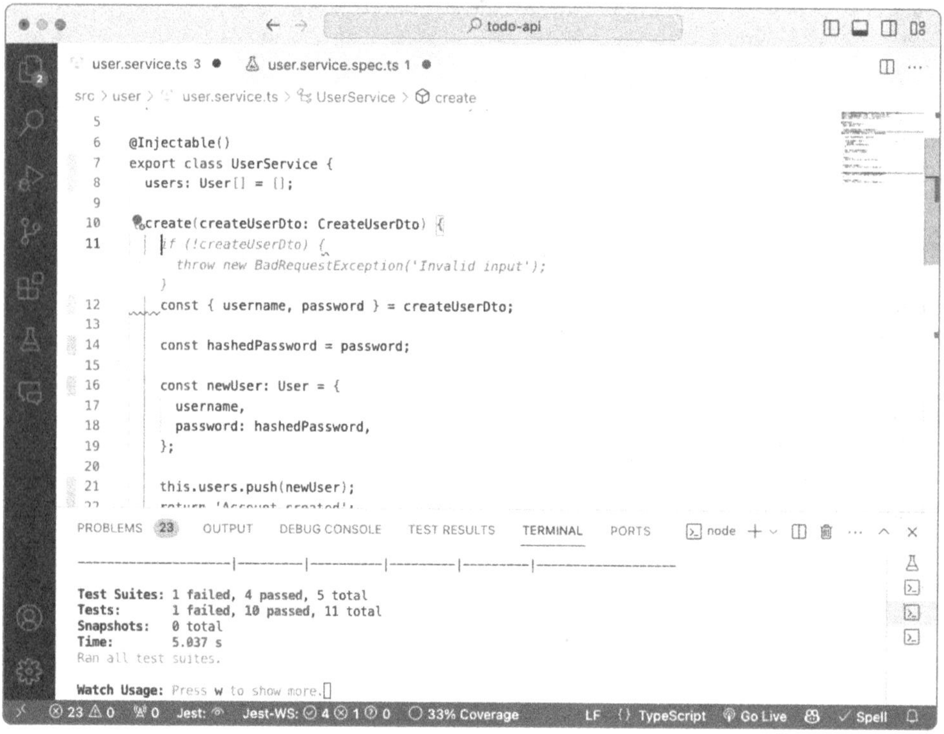

**Figure 7.6:** User service create method guard statement code suggestion

If you don't get a good suggestion from Copilot when adding a new line, you can try typing out the first part of the `if` statement or adding an import for the `BadRequestException` at the top of the file first.

After you accept this code from Copilot, you can save the file. With the guard statement in place, the null reference test should pass (see Figure 7.7).

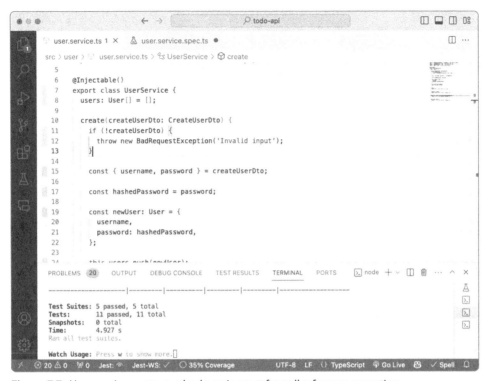

```
     5
     6    @Injectable()
     7    export class UserService {
     8      users: User[] = [];
     9
    10      create(createUserDto: CreateUserDto) {
    11        if (!createUserDto) {
    12          throw new BadRequestException('Invalid input');
    13        }
    14
    15        const { username, password } = createUserDto;
    16
    17        const hashedPassword = password;
    18
    19        const newUser: User = {
    20          username,
    21          password: hashedPassword,
    22        };
    23
```

```
Test Suites: 5 passed, 5 total
Tests:       11 passed, 11 total
Snapshots:   0 total
Time:        4.927 s
Ran all test suites.

Watch Usage: Press w to show more.
```

**Figure 7.7:** User service create method passing test for null reference exception

## Resolving Terminal Errors

You can perform many powerful tools and operations within the command-line interface (CLI). While CLI tools and commands can vastly improve the development experience, there are inevitably times that you will encounter an error and need to troubleshoot the issue and find a solution.

Often there are `--help` commands that will describe the command you are currently attempting to execute, but using the help documentation can sometimes be hard to read and may not fully articulate the bespoke needs of your problem.

Let's see how Copilot can assist you, using the integrated terminal in VS Code, to provide helpful assistance to errors you might encounter while using CLI tooling.

In this first example, let's look at checking out a branch for the test project. If you were to run the command `git checkout user-creation`, you will get an error if you have not yet created this branch (see Figure 7.8).

As you will see, you can use the quick-fix menu to access Copilot's `/explain` function, which will auto-apply the tag `#terminalLastCommand` to the chat prompt (see Figure 7.9).

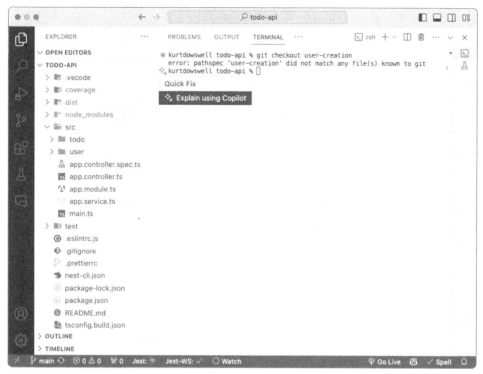

**Figure 7.8:** CLI error for the `git checkout` command

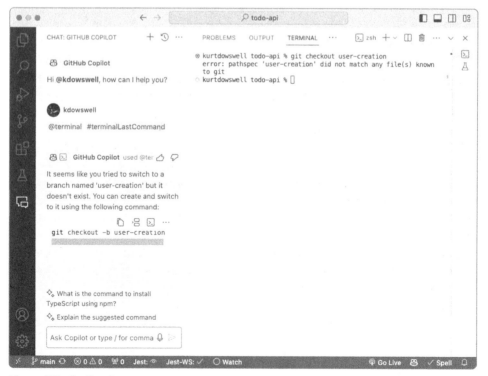

**Figure 7.9:** Copilot chat response

With this prompt, Copilot was able to determine that you have attempted to check out a branch that doesn't exist and provide you with a bespoke command-line statement with the appropriate flag to create and check out the branch at the same time.

## Conclusion

In this chapter, you saw how GitHub Copilot can assist you with the complexities of resolving syntax errors, smoothing over runtime exceptions, and overcoming terminal errors. Interacting with Copilot has enabled you to transform the debugging process from an isolated solo endeavor to a collaborative pair-programming debugging session.

As you move forward with the knowledge from this chapter, look for ways, unique to your codebase, that Copilot can assist you in having more bug-free days and clean builds!

# Code Refactoring with Copilot

In this chapter, you will learn how to use Copilot as a refactoring pair-programming assistant. While code refactoring tools such as VS Code language services and JetBrains ReSharper help you make safe refactors for your code, you can use Copilot as a pair programmer in your refactoring efforts. Copilot can assist you in exploring better ways to write your code and even assist you when making changes. You can download a copy of the starter project `todo-api-ch08-starter` in the Chapter 8 folder.

```
www.wiley.com/go/programminggithubcopilot
```

- Introducing Code Refactoring with Copilot
- Establishing the Example Project
- Refactoring Duplicate Code
- Refactoring Validators
- Refactoring Bad Variable Names
- Documenting and Commenting Code

## Introducing Code Refactoring with Copilot

*Code refactoring* is the process of modifying internal code without changing its external behavior. Before you begin refactoring code, you must have a test suite that covers your code to ensure that you do not modify your external behavior.

The goal in code refactoring is to increase the maintainability of your code and enhance its extensibility. Maintainable code is easy to understand, navigate, and modify. Extensible code is flexible and adaptable to the needs of your application as it advances over time.

You have seen how Copilot can assist you in creating new tests, functions, classes, and even entire program templates. We have not yet explored how Copilot can assist you in code refactoring. Traditionally, refactoring tools have been defined as tools that understand the parse tree of your application and are able to make precise modifications to your files. As we have discussed in this book, Copilot is founded on large language models that allow it to predict the next most likely token given the context that you have provided. Copilot interacts with your code more similarly to how you would edit code via text updates.

When using Copilot to assist you in code refactoring, you should not attempt to replace the existing integrated development environment (IDE) IDE tooling that helps with precise refactors such as function extraction and formatting tools.

While Copilot is capable of assisting in a variety of refactoring tasks, it is just as important to ensure that you are choosing the right tool for the right job when it comes to code refactoring. Copilot is here to help guide you through refactoring code even if you use other tools to do the refactoring. You can bounce ideas off Copilot for better solutions to your code organization, learn how you can reduce the complexity of functions, explore best practices in design patterns, and more.

## Establishing the Example Project

In this chapter, you'll start from an updated copy of the `todo-api` project with some additional code to allow you to explore what it would be like to refactor existing code in a project.

You can access the code in the Chapter 8 folder at the following URL:

`www.wiley.com/go/programminggithubcopilot`

The updated application programming language (API) has several additional features enabling you to showcase how you might refactor existing code in a real-world scenario.

The project now has a SQLite database using the TypeORM library to handle database transactions. We have also added logging to the `UserController`. In the `UserService`, we have added repository calls and validation logic. Lastly, unit and integration tests that have been added to give you a good starting point in exploring code refactoring with Copilot.

## Prerequisites

To follow along with this example, you will need to install the following prerequisites:

- Visual Studio Code:
  `https://code.visualstudio.com/download`

- GitHub Copilot extension:
  `https://marketplace.visualstudio.com/items?itemName=GitHub`
  `.copilot`

- Node.js:
  `https://nodejs.org/en/download`

- NestJS:
  `https://docs.nestjs.com/first-steps`

To get started with the `todo-api-ch08-starter` example project, download it from the link provided. Once you have this project downloaded, open the root folder in VS Code. Once the project is open, you should see the `todo-api` source files with a to-do and user resource.

Open the integrated terminal. At the project root, run the following command:

```
npm install
```

After installing the packages for the project, start the compilation mode watching for changes and compiling when the updates occur.

```
npm run start:dev
```

After this, you can open a second integrated terminal and run the following command:

```
npm run test:watchAll
```

You will now have unit tests triggered on each change that will output coverage results. You will continue using the VS Code extension Coverage Gutters. This extension uses the coverage output to show you which lines of code have been covered by the unit tests.

You can activate the "coverage gutters: watch" process via the command palette or via the right-click menu from any open editor.

When running the `npm run test:watchAll` command in the terminal, you may notice the NestJS error logs. Those are from the unit tests that are covering the `logger.error()` statements within the `user.controller.ts` class.

## Refactoring Duplicate Code

The first code refactoring you will explore is the reduction of duplicate code. In an API example like the to-do project, this can occur most commonly in things such as validation, error handling, logging, and authorization.

Let's look at the `UserController` class and see where you can reduce the duplicate code. In this controller, you will see that each function is handling the logging of an error that occurs and throwing that error after the logging has been completed (see Figure 8.1).

```
src > user > user.controller.ts > UserController > update
18    export class UserController {
52      @Get(':id')
53      async findOne(@Param('id') id: string) {
54        try {
55          return await this.userService.findOne({ id: +id } as FindOneUserDto);
56        } catch (error) {
57          // Log the error
58          this.logger.error(`Error finding user with ID ${id}: ${error.message}`);
59
60          // Rethrow the error
61          throw error;
62        }
63      }
64
65      @Patch(':id')
66      async update(@Param('id') id: string, @Body() updateUserDto: UpdateUserDto) {
67        try {
68          return await this.userService.update(+id, updateUserDto);
69        } catch (error) {
70          // Log the error
71          this.logger.error(`Error updating user with ID ${id}: ${error.message}`);
72
73          // Rethrow the error
74          throw error;
75        }
76      }
77
78      @Delete(':id')
79      remove(@Param('id') id: string) {
```

**Figure 8.1:** User controller error logging

In the `update()` function, you will see that you have the same logging code as you have in the `findOne()` function. This code is duplicated in each of the functions.

As mentioned at the beginning of this chapter, it is important to use IDE tooling for precise refactoring when possible. And, you must always have a solid test suite before you can refactor due to the risk of potentially breaking your external behavior with internal code changes.

The first step in your refactoring efforts in this controller will be to ensure that you have the external behaviors covered by your test suite. You can see from the previous figure that you have coverage on your `findOne()` method but not on the `update()` function. Let's see how Copilot can assist you in covering this function with unit tests to allow you to refactor with confidence.

## Adding Unit Tests

There are multiple ways you can get Copilot to assist you in writing unit tests for this function. In this section you will explore the different types of test creation methods you have with Copilot.

First let's use Copilot code completion by simply beginning the function in the test file (see Figure 8.2).

Because you have established well-formatted and functional unit tests before this method implementation, you get a great result from Copilot without having to add more context like inline comments or import statements.

For the next method to cover in the `UserController`, let's look at how inline chat can assist you in creating a unit test. First, highlight the code you would

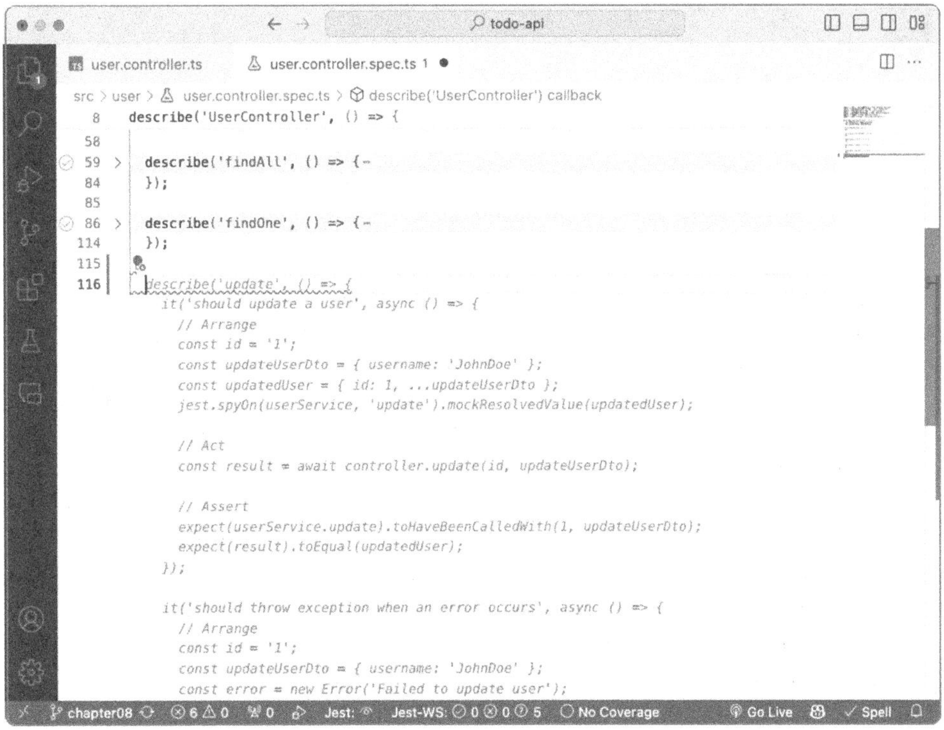

**Figure 8.2:** User controller test file with code completion for the update function

like to create tests for, then activate inline chat via the keyboard shortcut or the right-click menu. With the inline chat dialog active, type /**tests** in the dialog input (see Figure 8.3).

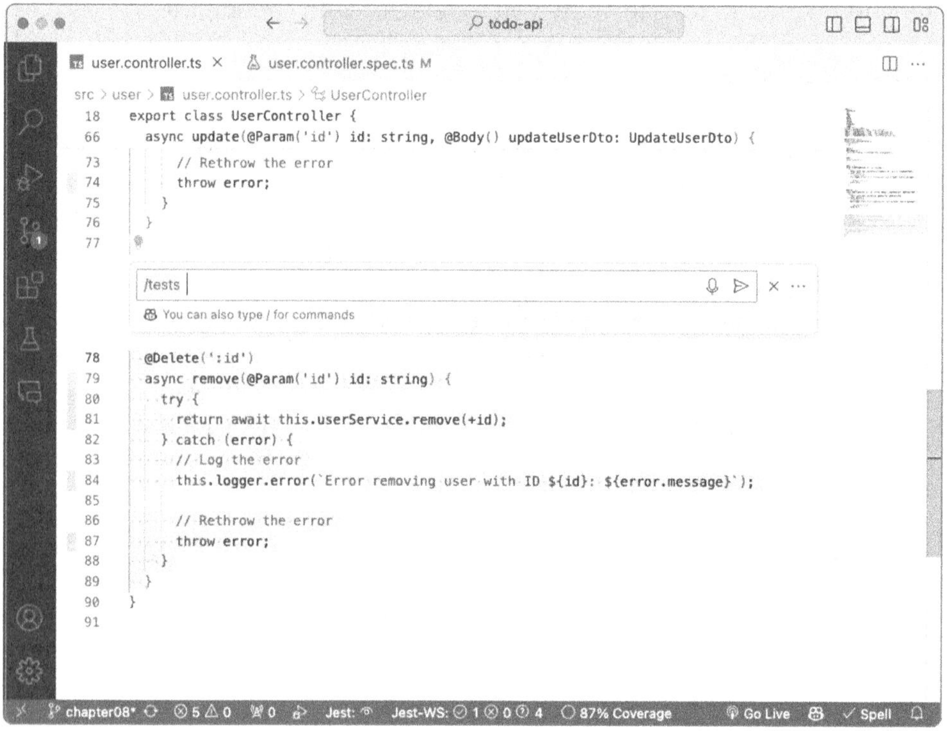

**Figure 8.3:** User controller inline chat tests prompt

After you send the tests prompt to Copilot, you will get a refactor preview window that allows you to review the changes that Copilot has made to your code and apply or discard them (see Figure 8.4).

Copilot has found that you have a user.controller.spec.ts file that covers the class that your remove() function is in. You can view the proposed refactor in detail by double-clicking the result and viewing the code.

After accepting this code, you may need to clean up the output due to the way the code was populated in the test file. From my experimentation, inline chat test creation does better when there are no existing tests in the corresponding test file. When tests do exist, you need to clean up the output slightly to get it to adhere to your class structure. This will most likely be altered in future updates, allowing for a more seamless code refactoring activity.

In this example, you will see Copilot reference "existing code" in a comment while not making the adjustment to my code file with the new code placed in the correct location (see Figure 8.5).

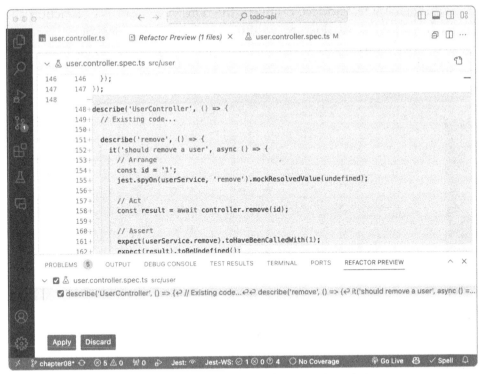

**Figure 8.4:** User controller inline chat tests prompt refactor preview window

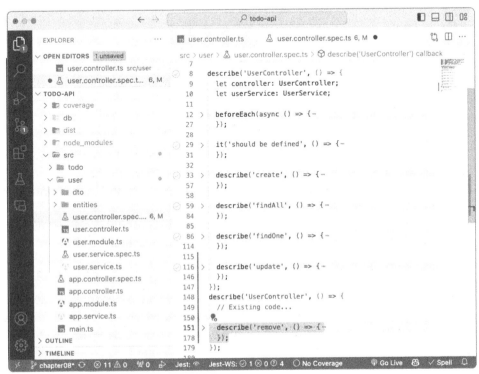

**Figure 8.5:** User controller tests remove function result from inline chat tests command

With the new test added, I will cut the remove `describe()` function and paste it within the existing `describe()` function for the `UserController` and remove the duplicate `describe()` function for the `UserController` on line 148. (see Figure 8.6).

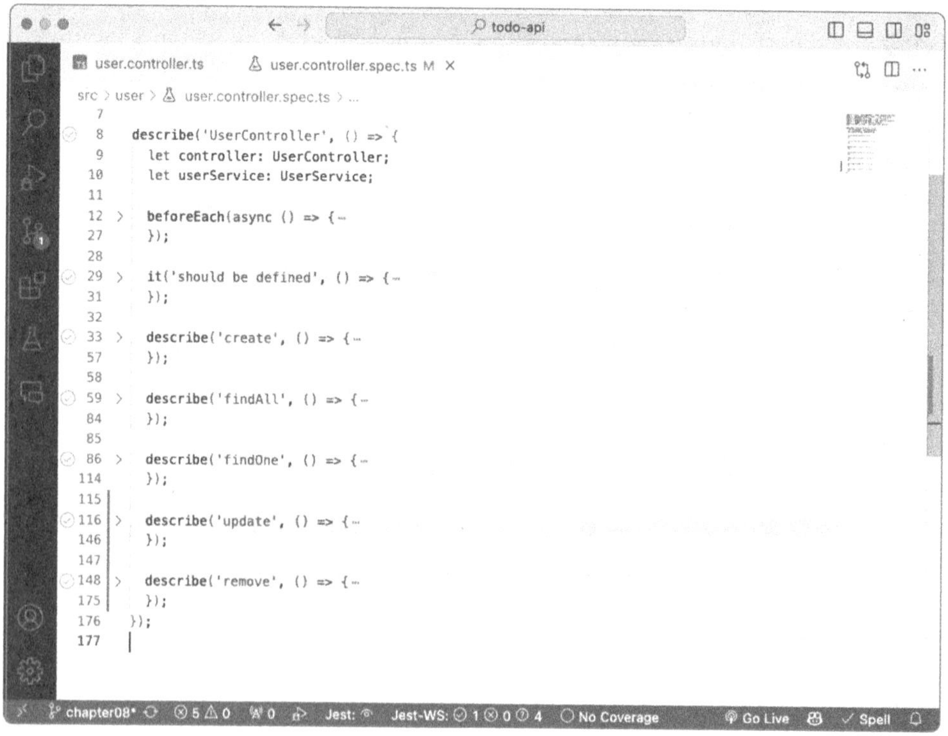

**Figure 8.6:** User controller tests file with adjustment from inline chat result

## Refactoring Duplicate Error Handling Code

Now that you have full coverage on the code you intend to refactor, you can head back to the `UserController`. You should see that you have all passing tests and, using the Coverage Gutters extension, see each line in the controller file is green.

Within this file, select all the code and activate the Copilot inline chat dialog. With the dialog open, type the following command (see Figure 8.7):

```
/fix add private handleError function to reduce code duplication
```

After submitting this request to Copilot, you should see a response indicating the proposed refactor along with an explanation of why Copilot feels this is a valid adjustment to your code (see Figure 8.8).

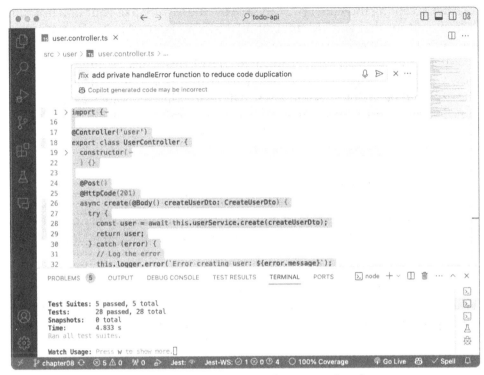

**Figure 8.7:** User controller code selected with inline chat prompt for refactor

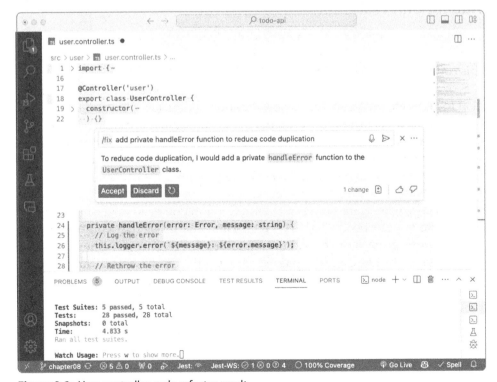

**Figure 8.8:** User controller code refactor result

After accepting this code, you can save the file to initialize your unit test run. You should see that you are still getting the same external behavior with your simplified controller error logging.

While there are many ways to log in to an API, this is just a simple example of how you can leverage Copilot to help you reduce your code while maintaining the expected behavior. In some cases, IDE refactoring tools such as the extract function could be a great solution. But when appropriate, as shown here, Copilot can help you adjust your code quickly and accurately.

# Refactoring Validators

Validation logic starts simple in a lot of projects but can quickly outgrow its container functions, causing increased complexity and reduced maintainability of the code.

The next focus area will be in the `user.service.ts` file. Here you have a `create()` method that has validation code for the username and password fields. While it is good to add guard clauses and validation for the user-provided input, placing large quantities of code with varied responsibilities in a single function will cause decreased maintainability. Let's explore how you can add tests and refactor this code with Copilot.

## Adding Unit Tests

In the `create()` method, you will find that you have a lot of validation logic that is not covered by the test suite. Let's start by generating some unit tests for this code using Copilot inline chat.

Select the validation code within the `create()` method and use Copilot inline chat to generate unit tests for these validation checks (see Figure 8.9).

This should generate unit tests placed under your existing `user.service` `.spec.ts` tests. While you can order things that best match your coding style, I prefer to have them nested under the create behavior. I also updated their container behavior to be called *validation* to provide a clear visual hierarchy of method testing (see Figure 8.10).

As always, when generating code with Copilot, you need to verify the output is accurate to your needs and is correct. There are times that you might need to refine your prompt or context to enable Copilot to give you a better result.

In my case, the test case for "password is less than 6 characters" failed due to the password generated by Copilot being valid. After modifying the password to five characters, the unit test passed as expected.

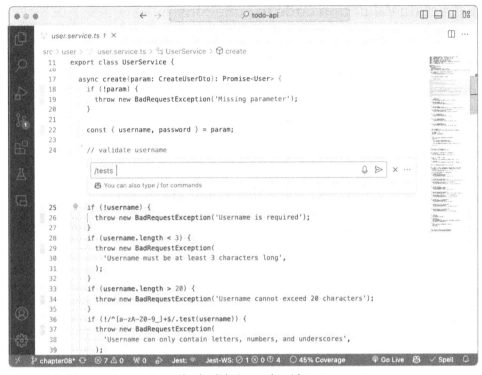

**Figure 8.9:** User service create method validation code with tests prompt

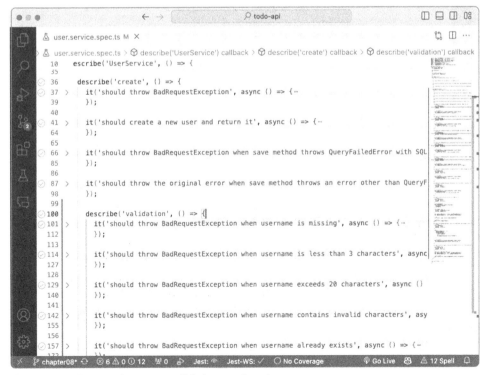

**Figure 8.10:** User service create validation test functions

## Extracting Validation Code to Functions

With the code coverage in place, you can now safely refactor the validation code. In this case, you should strive to reduce the complexity of your methods and keep that as single focused as possible. Let's use a built-in refactoring tool to extract the username validation code to a separate function via the code actions menu. This can be accessed via right-clicking the selected code, using the lightbulb shortcut in the VS Code sidebar margin, or using the keyboard shortcut (see Figure 8.11).

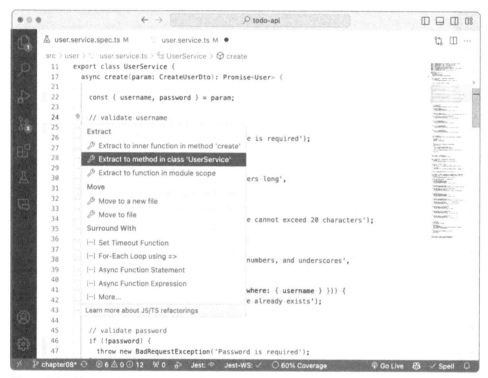

**Figure 8.11:** User service create user validation extract function

Choosing "Extract to method in class 'UserService,'" you are presented with naming options from Copilot. This targeted refactoring works great using the built-in refactoring tools. This example showcases how traditional refactoring tools can benefit Copilot to enable a robust refactoring experience.

After saving the file, the unit tests should have run and indicated that you have all passing results after the function extraction. With this code extracted, you can move on to extracting the password validation code as well (see Figure 8.12).

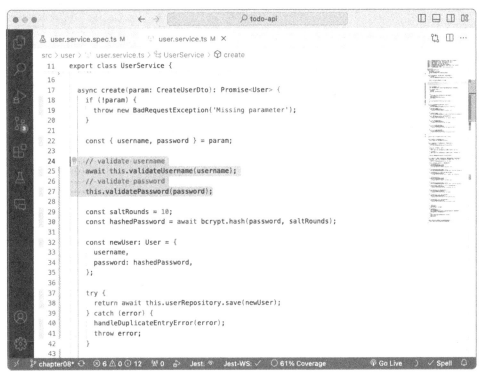

**Figure 8.12:** User service create user validation refactored result

Using this extract selected code tooling, continue to refactor the `create()` method. Extract the parameter validation to a function, extract the `bcrypt` hash password to a function, and finally extract the duplicate entry error code to a function. With these changes you should see a resulting `create()` method that is much more maintainable (see Figure 8.13).

While in this case you used built-in refactoring tools for the specific task of extracting code to functions, Copilot can assist you in going further and explore what more you could do that you might not have the knowledge of or have thought of on your own.

Let's open a chat with Copilot and see what other considerations you should make when refactoring validation code in your service functions. With a prompt like the following, you should get a detailed response from Copilot indicating some additional steps you can take and get example code bespoke to your model (see Figure 8.14):

```
What refactors would you suggest for the validation code in my service?
Should I consider using a different approach? #file:user.service.ts
```

**NOTE**  When using the `#file` variable within the Copilot chat, you must use the drop-down menu to select the file.

**Figure 8.13:** User service create method extended code refactoring result

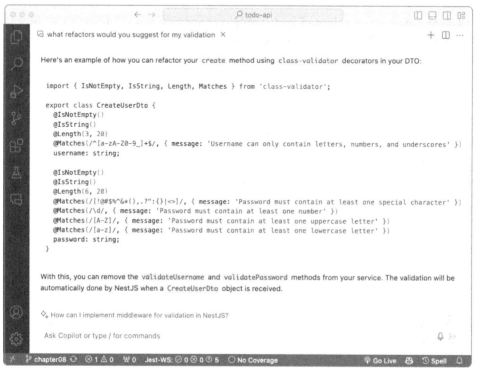

**Figure 8.14:** Copilot chat response to additional refactoring that could be done for validation code

*Use Middleware for Validation: You can use middleware to validate the request data before it reaches your service methods. This way, your service methods will only run if the request data is valid.*

*Use Decorators for Validation: In NestJS, you can use decorators like @IsString(), @IsNotEmpty(), @Length(), etc., from the class-validator package in your DTOs. This will automatically validate the incoming request data based on the decorators you've used.*

*Separate Validation to a Different Method or Class: If you don't want to use middleware or decorators, you can at least separate the validation code to a different method or even a different class. This will make your service methods cleaner and easier to read.*

*Use a Validation Library: There are many validation libraries available for TypeScript/ JavaScript like Joi, Yup, etc. These libraries provide a declarative way to define validation rules and can make your validation code cleaner and easier to manage.*

Interacting with Copilot to plan your refactoring techniques and get actionable results is a powerful tool. In this example, you can explore a variety of code refactoring options and choose the right solution for your needs.

## Refactoring Bad Variable Names

Many years ago, software was deployed on very small memory devices. Mainframe computers would run programs that were deployed using punch cards. On these programs, each line of the punch card represented a line of code. Therefore, storage was constrained, and techniques were established to reduce code size, such as short variable names and more.

In today's programming landscape, you have much higher memory footprints that can be utilized, and there is no reason to shortcut on things like variable naming length. So, let's use this to our advantage and ensure that our code has highly readable and accurate variable names.

In the following example, you have a function that is functional and covered by unit tests but has bad variable names. Let's see how Copilot can assist you in refactoring bad variable names.

First select the code that you would like to refactor. In this case, you will use Copilot inline chat to assist in fixing some bad variable names.

Enter the following prompt (see Figure 8.15):

```
/fix bad variable names
```

After submitting this request to Copilot, you will receive an inline refactor with an explanation of the suggested refactor (see Figure 8.16).

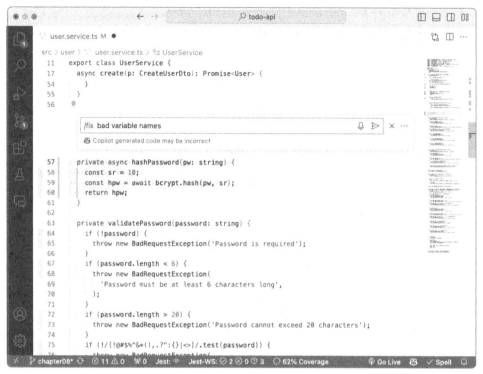

**Figure 8.15:** Copilot inline chat refactor bad variable names prompt

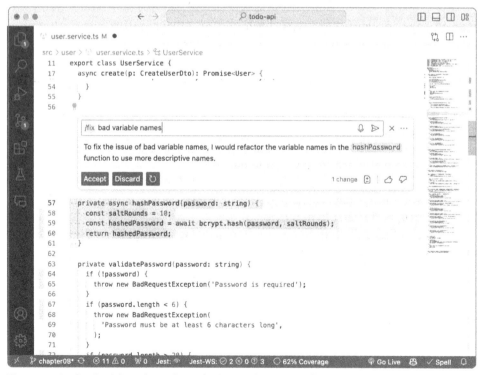

**Figure 8.16:** Copilot inline chat refactor bad variable names refactor result

There are many ways to accomplish renaming refactors in your code. When renaming variables, Copilot works best when targeting single-file updates. When you start to modify code that might have external dependencies, using our IDE-based tooling can ensure the reactor is accounting for the external file references and adjusting those files as well.

# Documenting and Commenting Code

You can add to the maintainability and accessibility of your code by providing additional documentation such as function and class descriptions. These give you quick insights into the behavior, inputs, and outputs of your code.

## Method Documentation

Let's explore how Copilot can assist you in documenting your code. With your user .service.ts file open, you can select all the lines in the class and activate Copilot inline chat. With the chat active, you can use the /doc command to give Copilot the context of your intent and assist you in a more accurate refactor (see Figure 8.17).

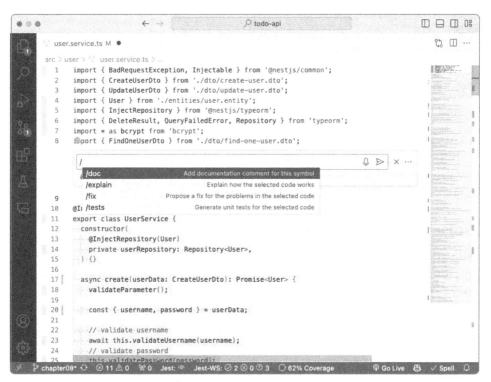

**Figure 8.17:** Copilot inline chat add documentation to user service class

After submitting this request to Copilot, you should get a response with the method descriptions for all the methods in the UserService class. You will see that you have seven changes you can cycle through and choose to accept or discard those suggested documentation blocks (see Figure 8.18).

**Figure 8.18:** Copilot inline chat add documentation to user service class result

This initial response from Copilot was great. Always review each of the modifications that Copilot provides and ensure they match the functionality.

You can now benefit from these documented methods and better understand the inputs, outputs, and expected behavior (see Figure 8.19).

## Project Documentation

With all the hard work you have put into your project, you need to make sure you document the overall project and allow other contributors to understand your project structure and features.

You will use Copilot chat to create a baseline readme.md file for the todo-api project. Opening the Copilot chat window, you can add the following command to get Copilot to generate documentation for you:

```
@workspace Please write a readme for my todo-api project.
```

After you submit this request to Copilot, you should get a result with bespoke details for your project (see Figure 8.20).

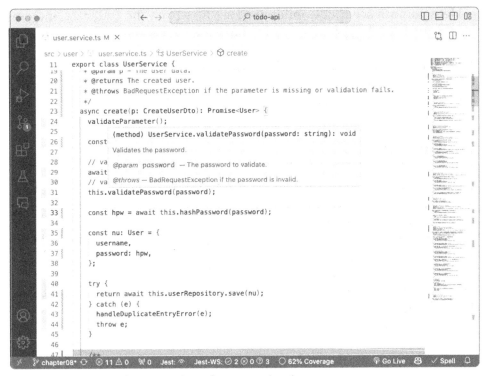

**Figure 8.19:** Function documentation refactor completed

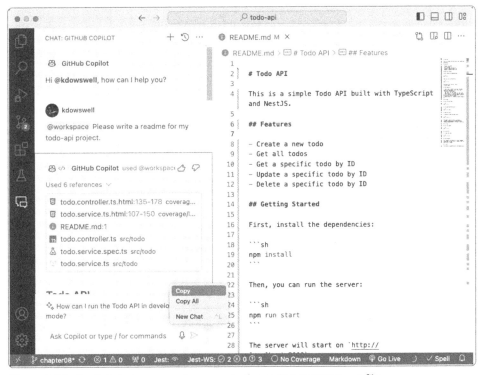

**Figure 8.20:** Copilot chat response to generate the project README.md file

Here you can see that Copilot used six files from the codebase and created a great starting point for you to have a useful and detailed descriptive README.md file.

From my testing, it seems the best way to get the generated markdown for the Copilot response is to right-click the response area and click Copy. This will allow you to paste the markdown in your project README.md file.

## Conclusion

This chapter touched on the history of refactoring code, the tools and techniques used today, and how you should best incorporate Copilot into your code refactoring workflow.

You looked at examples from a project that showcased Copilot's ability to assist you in creating a test suite to enable confident refactoring of code.

After establishing some tests, you explored how Copilot was able to assist in a variety of refactoring tasks, from duplicate code reduction to documentation. Through these examples, I hope you have seen how Copilot can be an asset to you as you refactor your codebases.

# Enhancing Code Security

In this chapter, you will be equipped with the ability to fully utilize GitHub Copilot to assist you in enhancing your code security. This chapter will outline the importance of security, how Copilot can assist you in learning about security vulnerabilities and best practices, and ways to apply that knowledge to your codebase to make corrective measures before releasing insecure code to your users.

- Detailing Code Security
- Establishing the Example Project
- Exploring Code Security
- Finding and Fixing Security Issues

## Detailing Code Security

With a steady increase of cyberattacks daily, security vulnerabilities in your code come at a high cost. Whether you are working on applications that host customer data or enable mission-critical operations for businesses and governments, you have a responsibility to create software solutions that do not compromise the integrity of the community that you support.

Organizations like the Open Worldwide Application Security Project (OWASP) help the technology community to track and identify the greatest known security vulnerabilities that exist in software applications today. OWASP, which has existed since 2001, is well-known for its top 10 application security vulnerability lists.

```
https://owasp.org/Top10
```

The OWASP top 10 list is a great start for teams to understand the most prominent security threats facing the software industry. While this information empowers developers to make changes to their code, it is important to implement a multifaceted security suite to protect against security threats.

> **NOTE**   Copilot is not intended to replace traditional static application security testing (SAST). Utilizing Copilot in conjunction with static and dynamic testing tools and processes is recommended to ensure your application is properly tested.

With the increasing complexity of modern web applications and the steady rise in security threats, application security has become a critical part in the software development life cycle (SDLC). The need for enhanced application security gave rise to the term *application security development operations (DevSecOps)*. Traditional security practices often struggle to keep up, leading to vulnerabilities being discovered late in the process or even after deployment, when they are costly and disruptive to fix. DevSecOps addresses this by integrating security practices directly into the SDLC. This "shift left" approach ensures that security is considered at every stage of development, from initial design through deployment and maintenance. Automated testing, continuous monitoring, and proactive threat modeling become integral parts of the process, enabling teams to catch and fix issues early when they are easier to manage.

In this chapter, you will learn how GitHub Copilot can be used to assist in producing secure code. This chapter will also detail how Copilot can be used to help you learn about security best practices and vulnerabilities specific to your codebase.

## Establishing the Example Project

The project used in this chapter will be a continuation of the `todo-api` project used for previous examples. You will see how Copilot can assist you in understanding security vulnerabilities and how you can mitigate them.

If you would like to follow along with this coding example, you can download a copy of the starter project `todo-api-ch09-starter` from the Chapter 9 folder.

```
https://www.wiley.com/go/programminggithubcopilot
```

## Prerequisites

To follow along with this example, you will need the following prerequisites installed:

- Visual Studio Code
  ```
  https://code.visualstudio.com/download
  ```
- GitHub Copilot extension
  ```
  https://marketplace.visualstudio.com/items?itemName=GitHub
  .copilot
  ```
- Node.js
  ```
  https://nodejs.org/en/download
  ```
- NestJS
  ```
  https://docs.nestjs.com/first-steps
  ```
- Jest extension
  ```
  https://marketplace.visualstudio.com/items?itemName=Orta
  .vscode-jest
  ```
- ESLint
  ```
  https://marketplace.visualstudio.com/items?itemName=dbaeumer
  .vscode-eslint
  ```

To get started with the `todo-api-ch09-starter` example project, download it from the link provided. Once you have this project downloaded, open the root folder in VS Code. Once you have the project open, you should see the `todo-api` source files.

Open the integrated terminal. At the project root, run the following command:

```
npm install
```

After installing packages for the project, start the compilation mode watching for changes and compiling when updates occur:

```
npm run start:dev
```

After this, you can open a second integrated terminal and run the following command:

```
npm run test:watch
```

## Exploring Code Security

A great place to start addressing code security with Copilot is by using chat. Let's open a new chat window and prompt Copilot to give us some best practices for securing a NestJS API (see Figure 9.1).

Prompt for NestJS API security:

```
What are some best practices for securing NestJS APIs?
```

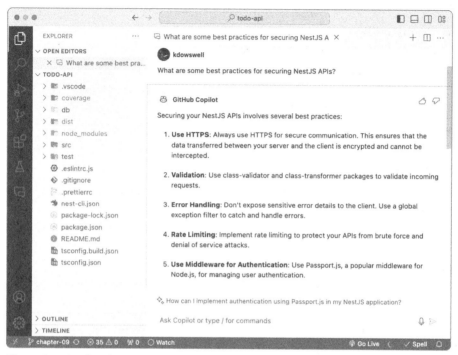

**Figure 9.1:** Copilot Chat response for best practices for NestJS APIs

You will see Copilot respond with a set of targeted security practices that would be a great start for a security audit of the application. The following are the security practices that Copilot suggested as best practices:

1. *Use HTTPS: Always use HTTPS for secure communication. This ensures that the data transferred between your server and the client is encrypted and cannot be intercepted.*

2. *Validation: Use class-validator and class-transformer packages to validate incoming requests.*

3. *Error Handling: Don't expose sensitive error details to the client. Use a global exception filter to catch and handle errors.*

4. *Rate Limiting: Implement rate limiting to protect your APIs from brute force and denial of service attacks.*

5. *Use Middleware for Authentication: Use Passport.js, a popular middleware for Node.js, for managing user authentication.*

6. *Use Guards for Authorization: Use NestJS Guards to manage user roles and permissions.*

7. *Use Helmet: Helmet can help protect your app from some well-known web vulnerabilities by setting HTTP headers appropriately.*

8. *Use CSRF Protection: If you're serving HTML with your NestJS server, you'll need CSRF protection. You can use the csurf middleware for this.*

9. *Update Dependencies: Regularly update your project dependencies to get the latest security patches.*

10. *Use Environment Variables for Sensitive Data: Never hard-code sensitive data. Use environment variables instead.*

Let's examine how you can take the conversation further to get actionable suggestions for some of these security controls.

## Using HTTPS

Continuing the conversation, ask Copilot the following:

```
How do I use HTTPS in a NestJS API?
```

With this request, Copilot will return detailed, step-by-step instructions for you to produce a certificate for testing purposes and make the appropriate modifications to the `main.ts` file of your application (see Figure 9.2).

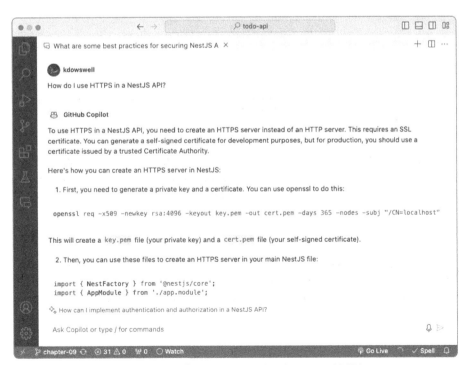

**Figure 9.2:** Copilot Chat response for how to use HTTPS in a NestJS API

## Implementing Validation

Up next, let's see what Copilot suggests for validation. Ask Copilot the following:

```
How to do input validation in a NestJS API?
```

With this request, Copilot will return another detailed response with specific instructions to implement this security control (see Figure 9.3).

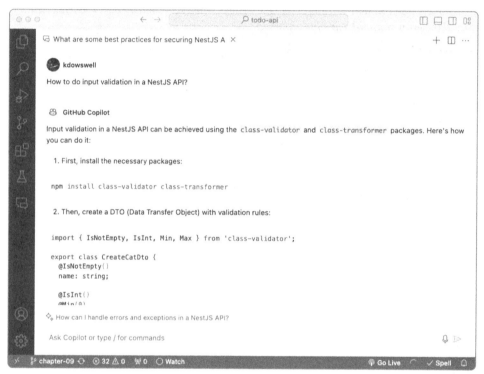

**Figure 9.3:** Copilot Chat response for how to do input validation in a NestJS API

In this case, you can see that Copilot gives necessary package installations, DTO object modifications, controller class update requirements, and instructions for implementing a global pipeline validator.

## Conclusion

As you can see from this example, with some basic questions about security, you can navigate the complexities of securing a modern API. Make sure to always verify the suggestions with Copilot if you are unsure of the suggested result.

# Finding and Fixing Security Issues

While it is valuable to gain insights and implement new security controls for an application, reviewing existing code and making security fixes is another area of focus to investigate.

Open the `user.service.ts` file. This file contains some security vulnerabilities. There is a weak hashing function in use. Also, there is a SQL injection vulnerability.

Begin a security audit of this specific file using Copilot Chat. In this chat prompt, you will indicate to Copilot that you would like to know about the security issues with the file provided. Using a prompt like the following:

```
What security issues are in this code? #file:user.service.ts
```

This request should give you a result indicating that the code has weak password hashing, potential SQL injection, error handling leaking sensitive data, lack of rate limiting, no salting of password, and password validation enhancements that are needed (see Figure 9.4).

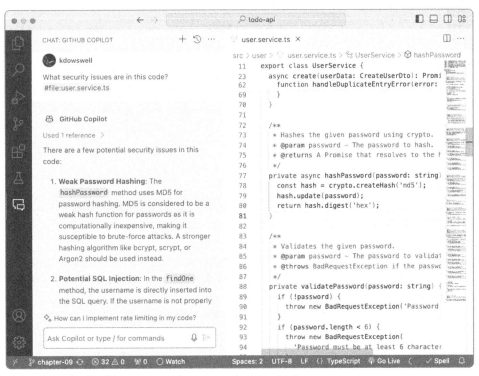

**Figure 9.4:** Copilot Chat response for user service security issues

Now that you have these insights into security issues that may need to be addressed, Copilot can continue to help as you navigate the modifications required to fix the security issues found.

## Fixing Weak Password Hashing

Using Copilot Chat, highlight the `hashPassword()` function and send a request to Copilot like the following (see Figure 9.5):

```
How do I fix the weak password hashing?
```

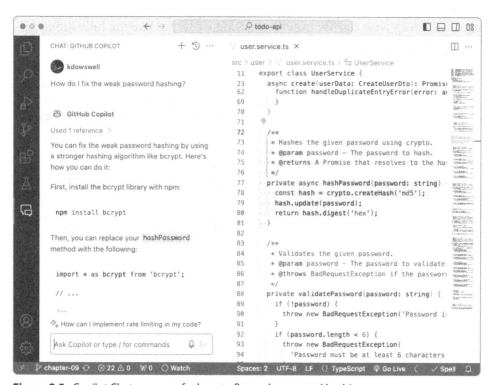

**Figure 9.5:** Copilot Chat response for how to fix weak password hashing

Copilot will provide the suggested package needed to enhance the hashing algorithm. The response from Copilot should also contain the steps required to implement security fix.

To implement the requested changes, run the following `npm install` command for the bcrypt package:

```
npm install bcrypt
```

Now, instead of navigating around the file to adjust imports, you can utilize Copilot inline chat to make the necessary adjustments to code. With the `hashPassword()` function selected, activate the Copilot inline chat.

You can then provide a request to Copilot using the /fix command to resolve the hashing refactor (see Figure 9.6).

```
/fix the hash password function to use bcrypt
```

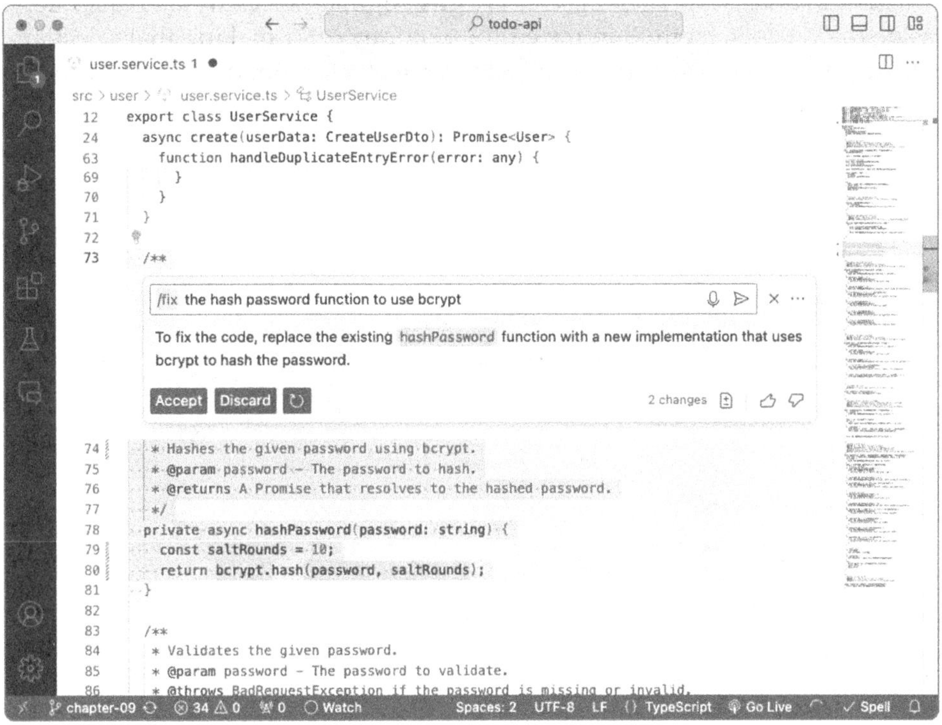

**Figure 9.6:** Copilot Chat response for how to fix weak password hashing

After Copilot processes the request, you should see a preview of the suggested refactors and an explanation for the adjustments that have been applied. In this case, two changes are provided. One change is for the function doing the password hashing, and the other change is to add the import for the bcrypt library.

> **NOTE**   When adjusting existing code with the Copilot inline chat, using the /fix command will be better suited to make multiple adjustments in the current file.

## Fixing SQL Injection

In the previous chat request, Copilot listed several potential security issues for review. The second response Copilot returned for review was the following:

*Potential SQL Injection: In the* findOne *method, the username is directly inserted into the SQL query. If the username is not properly sanitized, this could lead to SQL injection attacks. It would be safer to use parameterized queries or an ORM's built-in methods to avoid this.*

Within this response, you can see that Copilot identified that the `findOne` method had a potential SQL injection issue. After navigating to this code within the `user.service.ts` file, you will see that there is a query accepting a `username` parameter without being properly sanitized.

To fix this issue, Copilot inline chat is a great option. Select the `username` query inside the `findOne` method in the editor window. After making that selection, activate inline chat. You can then provide a request to Copilot like in Figure 9.7.

**Figure 9.7:** Copilot Chat response for how to fix SQL injection

Copilot has suggested that a change be made to use a parameterized query instead of a concatenated string. While there are several ways this could be mitigated, altering the code to use query parameters was the simplest modification.

## Conclusion

In this chapter, Copilot proved to be a powerful asset in the software development lifecycle when confronting security issues. Through practical application within the example project, you saw how Copilot not only identifies vulnerabilities but also guides the implementation of robust security measures. As you move forward, let the insights gained here inspire a deeper integration of Copilot into your security practices.

# Accelerating DevSecOps Practices

In this chapter, you will learn how Copilot can assist in several DevSecOps tasks. DevSecOps tasks can be complicated to learn and implement. With Copilot by your side, you will be empowered to create the necessary resources and actions that will get your application from concept to center stage.

- Detailing DevSecOps
- Simplifying Containers
- Automating Infrastructure as Code
- Streamlining CI/CD Pipelines

## Detailing DevSecOps

DevSecOps, short for development, security, and operations, is a software engineering culture and practice that aims to unify software development (Dev), security (Sec), and operations (Ops).

To practice DevSecOps, security needs to be considered at every phase of the software development life cycle (SDLC) (see Figure 10.1).

As you can see from Figure 10.1, in addition to the development tasks, the release, deployment, operation, and monitoring tasks all play a vital role in successful software delivery with security embedded at every task.

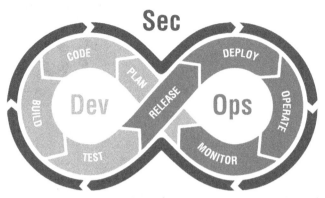

**Figure 10.1:** DevSecOps diagram detailing security considered at each stage of the DevOps cycle

Here are some key points:

- **Shift left on security:** This means introducing security as early as possible in the life cycle of app development. This is a significant change from traditional practices where security was often considered at the end of the development cycle ("shifting it left in the cycle").

- **Collaboration:** DevSecOps encourages increased communication and collaboration between the development, security, and operations teams.

- **Automation:** DevSecOps leverages automation and continuous integration/continuous deployment (CI/CD) tools to minimize the risk of human error and to facilitate the integration of security at all stages of development.

- **Continuous security:** Security measures are not just implemented during the development phase but throughout the entire lifecycle of the application, including during use and maintenance.

- **Responsibility:** In a DevSecOps culture, everyone involved in the development process is responsible for security, not just the security team.

In all these areas of DevSecOps, Copilot can be leveraged. Whether you are considering a CI/CD pipeline, security vulnerability scanning, or production monitoring, Copilot is there to gain insights, ask questions, and help create resources that will allow your application to take flight.

## Simplifying Containers

A container is a lightweight, stand-alone, and executable software package that includes everything needed to run a piece of software. This includes the code, a runtime, libraries, environment variables, and config files.

In this section, you will see how Copilot can assist in writing container configuration files and support running the application within a container.

## Creating a Container

Let's explore how Copilot can assist in creating a container to run a NestJS API. To showcase this capability, open a Copilot Chat window. After you have that open, you can enter a prompt to request help to create a container.

Request to Copilot (see Figure 10.2):

```
Help me create a production container for my NestJS API project.
```

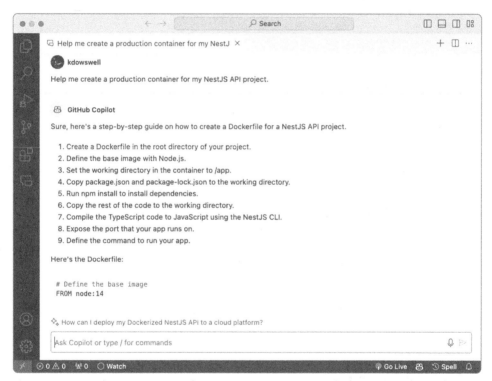

**Figure 10.2:** Copilot Chat response for how to create a container for a NestJS API

You will see Copilot respond with a Dockerfile and instructions on how to build and run the image.

Within this resulting Dockerfile, Copilot suggests the use of Node.js version 14. GitHub Copilot is trained on a large dataset of publicly available code, but it doesn't know specifics about which libraries or versions it was trained on. The base functionality of Copilot doesn't have the ability to access or retrieve information beyond its training data. With this functionality in mind, it is always important to ensure the version numbers and syntax match the current versions and syntax is matched to the needs you have. You can add context to Copilot with example files of current standards or library versions to get a generated output that aligns better with your needs.

Here is the Docker file that Copilot returned:

```
# Define the base image
FROM node:14

# Set the working directory
WORKDIR /app

# Copy package.json and package-lock.json
COPY package*.json ./

# Install dependencies
RUN npm install

# Copy the rest of your app's source code
COPY . .

# Compile TypeScript to JavaScript
RUN npm run build

# Expose the port your app runs on
EXPOSE 3000

# Define the command to run your app
CMD ["npm", "run", "start:prod"]
```

In addition, Copilot gave instructions on how to build and run the Docker image.

```
docker build -t my-nestjs-app .
docker run -p 3000:3000 my-nestjs-app
```

## Deploying a Container

Copilot has provided a great follow-up prompt given the initial question about a container for an API project. If you did not receive this prompt, you can submit the following to see how you could deploy a container to a cloud platform (see Figure 10.3).

Insert your cloud platform of choice to receive detailed instructions targeted to your specific needs.

Here is the request to Copilot:

```
How can I deploy my Dockerized NestJS API to a cloud platform?
```

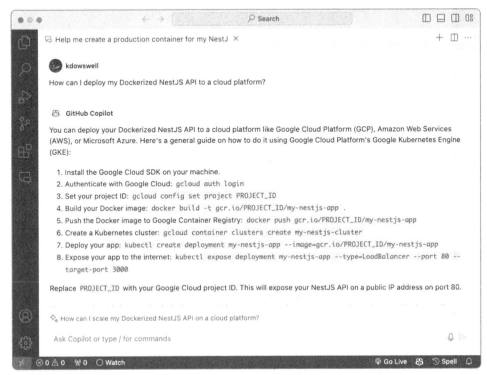

**Figure 10.3:** Copilot Chat response for how to deploy a Dockerized NestJS API to a cloud platform

## Applying Security Controls

While the stability of a "Dockerized" NestJS API is great to have a repeatable and scalable codebase, security should be considered for every task you complete in your DevOps responsibilities.

You can continue the conversation with Copilot to gain insights on which security controls can be applied to your image so that you can protect your application from security threats (see Figure 10.4).

Here is the request to Copilot:

```
What security controls can be applied to my Dockerized NestJS API?
```

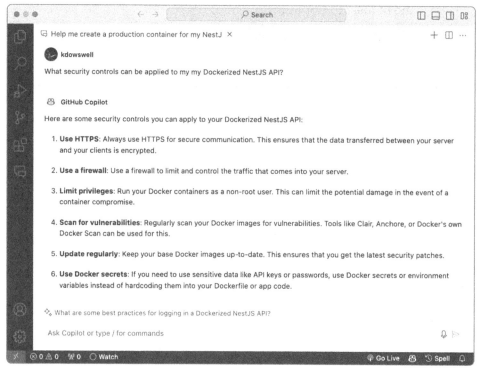

**Figure 10.4:** Copilot Chat response for what security controls can be applied to a Dockerized NestJS API

# Automating Infrastructure as Code

Like the advantages of containerization, infrastructure as code (IaC) allows for transparency, consistency, and automation of infrastructure required to run an application.

With a modern DevSecOps pipeline, multiple environments need to be provisioned and maintained for your application to be successfully developed, tested, scanned, staged, and released to production. Managing these distinct environments with manual configuration will quickly become troublesome, injecting a higher potential for defects and security vulnerabilities.

## Creating IaC

Starting with a basic request to Copilot, you can get a detailed outline and starter implementation for your application (see Figure 10.5).

Here is the request to Copilot:

```
Help me create a infrastructure as code for my NestJS API project.
```

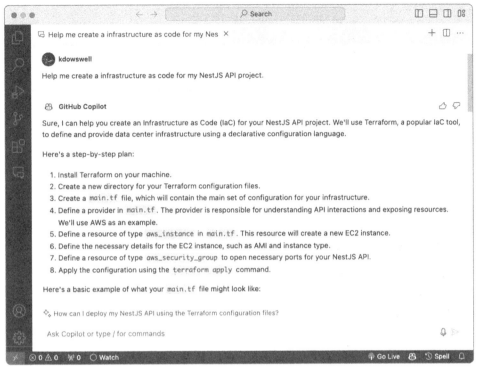

**Figure 10.5:** Copilot Chat response for what security controls can be applied to a Dockerized NestJS API

You will see Copilot respond with a detailed step-by-step plan to create your IaC using Terraform. Copilot should also suggest a basic example of a `main.tf` file that will provision the resources required for a NestJS API (see Figure 10.6). Here is the Terraform file:

```
provider "aws" {
  region = "us-west-2"
}

resource "aws_instance" "nestjs_api" {
  ami           = "ami-0c94855ba95c574c8" # This is an example, replace
with your AMI
  instance_type = "t2.micro"

  tags = {
    Name = "nestjs_api"
  }
}

resource "aws_security_group" "nestjs_sg" {
  name        = "nestjs_sg"
  description = "Allow inbound traffic"
```

```
ingress {
  from_port    = 3000
  to_port      = 3000
  protocol     = "tcp"
  cidr_blocks  = ["0.0.0.0/0"]
}

egress {
  from_port    = 0
  to_port      = 0
  protocol     = "-1"
  cidr_blocks  = ["0.0.0.0/0"]
}
}
```

## Deploying Code Using Terraform

As you saw previously, Copilot can assist in a deployment strategy to the cloud platform of your choosing. Now that Copilot has provisioned a starting point for your IoC, take the conversation to the next step to see how you can deploy your code with Terraform (see Figure 10.6).

Here is the request to Copilot:

```
How can I deploy my NestJS API using the Terraform configuration files?
```

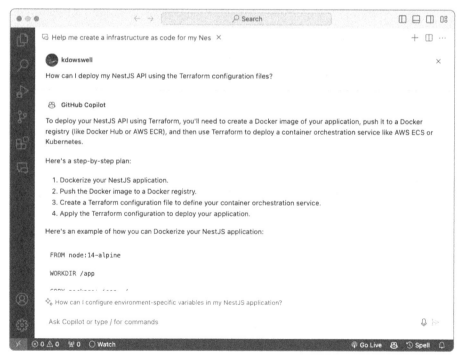

**Figure 10.6:** Copilot Chat response for how to deploy NestJS API using Terraform configuration files

This result from Copilot is a great starting point containing instructions on how to create a Docker image, publish the image, and create a Terraform configuration to facilitate container orchestration.

Here is the Terraform file:

```
provider "aws" {
  region = "us-west-2"
}

resource "aws_ecs_cluster" "nestjs_cluster" {
  name = "nestjs-cluster"
}

resource "aws_ecs_task_definition" "nestjs_task" {
  family                   = "nestjs-task"
  network_mode             = "bridge"
  requires_compatibilities = ["EC2"]
  cpu                      = "256"
  memory                   = "512"

  container_definitions = <<DEFINITION
  [
    {
      "name": "nestjs-container",
      "image": "<your-dockerhub-username>/nestjs-api",
      "essential": true,
      "portMappings": [
        {
          "containerPort": 3000,
          "hostPort": 3000
        }
      ]
    }
  ]
  DEFINITION
}

resource "aws_ecs_service" "nestjs_service" {
  name            = "nestjs-service"
  cluster         = aws_ecs_cluster.nestjs_cluster.id
  task_definition = aws_ecs_task_definition.nestjs_task.arn
  desired_count   = 1
}
```

## Applying Security Controls

Now that you have a strong start to a deployment process using Terraform, consider the security controls that can be applied to this process. Again, Copilot can assist in listing potential areas of security concern and help guide you in implementing those just like other deployment tasks you have seen so far.

Continue the conversation with a request to Copilot to get information about security controls that can be applied to this deployment process (see Figure 10.7).
Here is the request to Copilot:

```
What security controls should be added for this deployment process?
```

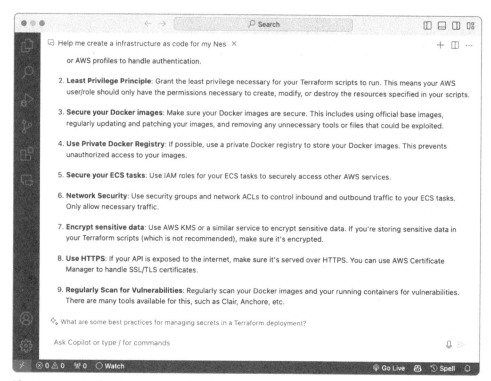

**Figure 10.7:** Copilot Chat response for what security controls should be added for this deployment process with Terraform

The result from Copilot helps guide you to critical security measures, such as securing AWS credentials, least privilege principle, securing Docker images, and more.

## Streamlining CI/CD Pipelines

An essential part of a good DevSecOps process is automation. Continuous integration (CI) and continuous delivery (CD) allow for software to be validated and deployed with repeatable actions.

*Continuous integration* is a software development practice where developers regularly merge their code change into a central repository. Generally, when code changes or pull requests are submitted to the repository, the submitted code is built, tested, and scanned for security vulnerabilities and code smells.

*Continuous delivery* is the practice of automating the entire software release process. With CD, you can deploy to production at any time. This ability enables you to release an updated version of your application code to any environment with automated triggers or release gates to ensure control for sensitive environments is maintained.

## Creating CI Pipeline

Starting with continuous integration to the source code repository, you will see how Copilot can support the creation of automated tasks that allow for quality contributions to your application codebase (see Figure 10.8).

Here is the request to Copilot:

```
Help me create a continuous integration pipeline for my NestJS API
project dev branch and pull request.
```

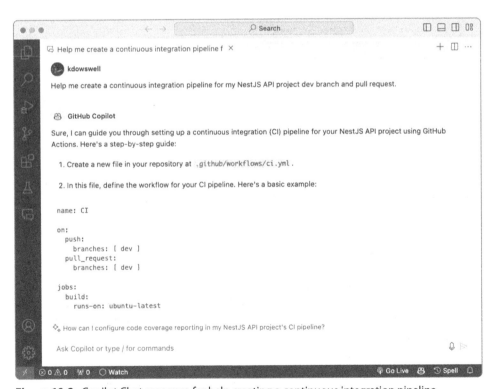

**Figure 10.8:** Copilot Chat response for help creating a continuous integration pipeline

This result from Copilot provides a good starting point for a GitHub Actions–based CI pipeline that will support listening for changes to your repository branch of choice, building the application, and running any tests that the application has.

Here is the GitHub workflow .yml file:

```
name: CI

on:
  push:
    branches: [ dev ]
  pull_request:
    branches: [ dev ]

jobs:
  build:
    runs-on: ubuntu-latest

    strategy:
      matrix:
        node-version: [12.x]

    steps:
    - uses: actions/checkout@v2
    - name: Use Node.js ${{ matrix.node-version }}
      uses: actions/setup-node@v2
      with:
        node-version: ${{ matrix.node-version }}
    - run: npm ci
    - run: npm run build --if-present
    - run: npm test
```

Like previous responses from Copilot, the Node.js version is not reflective of what would work for a modern NestJS API project today. So, as always, remember to review the output provided by Copilot for accuracy to the needs of your project.

## Adding Security Scanning

It is necessary to explore any security actions that can be taken for this DevOps task. You will see in this section how Copilot, using the existing context of the previous pipeline request, can assist in the addition of a valuable code scanning job (see Figure 10.9).

Here is the request to Copilot:

```
Can you help me set up security scanning of my code within my CI
pipeline?
```

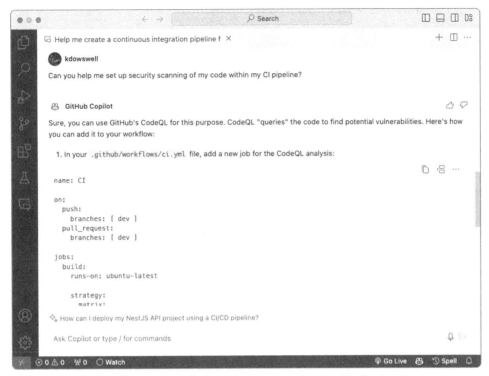

**Figure 10.9:** Copilot Chat response for help creating security scanning for a continuous integration pipeline

Copilot has responded with a great suggestion to include the GitHub CodeQL library. CodeQL is a semantic code analysis engine enabling the GitHub action `github/codeql-action/analyze` to run a series of queries against your code and report any security issues it has found. CodeQL is open-source, and the security findings that it reports are supported by the community of security experts continuing to expand the ability of the library as the security landscape changes year after year.

While the CodeQL library queries are open-source, the underlying engine is not licensed for commercial use. To use CodeQL in a commercial setting, you need to use GitHub Advanced Security.

Here is the updated GitHub workflow `.yml` file:

```
name: CI

on:
  push:
    branches: [ dev ]
  pull_request:
```

```yaml
      branches: [ dev ]

jobs:
  build:
    runs-on: ubuntu-latest

    strategy:
      matrix:
        node-version: [12.x]

    steps:
    - uses: actions/checkout@v2
    - name: Use Node.js ${{ matrix.node-version }}
      uses: actions/setup-node@v2
      with:
        node-version: ${{ matrix.node-version }}
    - run: npm ci
    - run: npm run build --if-present
    - run: npm test

  codeql:
    name: Run CodeQL
    runs-on: ubuntu-latest

    steps:
    - name: Checkout repository
      uses: actions/checkout@v2

    - name: Initialize CodeQL
      uses: github/codeql-action/init@v1
      with:
        languages: 'javascript'

    - name: Perform CodeQL Analysis
      uses: github/codeql-action/analyze@v1
```

## Creating CD Pipeline

Now that you have a CI GitHub Action established, the next thing needed is to release changes to environments for functional testing, pen testing, staging validation, and production delivery.

Create a new conversation with Copilot in a chat window and ask the following (see Figure 10.10):

```
Help me create a continuous deployment GitHub Action for my NestJS API
project dev branch merges. Create a Docker image, store the image, tag
it, and release to a development AWS EC2 environment.
```

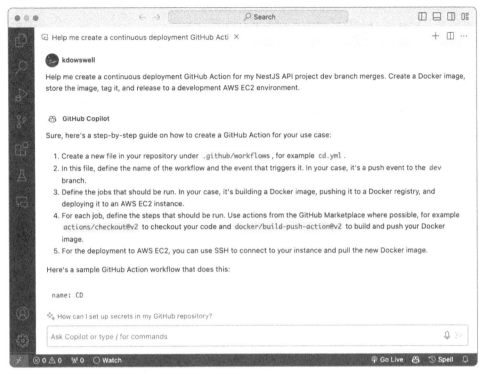

**Figure 10.10:** Copilot Chat response for help creating a continuous deployment action

This response from Copilot has detailed all the necessary steps in a GitHub Action that would enable your code to be built, published, and deployed. Here is the CD workflow .yml file:

```
name: CD

on:
  push:
    branches:
      - dev

jobs:
  build:
    runs-on: ubuntu-latest

    steps:
    - name: Checkout code
      uses: actions/checkout@v2

    - name: Set up Docker Buildx
      uses: docker/setup-buildx-action@v1
```

```
    - name: Login to DockerHub
      uses: docker/login-action@v1
      with:
        username: ${{ secrets.DOCKERHUB_USERNAME }}
        password: ${{ secrets.DOCKERHUB_TOKEN }}

    - name: Build and push
      uses: docker/build-push-action@v2
      with:
        context: .
        push: true
        tags: your-dockerhub-username/your-repo-name:latest

deploy:
  needs: build
  runs-on: ubuntu-latest

  steps:
  - name: executing remote ssh commands to deploy
    uses: appleboy/ssh-action@master
    with:
      host: ${{ secrets.HOST }}
      username: ${{ secrets.USERNAME }}
      key: ${{ secrets.SSH_KEY }}
      script: |
        docker pull your-dockerhub-username/your-repo-name:latest
        docker stop api-container || true
        docker rm api-container || true
        docker run -d --name api-container -p 80:3000 your-dockerhub-
  username/your-repo-name:latest
```

This continuous delivery workflow file is a great start for you finalizing the CI/CD process for a dev branch. Always remember to review and test code and scripts provided by Copilot.

## Conclusion

In this chapter, you saw how Copilot can be a great asset in the DevSecOps process, enabling you to do more and stay in the flow. Even with complicated tasks like infrastructure as code and security scanning in a DevOps pipeline, Copilot has your back and will always be ready to support you in your DevSecOps activities.

# CHAPTER 11

# Enhancing Development Environments with Copilot

In this chapter, you will discover how Copilot can assist you in a multitude of development environments. Whether you are running a command in the terminal or creating an enterprise application in Visual Studio, Copilot has you covered. Let's explore how you can get the most out of your IDE and enhance your development workflow with Copilot.

- Amplifying Visual Studio with Copilot
- Elevating Azure Data Studio with Copilot
- Boosting JetBrains IntelliJ IDEA with Copilot
- Enriching Neovim with Copilot
- Consulting Copilot in the GitHub CLI

## Amplifying Visual Studio with Copilot

Visual Studio is an integrated development environment (IDE) from Microsoft. Visual Studio allows developers to create enterprise-grade software for the Web, mobile, and cloud software solutions.

Visual Studio empowers developers with a vast number of project templates and tools to assist them in hitting the ground running in whichever technology stack they require.

While there are many different technologies that can be used in Visual Studio, using .NET in Visual Studio is where it really shines. .NET is an open-source, cross-platform framework for building modern apps and cloud services.

## Prerequisites

- GitHub Copilot license

  `https://github.com/features/copilot`

- Window OS

  `https://www.microsoft.com/software-download/windows11`

- Visual Studio

  `https://visualstudio.microsoft.com/downloads`

## Installing the GitHub Copilot Extension

With Visual Studio installed and opened, you can open the Extensions menu on the top toolbar and select Manage Extensions. With the Manage Extensions window open, search for *GitHub Copilot*. After submitting that search, you should see GitHub Copilot and GitHub Copilot Chat (see Figure 11.1).

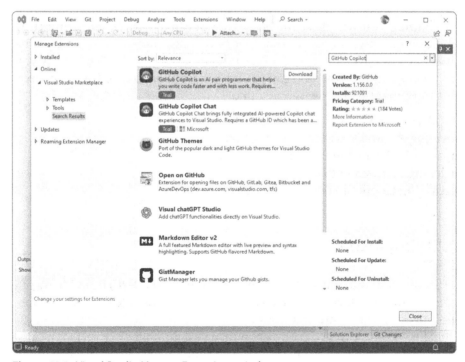

**Figure 11.1:** Visual Studio Manage Extensions window

For both the GitHub Copilot and GitHub Copilot Chat extensions, select Download. You will now be notified at the bottom of the extensions window that the changes will be scheduled, and modifications will begin when all Visual Studio windows are closed. Proceed to close all Visual Studio windows.

After closing Visual Studio, you will be prompted with a VSIX Installer window that will complete the installation of GitHub Copilot and GitHub Copilot Chat (see Figure 11.2).

**Figure 11.2:** Visual Studio GitHub Copilot extension installer

After completing the installation, open Visual Studio. When you have loaded the IDE, open the Accounts menu at the top right of the screen. From there, if you haven't already, add your GitHub account via the Add Another Account menu (see Figure 11.3).

**Figure 11.3:** Visual Studio Add GitHub Account menu

After following the steps to authenticate with GitHub, you should now be set up to use GitHub Copilot in Visual Studio.

## Exploring Code Completions

To explore code completes, create a console app. Start by opening the File menu at the top left, selecting the new menu, and then selecting the project menu. From here you can choose to create a console app. Name the project **PalindromeChecker**. Click Next to proceed. Then select create to initialize the project.

With the project open, you should see that Copilot is now enabled. Start by typing a top-level comment to the `Program.cs` file, as shown here:

```
// .net console application that checks if a string is a palindrome
```

As you start writing this comment, Copilot should start suggesting some text to complete it (see Figure 11.4).

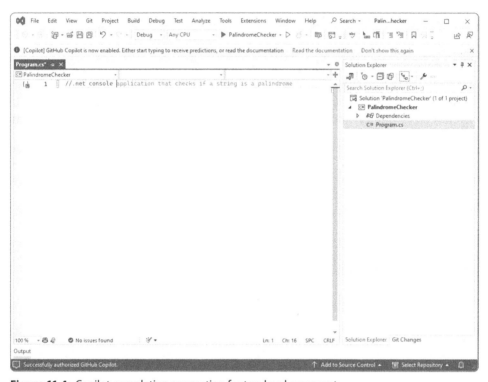

**Figure 11.4:** Copilot completion suggestion for top-level comment

After completing the top-level comment, add a second line to indicate the valid examples to help Copilot to provide the best result possible.

```
// valid examples: racecar, taco cat
```

With those comments now in place, enter two new lines to get another suggestion from Copilot. Within Visual Studio, you can also trigger a code completion via the keyboard shortcut. For more information on keyboard shortcuts and configuration of your Visuals Studio environment, check out the official documentation at the following URL:

```
https://docs.github.com/copilot/configuring-github-copilot/
configuring-github-copilot-in-your-environment?tool=visualstudio
```

Copilot will most likely suggest the statement using System;. After accepting that line, add another two lines to the file and wait for another code completion suggestion from Copilot. You should see Copilot attempting to complete a console program that has user input and checks if the input is a palindrome (see Figure 11.5).

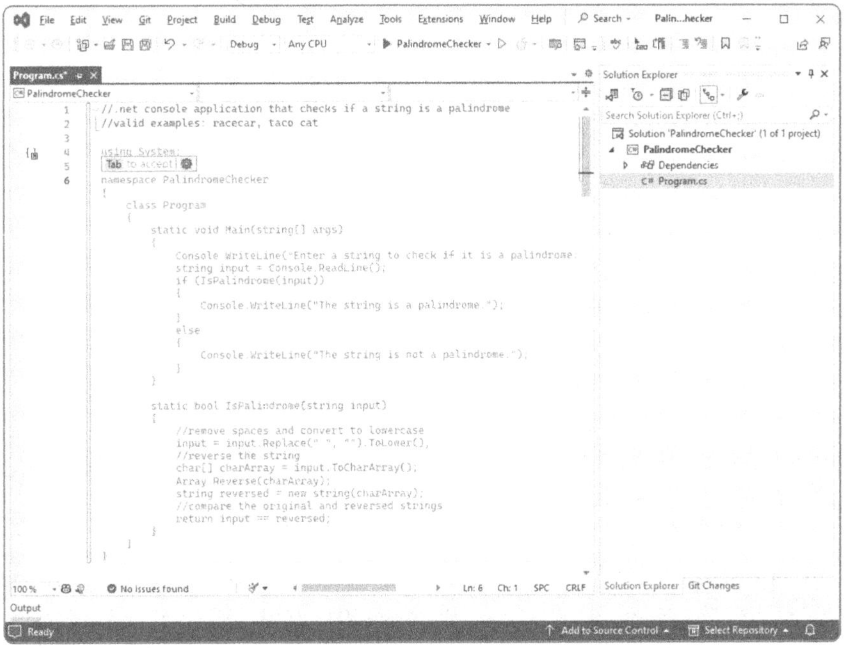

**Figure 11.5:** Copilot completion suggestion for top-level comment

After accepting this suggestion from Copilot, you can inspect the generated code and run the application to test.

## Chatting with Copilot

With the GitHub Copilot Chat extension installed, you can take your development experience to the next level with Copilot Chat. You can access the chat window via the view menu at the top left of the screen, using a keyboard shortcut, or by searching for Copilot Chat in the feature search tool in the top-right toolbar area.

After opening the chat view, you should see the ability to send a message to Copilot to start the conversation. Copilot Chat in Visual Studio supports slash commands for targeted context to assist Copilot in giving a great result. Visual Studio also supports tags that allow for targeted context for Copilot to know which files should be considered when giving you a response (see Figure 11.6).

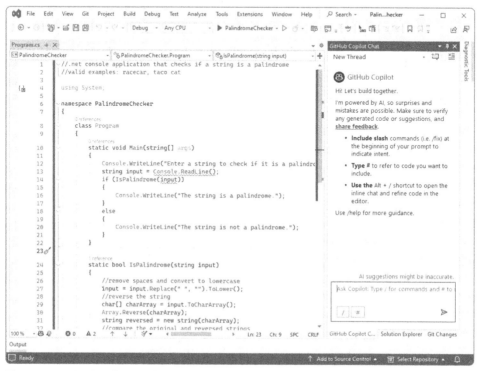

**Figure 11.6:** Copilot Chat window with greeting

GitHub Copilot Chat for Visual Studio does not currently have support for agents such as @workspace, @terminal, and @vscode. While the @workspace can be useful to automatically gain appropriate context for your prompt, you can achieve a similar effect by using multiple tagged files with #file in a prompt to allow for Copilot to have enough information to make a response that should consider many files within your project.

While agents are not present, you can trigger inline chat with Copilot right within your editor. You can right-click within the editor to trigger inline chat via the menu. Also, the preferred way is using the keyboard shortcut (Alt+/) (see Figure 11.7).

In this case, you can see inline chat in action by selecting the IsPalindrome function and activating inline chat. Select the /doc command. After selecting /doc, submit the request to Copilot. You should get a response with an inline code diff allowing you to review the changes made to the code and accept or cancel them (see Figure 11.8).

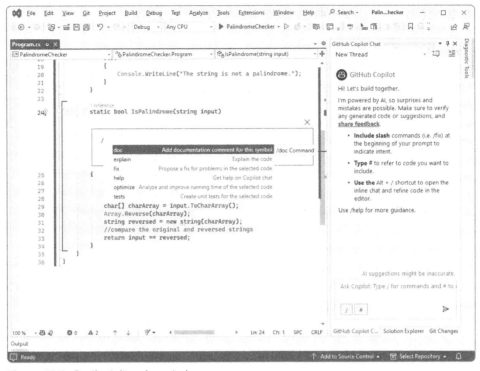

**Figure 11.7:** Copilot inline chat window

**Figure 11.8:** Copilot inline chat inline code diff

# Elevating Azure Data Studio with Copilot

Azure Data Studio is a cross-platform database tool that is built for database professionals who use SQL Server and Azure databases. Azure Data Studio supports both on-premises and cloud environments.

GitHub Copilot in Azure Data Studio only currently supports query completion. This can still be a huge productivity boost as you will see in the short demos that follow the setup processes.

## Prerequisites

- GitHub Copilot license
  https://github.com/features/copilot
- Azure Data Studio
  https://azure.microsoft.com/products/data-studio

## Installing the GitHub Copilot Extension

With Azure Data Studio installed and open, let's navigate to the Extensions panel on the Action Bar. You will find the Extensions panel identified by the "squares" icon.

Now follow these steps:

1. Open the Extensions panel.

2. Search for *GitHub Copilot*.

3. Within the GitHub Copilot extension result, click Install (see Figure 11.9).

After successfully installing the Copilot extension, you should see a pop-up in the lower-right corner of VS Code prompting you to sign in to GitHub. Please use this option to sign in. If that does not appear, you can check your login status via the account menu in the bottom-left corner of Azure Data Studio.

After following the login instructions with GitHub, you need to ensure that you have enabled GitHub Copilot globally via the bottom-right Copilot icon (see Figure 11.10).

## Constructing Database Schemas with Copilot

From a blank file, start with a top-level comment indicating your intent to create a SQL Server database schema.

```
-- SQL Server Database Schema
```

**Figure 11.9:** Azure Data Studio GitHub Copilot extension view

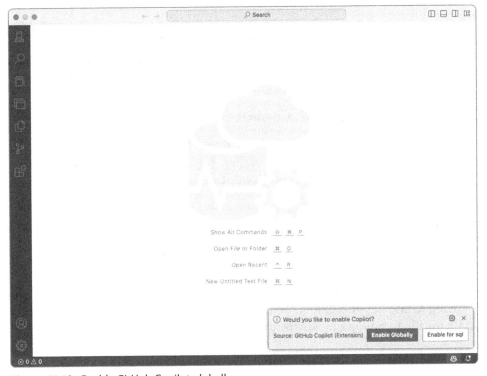

**Figure 11.10:** Enable GitHub Copilot globally

After that line, add another indicating some more instruction to Copilot to assist in query completion.

```
-- Create a database schema for a SQL Server database that will store
the following data:
```

After adding this line, add a new comment. In my case, Copilot quickly suggested a line indicating the database would store information about customers. Continue the new line comment creation until you have a few tables like this top-level comment:

```
-- SQL Server Database Schema
-- Create a database schema for a SQL Server database that will store
the following data:
-- 1. A table to store information about customers. Each customer has a
unique ID, a name, and an email address.
-- 2. A table to store information about products. Each product has a
unique ID, a name, and a price.
-- 3. A table to store information about orders. Each order has a unique
ID, a customer ID (from the customers table), a product ID (from the
products table), and a quantity.
```

With this comment in place, you can now proceed down two new lines and lead Copilot to initiate the database schema creation if it doesn't already start.

```
-- Create the customers table
```

With this comment, add a new line and then wait for a CREATE statement to be created. Repeat this new line process to the bottom of the file until you have three tables created for customers, products, and orders (see Figure 11.11).

## Inserting Test Data with Copilot

Extending this example further, let's see how Copilot can assist in creating test data for our new schema declared earlier. Add a comment after the last table with Insert as the first word, and Copilot should jump in to assist in the completion from here on out.

```
-- Insert some sample data into the customers table
```

Copilot will assist in writing the test data but will make you provide emails to ensure that it is not injecting any predicted emails that would be realistic.

After finishing two records of customer data, finishing that statement, and moving to another line, Copilot will assist with insert new test data. Add sample data for the remaining products and orders table (see Figure 11.12).

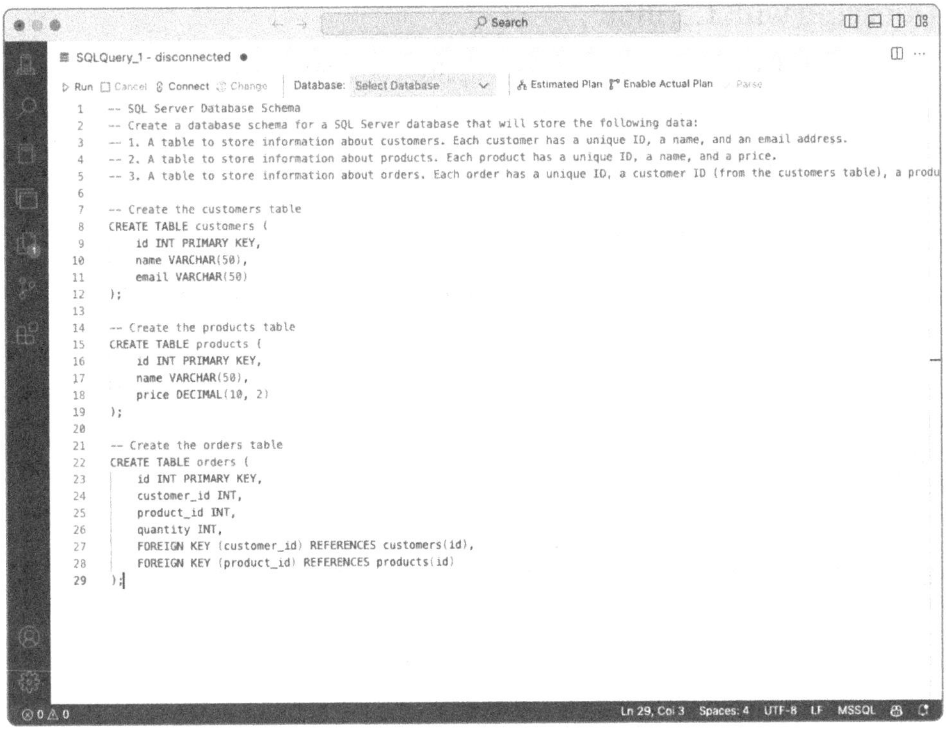

```
1   -- SQL Server Database Schema
2   -- Create a database schema for a SQL Server database that will store the following data:
3   -- 1. A table to store information about customers. Each customer has a unique ID, a name, and an email address.
4   -- 2. A table to store information about products. Each product has a unique ID, a name, and a price.
5   -- 3. A table to store information about orders. Each order has a unique ID, a customer ID (from the customers table), a produ
6
7   -- Create the customers table
8   CREATE TABLE customers (
9       id INT PRIMARY KEY,
10      name VARCHAR(50),
11      email VARCHAR(50)
12  );
13
14  -- Create the products table
15  CREATE TABLE products (
16      id INT PRIMARY KEY,
17      name VARCHAR(50),
18      price DECIMAL(10, 2)
19  );
20
21  -- Create the orders table
22  CREATE TABLE orders (
23      id INT PRIMARY KEY,
24      customer_id INT,
25      product_id INT,
26      quantity INT,
27      FOREIGN KEY (customer_id) REFERENCES customers(id),
28      FOREIGN KEY (product_id) REFERENCES products(id)
29  );
```

**Figure 11.11:** SQL Server database schema

```
16          id INT PRIMARY KEY,
17          name VARCHAR(50),
18          price DECIMAL(10, 2)
19      );
20
21      -- Create the orders table
22      CREATE TABLE orders (
23          id INT PRIMARY KEY,
24          customer_id INT,
25          product_id INT,
26          quantity INT,
27          FOREIGN KEY (customer_id) REFERENCES customers(id),
28          FOREIGN KEY (product_id) REFERENCES products(id)
29      );
30
31      -- Insert some sample data into the customers table
32      INSERT INTO customers (id, name, email) VALUES
33      (1, 'John Doe', 'test1@test.com'),
34      (2, 'Jane Smith', 'test2@test.com');
35
36      -- Insert some sample data into the products table
37      INSERT INTO products (id, name, price) VALUES
38      (1, 'Product A', 10.00),
39      (2, 'Product B', 20.00);
40
41      -- Insert some sample data into the orders table
42      INSERT INTO orders (id, customer_id, product_id, quantity) VALUES
        (1, 1, 1, 2),
        (2, 2, 2, 1);
        ...
```

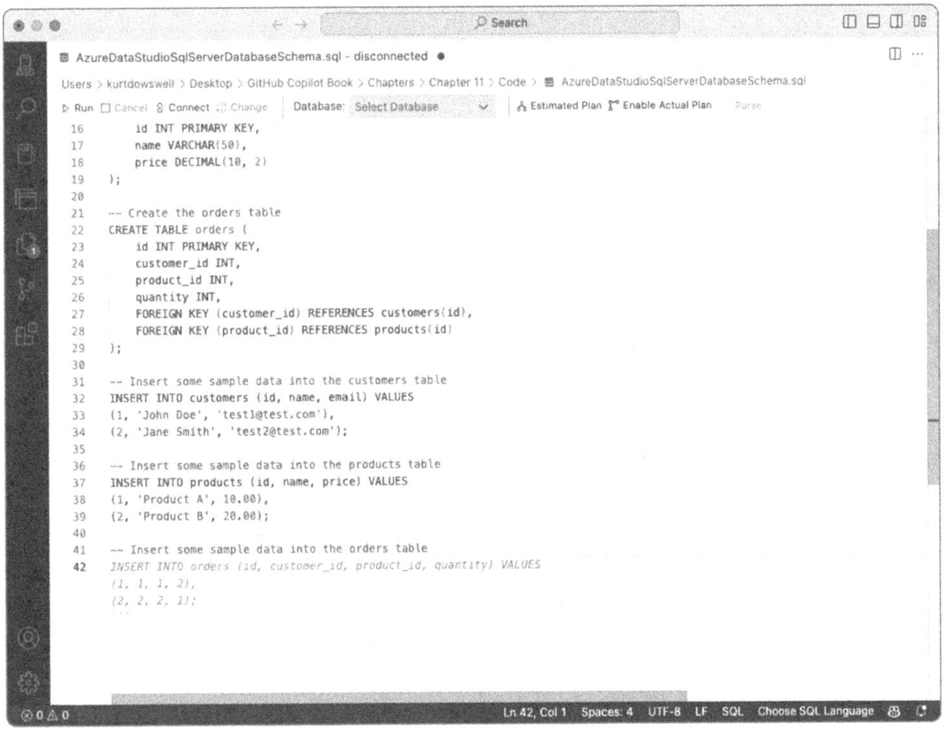

**Figure 11.12:** Copilot-assisted test data creation

## Querying with Copilot

Next, you will see how Copilot can amplify your database management tasks by creating a query on the tables that you just created and populated with data.

Continue to a new line after the test data inserts and add a comment starting with a query like the one shown here:

```
-- Query the orders table to get the total price of each order
```

After completing this comment, Copilot will again jump in to help you complete the SQL query you are wanting to write (see Figure 11.13).

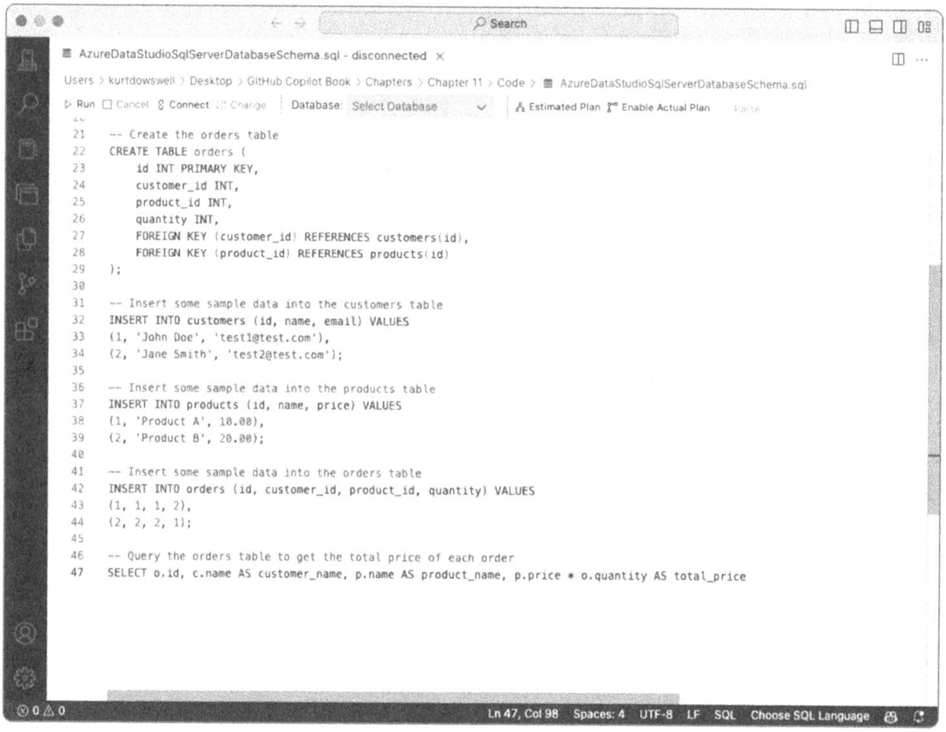

**Figure 11.13:** Copilot-assisted query creation

This example of GitHub Copilot within Azure Data Studio highlights the impressive skillset and how Copilot can assist in creating database schemas, constructing test data, and formulating complex queries.

Giving Copilot quality context is essential to the success of receiving quality responses. You can accomplish similar tasks in other IDEs. And by using skills like file tagging to reference database schema files, you can create queries in separate files and allow Copilot to access your database schema via a file reference.

# Boosting JetBrains IntelliJ IDEA with Copilot

IntelliJ IDEA by JetBrains is an IDE that supports the development of a multitude of programming languages. It focuses on the Java and Kotlin languages specifically.

In addition to the IntelliJ IDEA IDE, JetBrains offers many different IDEs that you can use Copilot within. Here are the current GitHub Copilot–compatible JetBrains IDEs:

- Android Studio
- AppCode
- Aqua
- CLion
- Code With Me Guest
- DataGrip
- DataSpell
- GoLand
- JetBrains Client
- MPS
- PhpStorm
- PyCharm
- Rider
- RubyMine
- RustRover
- WebStorm

To showcase GitHub Copilot in the JetBrains IDEs, in this section you will learn how GitHub Copilot can be leveraged to help you do more within IntelliJ IDEA.

## Prerequisites

- GitHub Copilot license
  https://github.com/features/copilot
- JetBrains IntelliJ IDEA
  https://www.jetbrains.com/idea/download

## Installing the GitHub Copilot Extension

After you have installed IntelliJ IDEA, open the IDE. In IntelliJ IDEA, you are greeted with a welcome screen. Here you can open the Plugins menu and search for *GitHub Copilot*. From here, select the search result and click Install (see Figure 11.14).

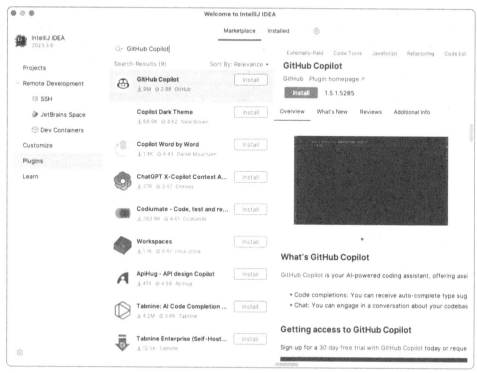

**Figure 11.14:** IntelliJ IDEA plugins search result screen with GitHub Copilot

After installing GitHub Copilot, you will be prompted to restart the IDE. Restart the IDE; after doing this, click New Project from the welcome page.

To see how Copilot can work within IntelliJ IDEA, let's create a `Palindrome Checker` Java project (see Figure 11.15).

After creating the project, you should see a prompt to sign in to GitHub at the bottom right. If you don't see this pop-up, you can also sign in via the welcome screen to the GitHub Copilot window accessible in the left menu (see Figure 11.16).

From this window or the Copilot icon on the bottom-right menu, sign in to your GitHub account using the steps outlined by the authentication prompt.

## Exploring Code Completions

After signing in to your GitHub account, you are ready to start using Copilot. Let's start with a top-level comment like you did in Visual Studio to see how you can use comments to direct Copilot to give you the type of program that you need.

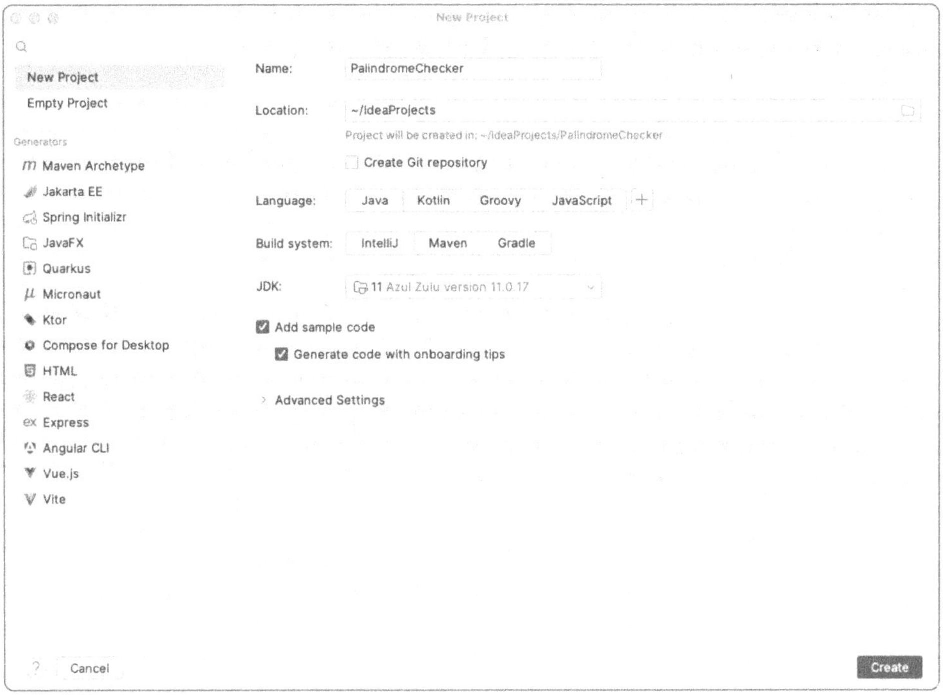

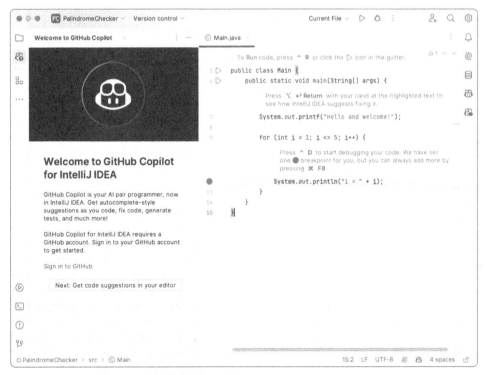

**Figure 11.15:** IntelliJ IDEA new project window

**Figure 11.16:** IntelliJ IDEA GitHub Copilot welcome

First, delete the contents of the `Main.java` file in your `PalindromeChecker` project. After deleting the contents, add a top-level comment like the following:

```
// Java console application that checks if a string is a palindrome
```

After completing the top-level comment, add a second line to indicate valid examples to help Copilot provide the best result possible.

```
// valid examples: racecar, taco cat
```

With those comments now in place, enter two new lines to get another suggestion from Copilot. Copilot will most likely suggest an import statement: `import java.util.Scanner;`. After accepting that line, add another two lines and wait for another code completion suggestion from Copilot. You should see Copilot attempting to complete a console program that has user input and checks if the input is a palindrome (see Figure 11.17).

**Figure 11.17:** Copilot completion suggestion for top-level comment

After accepting this suggestion from Copilot, you can inspect the generated code and run the application to test.

In my case, the resulting `isPalindrome` function did not include a statement to remove spaces and convert to lowercase like the C# example did.

To resolve this issue, add a comment to the isPalindrome function before the loop as follows:

```
// remove spaces and convert to lowercase
```

With this comment in place, add a new line and wait for Copilot to provide a code suggestion. After you accept the next line, you can run the application and test that the valid examples are returning the correct value (see Figure 11.18).

**Figure 11.18:** Programing the test result with new code

## Chatting with Copilot

In IntelliJ IDEA, Copilot Chat is installed automatically with the Copilot extension. To access Copilot Chat, you can use the GitHub Copilot Chat menu item on the right side of the IDE.

Let's explore how Copilot can assist in documenting the new function. Highlight the isPalindrome function. With this code selected, within the Copilot Chat window, use the /doc command. Send that request to Copilot.

With the documentation request sent to Copilot, you should see a resulting function within the chat window with detailed documentation added to the method signature and each line of code within the function (see Figure 11.19).

**Figure 11.19:** Copilot Chat result with documentation

Within the chat result, you can use the Insert Code Block At Cursor button at the top right of the generated code block in the response from Copilot. After doing this, the updated `isPalindrome` function with full documentation will be inserted into the editor.

Currently, inline chat is not supported in IntelliJ IDEA. But as you have seen, working with Copilot Chat in the windowed experience and transferring results to your editor is a breeze.

## Enhancing Neovim with Copilot

Neovim is a highly configurable text editor built to enable efficient text editing. It's an extension of Vim having many additional features designed to be helpful in editing source code for software applications.

While GitHub Copilot supports both Vim and Neovim, in this example we will be showcasing Neovim. In the installation section that follows, you will have access to the required installation commands to setup Copilot in either editor.

## Prerequisites

- GitHub Copilot license
  https://github.com/features/copilot
- Neovim
  https://neovim.io
- Node.js
  https://nodejs.org/en/download

## Installing the GitHub Copilot Extension

With Neovim or Vim installed, run one of the following commands according to your operating system and editor of choice to install the GitHub Copilot extension [1].

- Neovim on Linux or macOS:

  ```
  git clone https://github.com/github/copilot.vim.git \
     ~/.config/nvim/pack/github/start/copilot.vim
  ```

- Vim on Linux or macOS:

  ```
  git clone https://github.com/github/copilot.vim.git \
     ~/.vim/pack/github/start/copilot.vim
  ```

- Neovim on Windows via PowerShell:

  ```
  git clone https://github.com/github/copilot.vim.git `
     $HOME/AppData/Local/nvim/pack/github/start/copilot.vim
  ```

- Vim on Windows via PowerShell:

  ```
  git clone https://github.com/github/copilot.vim.git `
     $HOME/vimfiles/pack/github/start/copilot.vim
  ```

Start Neovim via the `nvim` command and run the following command:

```
:Copilot setup
```

After logging in to your GitHub account, you are now ready to enable Copilot. Run the following command to enable Copilot:

```
:Copilot enable
```

## Exploring Code Completions

Let's explore how GitHub Copilot can assist in writing a Node.js script within Neovim. Exit Neovim via the `:q` command. From your terminal, create a file called `dad-jokes.js`. On macOS, you can do this by running the following:

```
touch dad-jokes.js
```

On Windows, you can use the following:

```
echo. > dad-jokes.js
```

Open the `dad-jokes.js` file with Neovim with the following command:

```
nvim dad-jokes.js
```

After opening the file, Copilot should be enabled from the installation steps, so you can proceed to adding a top-level comment to the file. To start editing the file, press the i key to activate "insert" mode. Start by typing the following:

```
// Node.js script that fetches a random dad joke from the
icanhazdadjoke API
```

You will notice that Copilot, using the context of the filename, already completes the ending of the comment (see Figure 11.20). You can accept the request by hitting the Tab key.

**Figure 11.20:** Copilot completing a comment in Neovim

Add another comment to inform Copilot to use the `https` module:

```
// Use the https module to make a request to the API
```

After you have added the second comment, add two blank lines to the file. You should then be prompted with a code suggestion with the `https` variable declaration. Accept that line, and then add two more blank lines. Copilot should suggest a comment or function for fetching the dad joke (see Figure 11.21).

```
● ● ●                      Code — nvim dad-jokes.js • node — 90×31
// Node.js script that fetches a random dad joke from the icanhazdadjoke API
// Use the https module to make a request to the API

const https = require('https');

// Function to fetch a random dad joke
function fetchDadJoke() {
  // Make a request to the icanhazdadjoke API
  https.get('https://icanhazdadjoke.com/', {
    headers: {
      'Accept': 'application/json'
    }
  }, (res) => {
    let data = '';

    // Read the response data
    res.on('data', (chunk) => {
      data += chunk;
    });

    // Parse the JSON data
    res.on('end', () => {
      const joke = JSON.parse(data);
      console.log(joke.joke);
    });
  });
}
~
~
dad-jokes.js [+]                                              7,1        All
-- INSERT --
```

**Figure 11.21:** Copilot completing the `fetchDadJoke()` function

After accepting the `fetchDadJoke()` function, add two more blank lines and make a call to the `fetchDadJoke()` function. After you are done, your file should look like Figure 11.22.

With the export in place, hit the Esc key to stop editing. Now, save and quit the file via the `:wq` command.

After you are back in the terminal, run the following command to test the function (see Figure 11.23):

```
node dad-jokes.js
```

Now you can enjoy all the dad jokes you can handle thanks to Copilot! I hope this example shed light on just how useful Copilot can be in the context of Neovim/Vim.

For more extensive documentation, visit the DOC file for the Copilot Vim plugin.

```
https://github.com/github/copilot.vim/blob/release/doc/copilot.txt
```

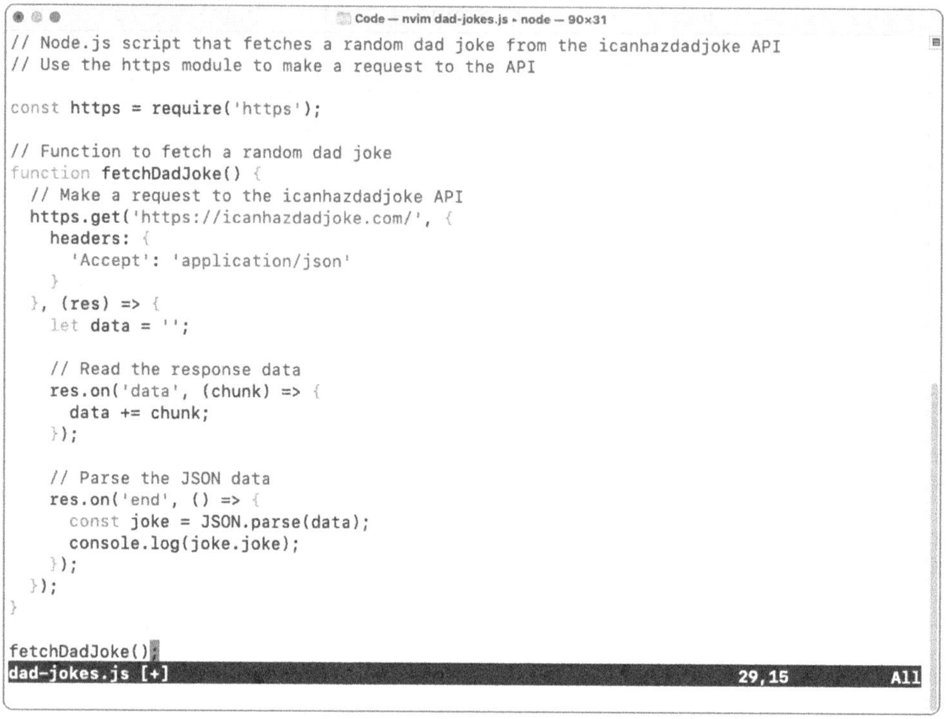
Code — nvim dad-jokes.js • node — 90×31
// Node.js script that fetches a random dad joke from the icanhazdadjoke API
// Use the https module to make a request to the API
const https = require('https');
// Function to fetch a random dad joke
function fetchDadJoke() {
// Make a request to the icanhazdadjoke API
https.get('https://icanhazdadjoke.com/', {
headers: {
'Accept': 'application/json'
}
}, (res) => {
let data = '';
// Read the response data
res.on('data', (chunk) => {
data += chunk;
});
// Parse the JSON data
res.on('end', () => {
const joke = JSON.parse(data);
console.log(joke.joke);
});
});
}
fetchDadJoke();
dad-jokes.js [+]
29,15
All

**Figure 11.22:** Copilot completing the `fetchDadJoke()` function

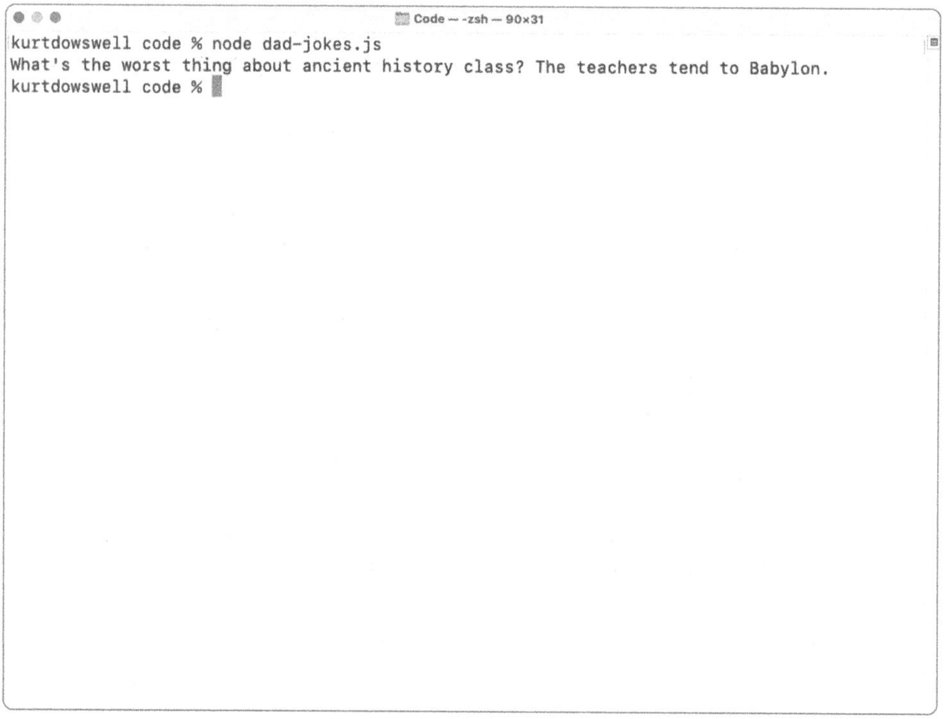
Code — -zsh — 90×31
kurtdowswell code % node dad-jokes.js
What's the worst thing about ancient history class? The teachers tend to Babylon.
kurtdowswell code %

**Figure 11.23:** Node.js call for dad jokes

# Consulting Copilot in the GitHub CLI

When running commands outside of an IDE, Copilot has you covered. With Copilot in the GitHub CLI, you have access to Copilot wherever you might be within your terminal activities.

In this section, you will see how easy it is to activate and interact with Copilot within the terminal.

## Prerequisites

- GitHub Copilot license
  ```
  https://github.com/features/copilot
  ```
- GitHub CLI
  ```
  https://cli.github.com
  ```

## Installing the GitHub Copilot Extension

After you have the GitHub CLI installed, make sure you are authenticated using the `gh auth login` command. Follow the login steps, and then you will be ready to install Copilot for the GitHub CLI.

To install the Copilot, run the following command:

```
gh extension install github/gh-copilot
```

If you want to upgrade your Copilot extension, you can run the `upgrade` command:

```
gh extension upgrade gh-copilot
```

Confirm you have installed or updated successfully by running the following (see Figure 11.24):

```
gh copilot
```

## Getting Suggestions with Copilot

You can get suggestions from Copilot by using the following command:

```
gh copilot suggest
```

> **NOTE**   The first time you run the `gh copilot suggest` function, you may be asked to allow GitHub to collect usage data to help improve the product. The data collected does not include your queries.

```
● ● ●                          ⬜ Code — -zsh — 90×31
kurtdowswell code % gh copilot
Your AI command line copilot.

Usage:
  copilot [command]

Examples:

$ gh copilot suggest "Install git"
$ gh copilot explain "traceroute github.com"


Available Commands:
  alias      Generate shell-specific aliases for convenience
  config     Configure options
  explain    Explain a command
  suggest    Suggest a command

Flags:
  -h, --help       help for copilot
  -v, --version    version for copilot

Use "copilot [command] --help" for more information about a command.
kurtdowswell code % ▊
```

**Figure 11.24:** Copilot in the GitHub CLI

This will provide you with multiple options. You can get generic shell command, gh command, or Git command assistance (see Figure 11.25).

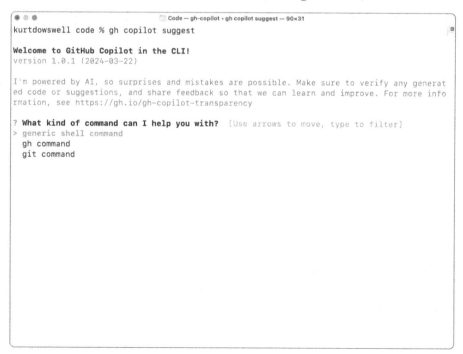

```
● ● ●                    ⬜ Code — gh-copilot · gh copilot suggest — 90×31
kurtdowswell code % gh copilot suggest

Welcome to GitHub Copilot in the CLI!
version 1.0.1 (2024-03-22)

I'm powered by AI, so surprises and mistakes are possible. Make sure to verify any generat
ed code or suggestions, and share feedback so that we can learn and improve. For more info
rmation, see https://gh.io/gh-copilot-transparency

? What kind of command can I help you with?  [Use arrows to move, type to filter]
> generic shell command
  gh command
  git command
```

**Figure 11.25:** Copilot suggest command result

In this case, you will see how Copilot can help you find how to search for a file that contains a specific string (see Figure 11.26).

```
● ○ ●                    Code — gh-copilot · gh copilot suggest — 90×31
kurtdowswell code % gh copilot suggest

Welcome to GitHub Copilot in the CLI!
version 1.0.1 (2024-03-22)

I'm powered by AI, so surprises and mistakes are possible. Make sure to verify any generat
ed code or suggestions, and share feedback so that we can learn and improve. For more info
rmation, see https://gh.io/gh-copilot-transparency

? What kind of command can I help you with?
> generic shell command

? What would you like the shell command to do?
> How to find a file that contains the string "joke"?

Suggestion:

  grep -r "joke" .

? Select an option  [Use arrows to move, type to filter]
> Copy command to clipboard
  Explain command
  Execute command
  Revise command
  Rate response
  Exit
```

**Figure 11.26:** Copilot `suggest` generic shell command result

With this result, you can do many actions. You can copy, explain, execute, revise, rate, or exit from the result.

Figure 11.27 shows the result if you explain the command and then execute it.

In this result, you can see that Copilot provided a great explanation of the command. Also, when attempting to directly run the command from Copilot's CLI, there was an issue because of not having the `ghcs` alias set up. You will see how this is configured at the end of this section.

You can also provide the Copilot `suggest` feature with the command you want help with from the first step like this:

```
gh copilot suggest "Task that you want to run"
```

## Explaining Commands with Copilot

To get insights about a particular command that you would like to know more about, you can use the `explain` feature.

```
gh copilot explain
```

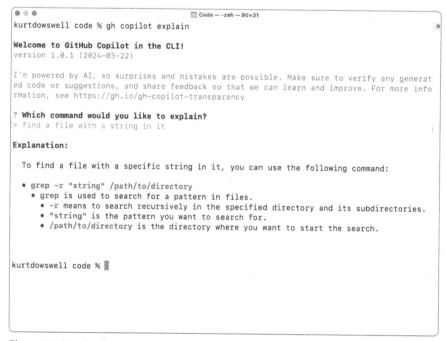

```
● ● ●                          🖵 Code — -zsh — 90×31
  grep -r "joke" .

? Select an option
> Explain command

Explanation:

  • grep -r "joke" . searches for the term "joke" recursively in all files and directories
  starting from the current directory.
    • -r or --recursive searches for the term in all files and directories recursively.
    • "joke" is the search term that we are looking for.
    • . specifies the starting directory for the search, which in this case is the current
    directory.


? Select an option
> Execute command

Without using the `ghcs` alias or `-s,--shell-out` flag, the suggested command will be cop
ied to your clipboard for you to paste and execute.

Command copied to clipboard!
kurtdowswell code % grep -r "joke" .
./dad-jokes.js:// Node.js script that fetches a random dad joke from the icanhazdadjoke AP
I
./dad-jokes.js:// Function to fetch a random dad joke
./dad-jokes.js:  // Make a request to the icanhazdadjoke API
./dad-jokes.js:  https.get('https://icanhazdadjoke.com/', {
./dad-jokes.js:       const joke = JSON.parse(data);
./dad-jokes.js:       console.log(joke.joke);
kurtdowswell code % ▊
```

**Figure 11.27:** Copilot explains and executes the generic shell command.

This will initiate a similar experience as the `suggest` feature but is focused only on providing you with an explanation of the command instead of the ability to run it directly from the result (see Figure 11.28).

```
● ● ●                          🖵 Code — -zsh — 90×31
kurtdowswell code % gh copilot explain

Welcome to GitHub Copilot in the CLI!
version 1.0.1 (2024-03-22)

I'm powered by AI, so surprises and mistakes are possible. Make sure to verify any generat
ed code or suggestions, and share feedback so that we can learn and improve. For more info
rmation, see https://gh.io/gh-copilot-transparency

? Which command would you like to explain?
> find a file with a string in it

Explanation:

  To find a file with a specific string in it, you can use the following command:

  • grep -r "string" /path/to/directory
    • grep is used to search for a pattern in files.
      • -r means to search recursively in the specified directory and its subdirectories.
      • "string" is the pattern you want to search for.
      • /path/to/directory is the directory where you want to start the search.


kurtdowswell code % ▊
```

**Figure 11.28:** Copilot `explain` command result

## Setting Up Aliases for Copilot

To make interacting with Copilot easier, it is a great idea to set up aliases for Copilot in the CLI. This can be accomplished by running one of the following commands based on the shell that you are using [2].

### *Bash*

```
echo 'eval "$(gh copilot alias -- bash)"' >> ~/.bashrc
```

### *PowerShell*

```
$GH_COPILOT_PROFILE = Join-Path -Path $(Split-Path -Path $PROFILE
-Parent) -ChildPath "gh-copilot.ps1"
gh copilot alias -- pwsh | Out-File ( New-Item -Path $GH_COPILOT_PROFILE
-Force )
echo ". $GH_COPILOT_PROFILE" >> $PROFILE
```

### *Zsh*

```
echo 'eval "$(gh copilot alias -- zsh)"' >> ~/.zshrc
```

After you have updated your configuration file, close your shell and re-open it. You will then have access to use the ghcs and ghce aliases.

# References

[1] GitHub, "GitHub Copilot for Vim and Neovim" 2024. [Online]. Available: https://github.com/github/copilot.vim

[2] GitHub, "Using GitHub Copilot in the CLI" 2024. [Online]. Available: https://docs.github.com/en/copilot/github-copilot-in-the-cli/using-github-copilot-in-the-cli

# Conclusion

In review, I hope this chapter has given you insights into just how helpful GitHub Copilot is in development environments. The team at GitHub is continuing to innovate, taking Copilot to more places to assist engineers where they work best.

# CHAPTER 12

# Universal Conversion with GitHub Copilot

In this chapter, you will discover the compelling use of GitHub Copilot for universal conversion in software development. Copilot can assist in translating languages, frameworks, libraries, databases, or CI/CD pipelines.

With Copilot by your side, you are empowered to transition between technologies with incredible speed. This opportunity to use the technologies that you require with speed and accuracy is a game-changing capability.

Let's jump to the examples of how Copilot can supercharge your development workflow when translation is required.

- Translating Natural Language to Programming Languages
- Converting JavaScript Components
- Simplifying CSS Styles
- Enhancing Non-Typed Languages with Types
- Transitioning Between Frameworks and Libraries
- Converting Object-Oriented Languages
- Migrating Databases
- Transitioning CI/CD Platforms
- Modernizing Legacy Systems

# Translating Natural Language to Programming Languages

Copilot, with its ability to understand a vast number of natural languages and programming languages, can facilitate the creation of software solutions simply by describing the need you have in natural languages.

Here you will see how Copilot can create a function with a requirement in English using the Gherkin syntax (see Figure 12.1).

Here is a top-level comment:

```
/**
Feature: Two Sum
  As a user
  I want to find two numbers in an array that add up to a specific
target number
  So that I can solve my problem

  Scenario: Find two numbers that add up to the target
    Given an array of integers
    And a target integer
    When I pass the array and target to the twoSum function
    Then it should return the indices of the two numbers that add up to
the target
  **/
```

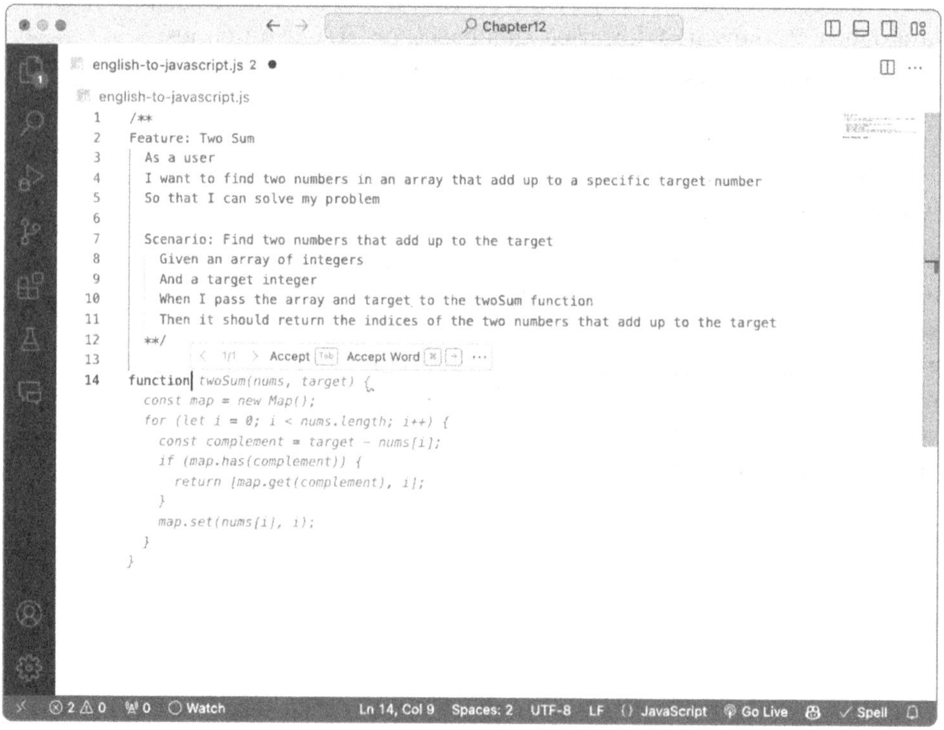

**Figure 12.1:** English to JavaScript

As demonstrated here, Copilot offers significant benefits for streamlining the software development process through its capacity to translate feature requirements directly into both code and corresponding test cases. By directly converting specifications into executable code, Copilot substantially accelerates development, minimizing the initial coding effort required from developers. This feature also promotes a test-driven development approach so developers can automatically generate test cases that align with the specified requirements. Such automation ensures that the newly written code is immediately validated, enhancing the overall code quality, and reducing the likelihood of bugs.

Looking at the inverse of this process, the /explain command is a great example of how Copilot can translate code back to natural language. You can see with this example using the /explain command; Copilot gives a detailed step-by-step breakdown of the function that was just created using natural language (see Figure 12.2).

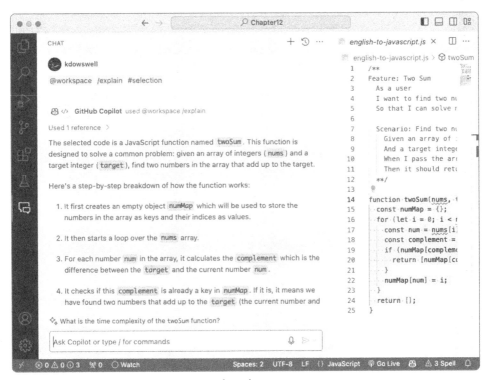

**Figure 12.2:** Copilot /explain command results

Copilot's ability to explain code in natural language is an invaluable feature for exploring and becoming more confident in an unfamiliar codebase. In addition to the initial explanation that Copilot gives when you request an explanation, you can continue the conversation to gain clarity about specific technologies, syntaxes, and more.

## Converting JavaScript Components

In the world of JavaScript, there are seemly endless numbers of front-end frameworks. In this example of translation, you will see how well Copilot can assist you in converting a component from one framework to another.

Imagine you have a requirement to create a design system that supports all major front-end frameworks. How long would it take you to convert each of those components to other frameworks? This extremely laborious task would take a long time if it weren't for Copilot. Let's explore how you can convert a React.js button component to Angular (see Figure 12.3).

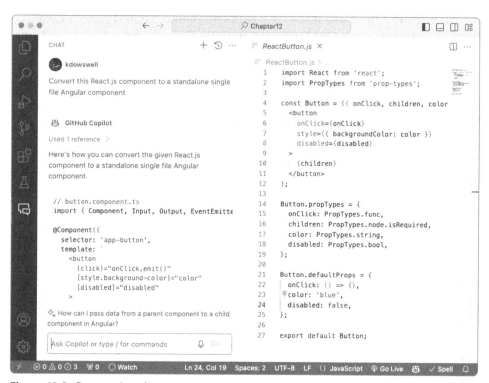

**Figure 12.3:** React to Angular

If you would like to follow along with this coding example, you can download a copy of the starter `ReactButton.js` component in the Chapter 12 folder.

```
https://www.wiley.com/go/programminggithubcopilot
```

Here is the request to Copilot:

```
Convert this React.js component to a single file Angular component.
```

Here you can see that Copilot created an Angular button component that has the appropriate naming convention of the file noted and file structure that is best practice for Angular and applies indention correctly. Figure 12.4 shows the resulting Angular button component.

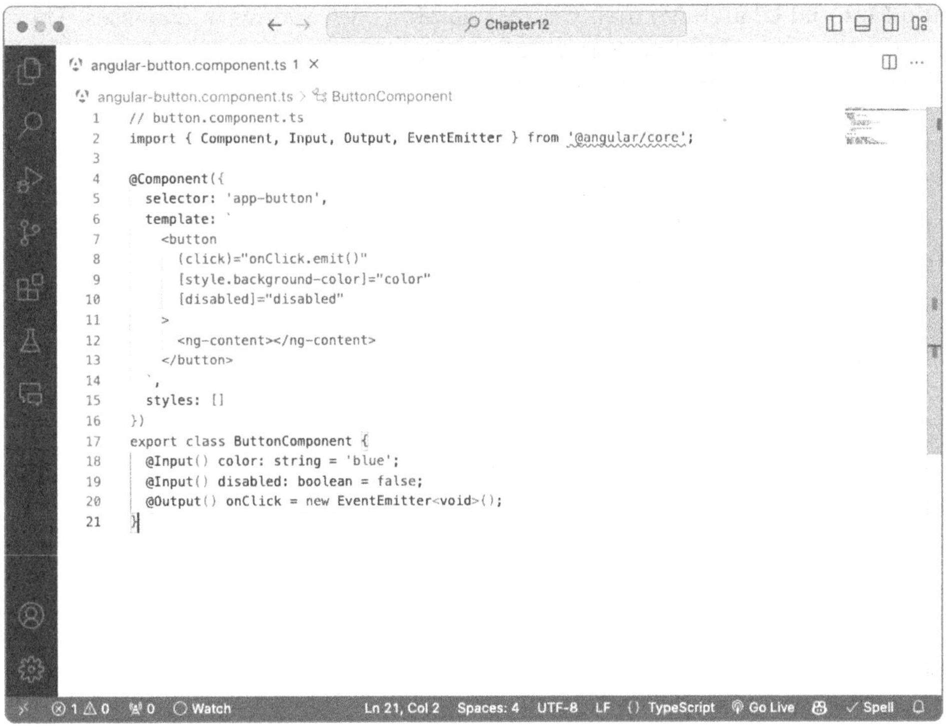

```
// button.component.ts
import { Component, Input, Output, EventEmitter } from '@angular/core';

@Component({
  selector: 'app-button',
  template: `
    <button
      (click)="onClick.emit()"
      [style.background-color]="color"
      [disabled]="disabled"
    >
      <ng-content></ng-content>
    </button>
  `,
  styles: []
})
export class ButtonComponent {
  @Input() color: string = 'blue';
  @Input() disabled: boolean = false;
  @Output() onClick = new EventEmitter<void>();
}
```

**Figure 12.4:** React to Angular

This could be extended to any other component type that you might need to convert. Also, this concept can apply to any of the popular front-end frameworks like Vue.js, Svelte, Ember.js, and more.

## Simplifying CSS Styles

Cascading Style Sheets (CSS) is an essential part of web applications. CSS allows for developers to describe the look and formatting of a document written in HTML.

Copilot can assist in writing CSS to help you produce designs faster than ever. In addition, Copilot can also help you convert CSS styles from one format to another. The style sheet adjustments can be daunting for programmers who are not well versed in front-end technologies. Copilot is here to help you every step of the way to simplify your CSS workflow.

## Converting Between CSS Frameworks

There are a lot of great options to help give you a starting point for your designs. Frameworks like Bootstrap, Tailwind CSS, Foundation, Sematic UI, and Material UI all have their distinct naming conventions and classes. They have a lot of overlapping features. So, when you want to move from one of these frameworks to another, it is possible, but the level of effort can be very high due to the massive sprawl of class names that can be spread throughout your codebase.

In this section, you will see how you can translate pure CSS to a framework and then translate from one framework to another. Let's look at an example create profile HTML page (see Figure 12.5).

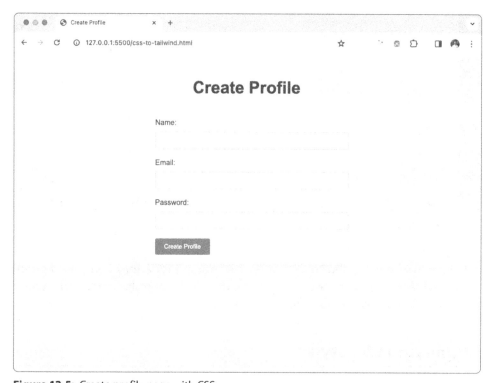

**Figure 12.5:** Create profile page with CSS

If you would like to follow along with this coding example, you can download a copy of the starter `css-to-tailwind-starter.html` file in the Chapter 12 folder.

```
https://www.wiley.com/go/programminggithubcopilot
```

This screen consists of a name, email, password, and Create Profile button. The form input is in a form tag that is aligned center with a header above it. All of this is currently done with inline CSS (see Figure 12.6).

**Figure 12.6:** Create profile HTML source file

You can see that there are many lines of styles per HTML tag supporting this design and layout. With Copilot's help, you can convert this page to use a framework like Tailwind CSS to clean up this markup and make the page much more maintainable.

To do this, open a chat window with the HTML file open. Send a request to Copilot like the following:

```
Convert this html page to use Tailwind CSS #file:css-to-tailwind.html
```

This request should result in a fully formed HTML page that utilizes Tailwind CSS in place of the pure CSS attributes (see Figure 12.7).

After getting this result, copy the contents of the Tailwind CSS version to the HTML file. You will notice this is a much more consolidated and cleaner file.

You can then open the HTML file in a browser to see the updated look (see Figure 12.8).

In addition to the source file improvements, you should notice that the style updates to the input boxes, button, padding, and colors are all subtly improved. This is because frameworks like Tailwind CSS and others have great defaults that give you a nice look right out of the box.

Now, you can take this further by exploring what other UI frameworks Copilot can assist in translating to. In this case, with the HTML file open, send another

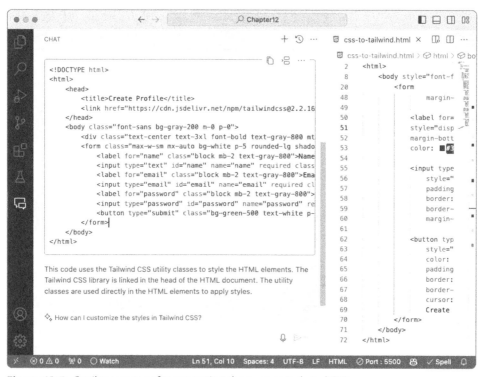

**Figure 12.7:** Copilot response for converting the page to Tailwind CSS

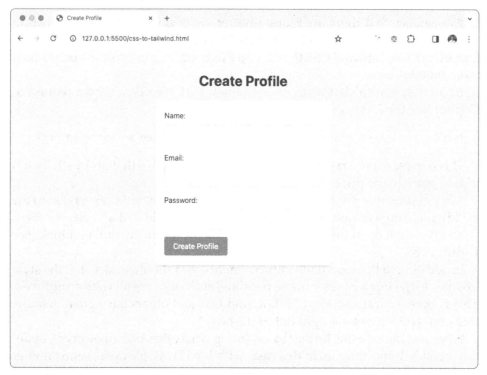

**Figure 12.8:** Create profile page with Tailwind CSS

request to Copilot for an HTML page using Bootstrap like the following (see Figure 12.9):

```
Convert this html page to use Bootstrap
```

**Figure 12.9:** Copilot response for converting the page to Bootstrap

You can see that due to the visibility of Tailwind CSS lines within the editor, you do not need to use the #file tag to give the entire context of the file. In addition, the generated HTML for the Bootstrap framework aligns to the required structure for the Bootstrap CSS class attributes to function properly.

After you have reviewed the generated HTML, add it to the editor in place of the previous HTML and open it in a browser to inspect the differences (see Figure 12.10).

With this design, you still have the same general layout, with the header above a centered card that has a drop shadow applied. A larger change between the two frameworks is the lack of a gray background. There are color classes that should assist this within Bootstrap if you would like to make further modifications to the file. Lastly, the Create Profile button is spanning the entire width of the form input area.

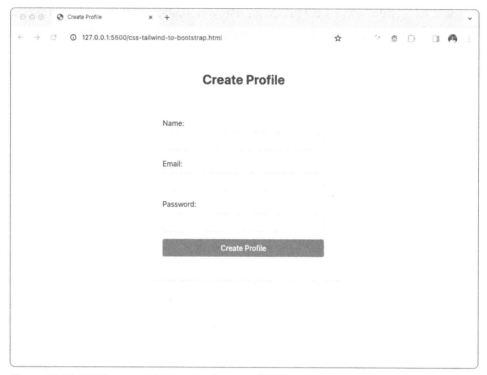

**Figure 12.10:** HTML page with Bootstrap framework powering design and layout

# Enhancing Nontyped Languages with Types

While nontyped languages are great at allowing for a fast and fluid development, adding type safety is a great way to do this when you need to stabilize your code; The following are all possible conversions from nontyped languages to typed languages:

- JavaScript to TypeScript
- Python to Cython
- Ruby to Crystal
- PHP to Hack
- Clojure to ClojureScript
- Erlang to Alpaca
- Lua to Typed Lua
- R to Slang
- Perl to Raku
- Groovy to Java

In this section, you will see some of these translations and how you can easily enhance your nontyped language with Copilot.

## JavaScript to Typescript

Let's look at how Copilot can help convert JavaScript to TypeScript. In this example, there is a `calculateTotal` function that has an input of items and discount properties and should return the calculated total.

```
function calculateTotal(items, discount) {
    let total = 0;
    for (let i = 0; i < items.length; i++) {
        total += items[i].price;
    }
    total -= total * (discount / 100);
    return total;
}
```

There are several potential issues that could arise when not using TypeScript in this function. First, type safety when using the input parameters items and discount is not present. So, if a developer accidentally passes a single item into the method instead of an array, there would be a runtime error. Also, for the discount parameter, if a developer later passes a non-numeric value, there would be a runtime error. While these things can be checked with unit tests, adding another layer of safety on your code can help identify issues quickly and keep the maintainability of your code higher.

To convert this function to typescript, let's use inline chat. You can also use chat within the window, but for this purpose I will be demonstrating an inline refactor.

Start by selecting the function. After making the selection, activate inline chat. Send a request to Copilot to convert the file to TypeScript with the `fix` command (see Figure 12.11):

```
/fix convert the file to TypeScript
```

After making this conversion, you would need to update your project to use TypeScript. As stated earlier, nontyped languages offer an ease of use because of their simplicity and an ease of execution. With the addition of types, it is now a requirement to do a few additional steps to get your code to compile and execute.

For assistance in these remaining steps, you can turn to Copilot. Start a new window chat and ask Copilot the following:

```
How can I update my JavaScript project to use TypeScript?
```

After sending this request, you should get a detailed step-by-step guide to implementing TypeScript for your project (see Figure 12.12).

**Figure 12.11:** Calculate total function converted to TypeScript

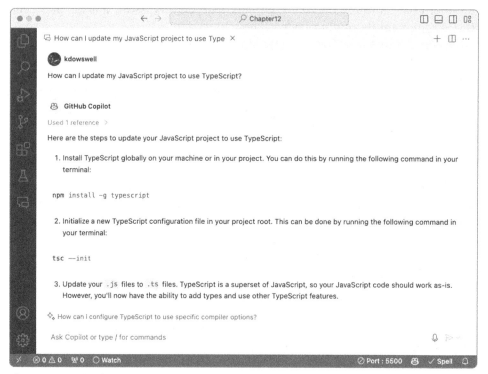

**Figure 12.12:** Copilot response on how to update a JavaScript project to Typescript

# Transitioning Between Frameworks and Libraries

In this section, you will discover how Copilot can help transition between object-oriented frameworks and libraries, which are both examples of reusable code. Libraries are generally categorized as a collection of functions and methods that perform specific tasks. A framework, on the other hand, dictates the structure of your application in addition to providing utilities and libraries.

The examples will be of specific libraries and frameworks, but due to the ability of Copilot as a universal translation assistant, you can apply these concepts to your specific libraries and frameworks.

## Pandas to Polars

An example of when you might need to translate from one library to another is when you might have some code that does a process for you that needs to be modernized for performance considerations. In Python, a popular data processing library called Pandas is heavily used. While this library is great, when you are working with large data sets, performance issues could become an issue, and you might need to consider another option. Here you will see how you can leverage Copilot to convert a Python Pandas data processing application to use Polars. Polars is a performance-first data processing library that has benchmarking tests indicating speed improvements of up to 50x in performance; compared to Pandas, speed tests from the independent TPC-H Benchmark indicate a 30x performance improvement over Pandas [1].

Starting from a simple data processing application in Python using Pandas, you will see how quickly Copilot can assist in translating to Polars.

If you would like to follow along with this coding example, you can download a copy of the starter `pandas-to-polars.py` file in the Chapter 12 folder.

```
https://www.wiley.com/go/programminggithubcopilot
```

Here is the starting Python application:

```
import pandas as pd

# Load a large CSV file
df = pd.read_csv('large_file.csv')

# Perform a groupby operation
grouped = df.groupby('column1').sum()

# Sort the result
sorted_df = grouped.sort_values('column2', ascending=False)

# Display the result
print(sorted_df)
```

From this starting point, select the application code and use the chat window to ask Copilot to convert the application to use Polars (see Figure 12.13). Here is the request to Copilot:

```
Convert application to use Polars #editor
```

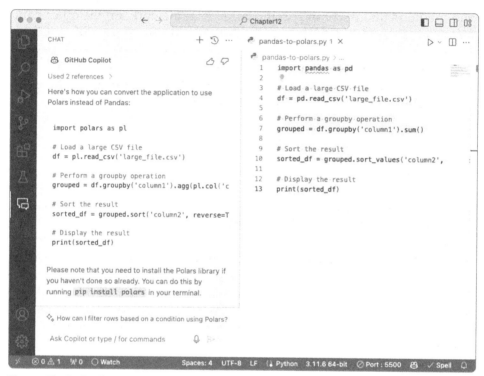

**Figure 12.13:** Copilot response on how to convert an application to use Polars

From here, you can use the Inject Code At Cursor option from the window chat result to apply the new code to the editor.

As you will see in this resulting Polars code, there are slight adjustments to the methods and parameter syntax for interacting with the dataset.

Here is the completed Python application with Polars:

```python
import polars as pl

# Load a large CSV file
df = pl.read_csv('large_file.csv')

# Perform a groupby operation
grouped = df.groupby('column1').agg(pl.col('column1').sum())
```

```
# Sort the result
sorted_df = grouped.sort('column2', reverse=True)

# Display the result
print(sorted_df)
```

With this conversion now completed, you can proceed to installing the appropriate library as Copilot indicated in the chat response and enjoy the speed improvements when dealing with your large dataset.

## Express.js to Koa.js

Express.js has long been the go-to framework for developing web applications in Node.js. It is simple, is unopinionated, and has a large community with a rich ecosystem of middleware. However, as JavaScript and Node.js have evolved, new frameworks have emerged that take advantage of newer features to offer a more modern and streamlined development experience.

One such framework is Koa.js. Developed by the same team behind Express, Koa.js leverages async functions to eliminate callbacks and significantly improve error handling. Koa is also modular, enabling for a leaner more dynamic offering.

In this section, you will discover how in the process of modernizing your framework-dependent applications, Copilot can assist in updating your code to ensure the functionality is preserved while giving you the benefits of modern advancements made by new frameworks.

If you would like to follow along with this coding example, you can download a copy of the starter express-to-koa.js file in the Chapter 12 folder.

```
https://www.wiley.com/go/programminggithubcopilot
```

Here is how to start the application using the Express.js framework:

```javascript
const express = require('express');

const app = express();
const port = 3000;

app.use((req, res, next) => {
    console.log(`Request URL: ${req.url}`);
    next();
});

app.get('/', (req, res) => {
    res.send('Hello World!');
});

app.listen(port, () => {
    console.log(`Example app listening at http://localhost:${port}`);
});
```

Using Copilot Chat, let's see how you can translate this application to Koa.js. Start by opening a window chat and request Copilot to convert the application to use Koa.js (see Figure 12.14).

Here is the request to Copilot:

```
Convert application to use Koa.js #editor
```

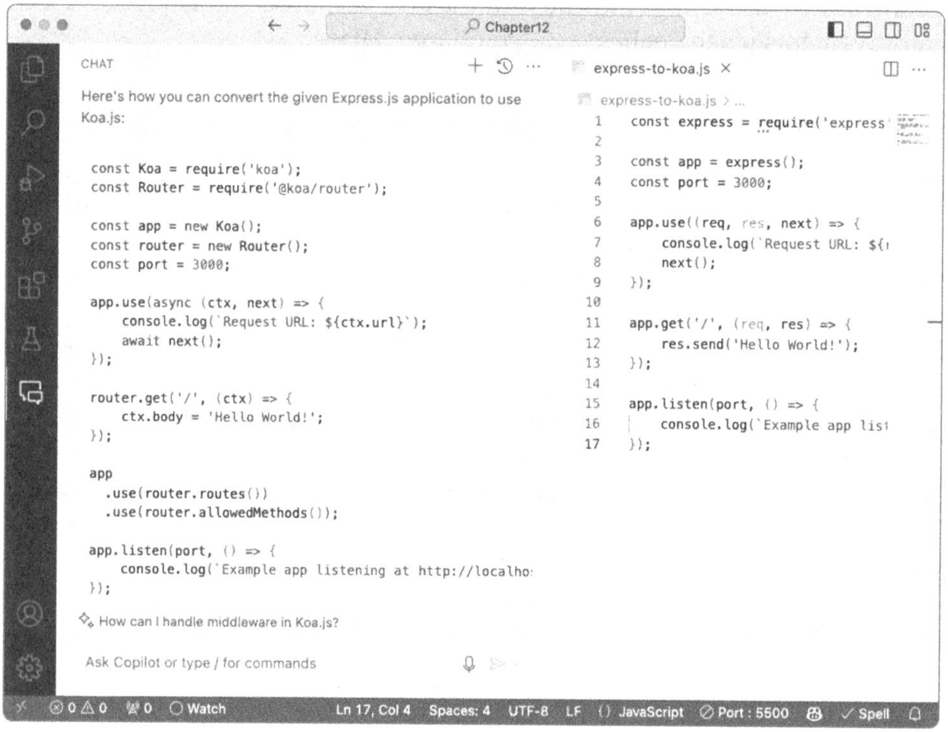

**Figure 12.14:** Copilot response on how to convert application to use Koa.js

From here, you can take this application code using Koa.js and apply it to your editor. There are several differences here from the use of a Koa router library to async functions. With Copilot, you can remove the burden of making each individual edit to your application code when migrating frameworks as you have seen here.

Here is the completed Node.js application using Koa.js:

```
const Koa = require('koa');
const Router = require('@koa/router');

const app = new Koa();
const router = new Router();
const port = 3000;
```

```
app.use(async (ctx, next) => {
    console.log(`Request URL: ${ctx.url}`);
    await next();
});

router.get('/', (ctx) => {
    ctx.body = 'Hello World!';
});

app
  .use(router.routes())
  .use(router.allowedMethods());

app.listen(port, () => {
    console.log(`Example app listening at http://localhost:${port}`);
});
```

# Converting Object-Oriented Languages

Converting from one language to another can arise from a variety of situations. Sometimes language support will diminish over time, and companies supporting them will shift focus to a new language and framework stack that developers need to migrate to so that they can continue to receive the latest feature updates and security fixes.

In this section, you will see how well Copilot can assist in the translation from one language to another.

## Objective-C to Swift

For years, the preferred language to create macOS and iOS applications was Objective-C. While this language allowed for a great ecosystem of applications to be developed and tooling to be created, modernization efforts for the Apple ecosystem resulted in the creation of the Swift programming language. As a result, the developer community began to have more and more reasons to migrate to Swift because of its continued feature enhancements and first-class support.

Let's look at an example of an Objective-C class that Copilot can assist in translating to Swift.

If you would like to follow along with this coding example, you can download a copy of the starter `Person.m` file in the Chapter 12 folder.

```
https://www.wiley.com/go/programminggithubcopilot
```

Here is the starting class file written in Objective-C:

```objc
#import <Foundation/Foundation.h>

@interface Person : NSObject

@property (nonatomic, strong) NSString *firstName;
@property (nonatomic, strong) NSString *lastName;

- (instancetype)initWithFirstName:(NSString *)firstName
lastName:(NSString *)lastName;
- (void)printFullName;

@end

@implementation Person

- (instancetype)initWithFirstName:(NSString *)firstName
lastName:(NSString *)lastName {
    self = [super init];
    if (self) {
        _firstName = firstName;
        _lastName = lastName;
    }
    return self;
}

- (void)printFullName {
    NSLog(@"%@ %@", self.firstName, self.lastName);
}

@end
```

In this example, you will see how Copilot can translate code using inline comments to drive code completion for the translation task. This may not be the ideal method for translating a class file, but I wanted to showcase another option if you are in an IDE without chat support but would still like to translate a class file.

In an editor window, add the following two blank lines after the Objective-C Person object and input a comment like the following:

```
// Convert the above code to Swift
```

After inputting that comment, you can proceed to the next line; in my case Copilot suggests a name for the `Person.swift` file we want to create. After adding a new line after that, you should get an import for the Foundation library. Add that line, and add two more blank lines after the import. This should trigger Copilot to suggest a completion for the `Person` class (see Figure 12.15).

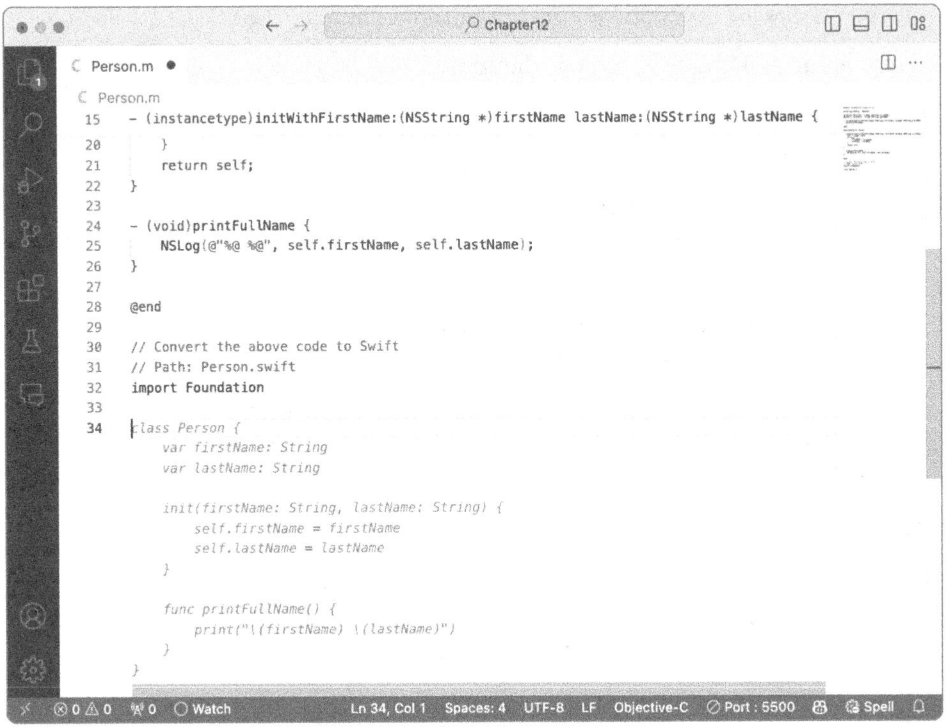

**Figure 12.15:** Copilot code suggestion for person object in Swift

# Migrating Databases

Migrating databases can be a huge effort. Although there are great tools to assist in large portions of migrations, there are still some manual tasks that Copilot can assist with. Whether you are moving from MySQL, PostgreSQL, SQL Server, or Oracle Database, you can lean on your pair-programming assistant GitHub Copilot to help you along the way.

In this section, you will learn how Copilot can assist with general database conversion tasks.

## SQL Server to PostgreSQL

When migrating to a new database, there are many conversion options. In the case of migrating to PostgreSQL, the `pgloader` CLI tool assists in many of the migration tasks required like table schemas, data imports, and basic indexing. In this basic example, you will see how Copilot can translate the schema, insert statements, and stored procedures from SQL Server to PostgreSQL.

If you would like to follow along with this coding example, you can download a copy of the starter `sql-server.sql` file in the Chapter 12 folder.

```
https://www.wiley.com/go/programminggithubcopilot
```

Here is the starting SQL Server database:

```
-- SQL Server
CREATE TABLE Employees (
    ID INT IDENTITY(1,1) PRIMARY KEY,
    FirstName NVARCHAR(50),
    LastName NVARCHAR(50)
);

INSERT INTO Employees (FirstName, LastName)
VALUES ('John', 'Doe'), ('Jane', 'Doe');

SELECT TOP(1) FirstName + ' ' + LastName AS FullName
FROM Employees
ORDER BY ID;

CREATE PROCEDURE GetFullName @ID INT AS
BEGIN
    SELECT FirstName + ' ' + LastName AS FullName
    FROM Employees
    WHERE ID = @ID;
END;

EXEC GetFullName 1;
```

Using Copilot Chat, you can make quick work of a small, targeted conversion. With the SQL Server database file open, request that Copilot convert to PostgreSQL.

```
Convert from SQL Server to PostgreSQL
```

After sending this request to Copilot, you should get a resulting PostgreSQL file that you can use as a baseline to your migration efforts (see Figure 12.16).

As mentioned, there are great tools that can support large migration efforts, but sometimes the ease of use with Copilot for targeted migrations can be a much better option. Also, a tool like `pgloader` does not migrate SQL Server stored procedures to PostgreSQL functions. This is a great area to get Copilot to assist and quickly migrate those files to your new database.

## Transitioning CI/CD Platforms

Transitioning between continuous integration/continuous delivery (CI/CD) platforms in software development is an important strategic decision that can significantly impact the efficiency, scalability, and reliability of the software development process.

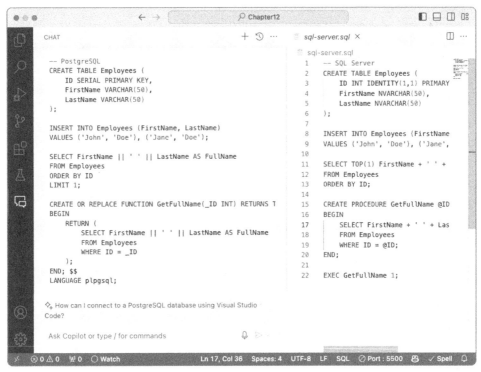

**Figure 12.16:** Copilot response for SQL Server to PostgreSQL migration

When transitioning to a new CI/CD platform, the files that define CI/CD pipelines are invaluable assets. These files, typically scripted in YAML or JSON, contain detailed descriptions of the build, test, and deployment processes that software goes through from development to production. Utilizing these files effectively can facilitate a smoother transition to a new platform, and tools like GitHub Copilot can significantly enhance this process by assisting in translating and adapting these infrastructure files to your target CI/CD platform.

In this example, Copilot will be used to translate the .yaml file for an Azure DevOps pipeline to GitHub Actions. The example will showcase a Copilot Chat conversation that references an Azure DevOps pipeline file for context.

If you would like to follow along with this coding example, you can download a copy of the starter ado.yaml file in the Chapter 12 folder.

```
https://www.wiley.com/go/programminggithubcopilot
```

Here is the chat request to Copilot to convert an Azure DevOps pipeline file to GitHub Actions:

```
Convert this Azure DevOps pipeline file to GitHub Actions:

trigger:
- master
```

```
pool:
  vmImage: 'windows-latest'

variables:
  solution: '**/*.sln'
  buildPlatform: 'Any CPU'
  buildConfiguration: 'Release'

steps:
- task: NuGetToolInstaller@1

- task: NuGetCommand@2
  inputs:
    restoreSolution: '$(solution)'

- task: VSBuild@1
  inputs:
    solution: '$(solution)'
    msbuildArgs: '/p:DeployOnBuild=true /p:WebPublishMethod=Package
/p:PackageAsSingleFile=true /p:SkipInvalidConfigurations=true
/p:DesktopBuildPackageLocation="$(build.artifactStagingDirectory)\
WebApp.zip"
/p:DeployIisAppPath="Default Web Site"'
    platform: '$(buildPlatform)'
    configuration: '$(buildConfiguration)'

- task: VSTest@2
  inputs:
    platform: '$(buildPlatform)'
    configuration: '$(buildConfiguration)'

- task: PublishBuildArtifacts@1

- task: AzureRmWebAppDeployment@4
  inputs:
    ConnectionType: 'AzureRM'
    azureSubscription: 'Your Azure Subscription'
    appType: 'webApp'
    WebAppName: 'Your Web App Name'
    packageForLinux: '$(build.artifactStagingDirectory)/**/*.zip'
```

After sending this request to Copilot, you should get a result that details the resulting GitHub Actions workflow file and indicates any manual updates that might be needed due to different build dependencies (see Figure 12.17).

As you can see from this example, both platforms allow .yaml file formats, but the structure and keywords are different. Azure DevOps Pipelines use a more linear structure, while GitHub Actions use a more nested structure. GitHub Actions also make extensive use of "actions," which are reusable pieces of code.

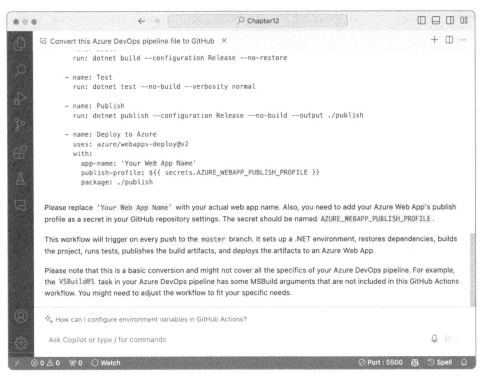

**Figure 12.17:** Copilot response for Azure DevOps pipeline file to GitHub Actions

# Modernizing Legacy Systems

Legacy systems can be a liability for businesses due to increased vulnerability to security threats, maintenance challenges, and the inability to adapt to evolving business needs. Transitioning from these outdated systems to newer technologies can significantly decrease risk exposure, enhance business agility, and maintain competitiveness. This modernization enables organizations to innovate more effectively and meet changing customer demands.

In this section, you will learn how Copilot can assist in modernizing legacy systems using languages such as COBAL or Fortran. Using Copilot to modernize legacy applications can significantly reduce the effort it would take to do a legacy system modernization with traditional tooling.

## Modernizing a COBAL Program

In this section, you will see how Copilot can assist in modernizing a legacy COBAL program. The example program connects to a DB2 database, declares a cursor for a SELECT statement that retrieves data from the CUSTOMERS table, and then opens the cursor. It fetches rows from the cursor until there are no more rows to fetch, displaying the ID, name, and balance for each row. When it's done, it closes the cursor and disconnects from the database.

If you would like to follow along with this coding example, you can download a copy of the starter `CustomerBalanceDisplay.cob` file in the Chapter 12 folder.

https://www.wiley.com/go/programminggithubcopilot

Here is the COBAL program to be modernized:

```
IDENTIFICATION DIVISION.
PROGRAM-ID. CustomerBalanceDisplay.

DATA DIVISION.
WORKING-STORAGE SECTION.
01  WS-ID         PIC 9(5).
01  WS-NAME       PIC X(20).
01  WS-BALANCE    PIC 9(5)V99.
01  WS-EOF        PIC X VALUE 'N'.

EXEC SQL INCLUDE SQLCA END-EXEC.

PROCEDURE DIVISION.
Begin.
    EXEC SQL
        CONNECT TO DB2
    END-EXEC.

    EXEC SQL
        DECLARE C1 CURSOR FOR
            SELECT ID, NAME, BALANCE
            FROM CUSTOMERS
    END-EXEC.

    EXEC SQL
        OPEN C1
    END-EXEC.

    PERFORM UNTIL WS-EOF = 'Y'
        EXEC SQL
            FETCH C1 INTO :WS-ID, :WS-NAME, :WS-BALANCE
        END-EXEC
        IF SQLCODE NOT = 0
            MOVE 'Y' TO WS-EOF
        ELSE
            DISPLAY WS-ID " " WS-NAME " " WS-BALANCE
        END-IF
    END-PERFORM.

    EXEC SQL
        CLOSE C1
```

```
    END-EXEC.

    EXEC SQL
        DISCONNECT DB2
    END-EXEC.

    STOP RUN.
```

Let's see how Copilot can convert this legacy program to a C# equivalent. Start by opening VS Code with the `CustomerBalanceDisplay.cob` file opened. After having that file open, start a new chat with Copilot and send a request like the following:

```
Convert this COBAL program to C#. #file:CustomerBalanceDisplay.cob
```

After sending this request, you should get a result from Copilot that matches something like the following program file:

```
using System;
using System.Data;
using IBM.Data.DB2;

namespace DB2Example
{
    class Program
    {
        static void Main(string[] args)
        {
            string connectionString = "your_connection_string_here"; //
replace with your DB2 connection string

            using (DB2Connection connection = new
DB2Connection(connectionString))
            {
                connection.Open();

                using (DB2Command command = new DB2Command("SELECT ID,
NAME, BALANCE FROM CUSTOMERS", connection))
                {
                    using (DB2DataReader reader = command.Execute
Reader())
                    {
                        while (reader.Read())
                        {
                            int id = reader.GetInt32(0);
                            string name = reader.GetString(1);
                            decimal balance = reader.GetDecimal(2);

                            Console.WriteLine($"{id} {name} {balance}");
                        }
```

```
                    }
                }

            connection.Close();
            }
        }
    }
}
```

In this program, you can see that Copilot did a great job preserving the functionality of the legacy COBAL application while modernizing the codebase to C#. Because no additional instructions were given, Copilot determined we most likely wanted to preserve the DB2 database connection. In some cases, you might want to migrate to a new database technology as well. In this next example, you will see how Copilot can also implement a new database technology and migrate the code functionality all at the same time.

Start this by sending a new request to Copilot like the following:

```
Convert this COBAL program to C#. Use SQL Server and Entity Framework.
#file:CustomerBalanceDisplay.cob
```

With this request, you are specifying the original request to convert the program to C#. In addition, you can layer on additional instructions to use SQL Server and the Entity Framework. It is important not to try to get Copilot to do conflicting tasks or overload your requests. In this example, it works out well to convert the database connection code and program code simultaneously. Using this request, you should get a result that describes the Entity Framework class and context files and an updated `CustomerBalanceDisplay` program file (see Figure 12.18).

In addition to the instructions and Entity Framework class files, Copilot should respond with the updated program class, resulting in something like this:

```
public class Program
{
    public static void Main(string[] args)
    {
        using (var context = new CustomerContext())
        {
            var customers = context.Customers.ToList();

            foreach (var customer in customers)
            {
                Console.WriteLine($"{customer.Id} {customer.Name}
{customer.Balance}");
            }
        }
    }
}
```

**Figure 12.18:** Copilot response for converting COBAL program and DB2 to SQL Server

With the help of Copilot, this program becomes more maintainable and easier to read. Using the Entity Framework has reduced the program code significantly. Using this framework also gives type safety when working with database objects enhancing the stability of the program.

## Conclusion

In this chapter, you explored the transformative capabilities of Copilot in facilitating seamless transitions across a multitude of technical landscapes. When converting languages, frameworks, libraries, databases, or CI/CD pipelines, Copilot not only accelerates the adoption of new technologies but also enhances the development workflow with unparalleled speed and accuracy. Through various examples, you saw how Copilot can be leveraged to do the following:

- Translate natural languages into programming languages, simplifying the bridge between concept and implementation.
- Convert JavaScript components, making the shift between different JavaScript frameworks less daunting.

- Simplify CSS, aiding in faster design production and conversion between CSS formats, thus streamlining front-end development tasks.

- Enhance nontyped languages with types, such as converting JavaScript to TypeScript, to improve code reliability and maintainability.

- Facilitate the transition between different frameworks and libraries, whether they are object-oriented or function-based, ensuring that applications remain robust and up to date.

- Assist in database migrations and general database conversion tasks, supporting the back-end aspect of development projects.

- Simplify the transition between different CI/CD platforms, as demonstrated by converting Azure DevOps pipeline files to GitHub Actions, ensuring that integration and deployment processes remain efficient.

- Modernize legacy systems like COBAL programs to current languages and frameworks like C# and Entity Framework to facilitate more maintainable, readable, and resilient applications.

The diverse examples provided illustrate Copilot's role as an indispensable tool in modern software development, enabling developers to navigate the complexity of technological evolution with ease. As we move forward, the ability of Copilot to assist in translating and transitioning across technologies will undoubtedly continue to be a game-changer, fostering innovation and efficiency in the development process.

## Reference

[1]  Polars, 2024. "Updated TPC-H benchmark results," `https://pola.rs/posts/benchmarks`

# Key Insights and Advanced Use Cases for GitHub Copilot

## In This Part

# Considering Responsible AI with GitHub Copilot

In this chapter, you will learn about responsible AI, what AI regulations are being established by governments, how GitHub Copilot implements responsible AI principles, and what you should consider when adopting AI-powered tools like GitHub Copilot.

- Introducing Responsible AI
- Examining How GitHub Copilot Implements Responsible AI
- Programming with AI Responsibly

## Introducing Responsible AI

Responsible artificial intelligence (responsible AI) refers to the practice of creating, evaluating, and implementing AI technologies in a manner that is safe, reliable, and aligned with ethical principles.

In recent years, a plethora of AI tools have emerged. With this surge in AI-powered tools and mass adoption of AI tooling at a global scale, responsible AI has never been more important.

The concept of AI has been around since the 1950s, but only recently has the convergence of hardware, software, and data combined to produce the rapid advancements seen today with tools like GitHub Copilot. This convergence of technological advancements to produce such powerful tools has amplified the need for responsible AI standards.

The following sections, which examine how GitHub Copilot implements responsible AI, will detail these responsible AI standards—which consist of fairness, reliability and safety, privacy and security, inclusiveness, transparency, and accountability.

## Responsible AI Regulation

The European Union AI Act is setting the stage globally for the adoption of responsible AI practices [1]. Once in force, the act will impact companies building, selling, and marketing AI in the EU. Due to the Brussels effect, a term that is used to describe an incentive for companies to adhere to regulatory standards in a particular market, I predict that other countries will essentially copy and paste the act for their own use. The act focuses on establishing an AI risk threat level that declares banned applications and sets requirements for high-risk systems, as well as establishing transparency requirements and implementing measures to support innovation while protecting citizens of the EU. Fines for violations of the EU AI Act can be as high as 7% of a company's global revenue, making this not only the first but the most serious regulation on AI.

In the United States, the White House has established a blueprint for an AI Bill of Rights, a nonbinding set of responsible AI considerations meant to generate conversation around establishing protections for U.S. citizens and residents in the same way the Constitutional Bill of Rights establishes protections [2]. President Biden also signed an AI Executive Order, which establishes requirements for the safe implementation and monitoring of AI systems in the U.S. federal government. This Executive Order was the first government-wide establishment of responsible AI requirements by a major global power.

Together, these major pieces of regulation, while incomplete and noncomprehensive, highlight that global leaders are seeing the importance of clear guidance and regulations that ensure their citizens are protected and benefit positively from the advancements in AI.

## Examining How Copilot Implements Responsible AI

As a company in the Microsoft ecosystem, GitHub has reaped the benefits of Microsoft's responsible AI leadership and processes, which have been established to ensure that Microsoft and its subsidiaries build, deploy, and use AI responsibly. Microsoft has established responsible AI principles across six categories: fairness, reliability and safety, privacy and security, inclusiveness, transparency, and accountability [3].

The GitHub Copilot Trust Center is a great resource that provides videos, FAQs, and resources specific to GitHub Copilot, which can help you understand some important information that individuals and organizations should consider when adopting GitHub Copilot into their development workflow [4].

In this section, you will learn how GitHub's dedication to responsible AI shows up across the six Microsoft responsible AI principles. The following examples do not represent an exhaustive list of GitHub's implementations of responsible AI considerations into the product but provide insight into some of the intentional responsible AI decisions made in the development of the product.

## Fairness

The idea behind the fairness principle is that "AI systems should treat all people fairly" [6]. One example of fairness considered by the GitHub Copilot team is ensuring that the tool operates in languages other than English. In developing the tool, the GitHub team ensured that natural language support was established for a large set of languages. The default language can be adjusted in the extension settings for Copilot (see Figure 13.1).

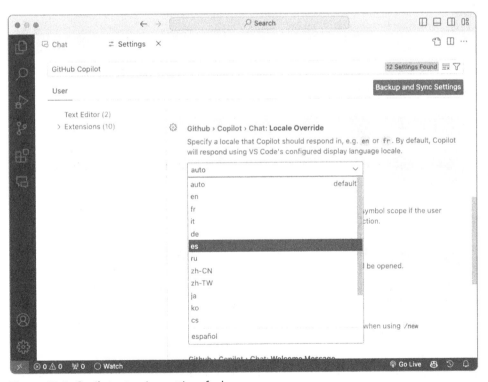

**Figure 13.1:** Copilot extension settings for language

In Figure 13.2, you can see how, when setting a default response language for Copilot, you will receive responses specific to the locale.

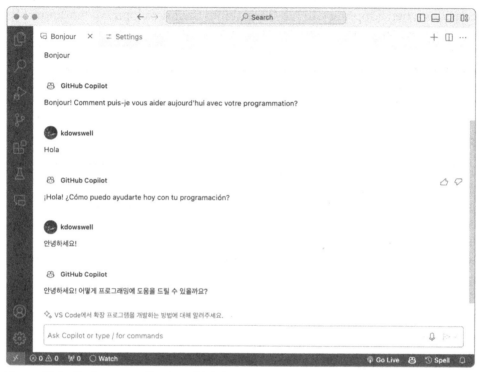

**Figure 13.2:** Copilot responding in multiple languages

In addition to language support, GitHub Copilot prioritizes support for accessibility. By intentionally supporting keyboard-only and screen reader users, GitHub Copilot empowers people with disabilities to contribute effectively to their projects.

## Reliability and Safety

Microsoft believes that "All AI systems should perform reliably and safely" [6]. Building trust in AI systems requires the systems to function reliably, safely, and consistently. They must perform as intended, safely manage unexpected conditions, and be resilient to malicious requests.

*Red teaming* is the practice of adopting an adversarial approach to identify vulnerabilities in the reliability and safety of a software system. Companies hire teams with the express purpose of identifying and exploiting vulnerabilities in the product. This allows the product team to shore up the vulnerabilities before the product, or updates to the product, are released. GitHub performs extensive red teaming to ensure Copilot can respond safely when provided with malicious requests.

In addition to red teaming, GitHub has an extensive bug bounty program that allows for talented security researchers to submit bugs they find within the GitHub services [5].

An example of this built-in protection is when a user might request detailed information on how to perform a cross-site scripting attack. Copilot will resist providing information on this topic (see Figure 13.3).

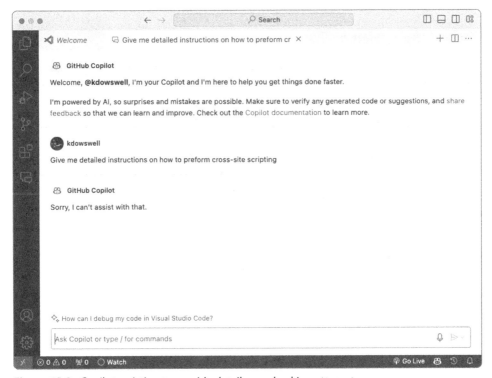

**Figure 13.3:** Copilot resisting to provide details on a hacking attempt

## Privacy and Security

Privacy and security are absolutely critical, especially in the digital age when so much information is available, or can be made available, to AI systems. This responsible AI principle establishes that "AI systems should be secure and respect privacy. [6].

### *Data Protection*

GitHub Copilot is compliant with the General Data Protection Regulation (GDPR). GDPR is Europe's data privacy and security law. This regulation works to protect consumer data and enforce fines on companies that do not have their data privacy and security standards in place.

For business and enterprise users, data used for GitHub Copilot code suggestions and chat responses are not stored in persisted storage. Instead, this data is kept in memory only for the duration of the API request. Once that is completed, the request data is cleared. Also, to further ensure your session data is protected, GitHub does not log user request data.

For individual plan users, prompts and suggestions are retained by default unless you disable code snippet collection in your settings.

### Vulnerability Prevention System

GitHub Copilot employs a vulnerability prevention system that inspects generated code suggestions for security vulnerabilities before returning the suggestion to you. This prevention mechanism checks common security vulnerabilities in the suggestions such as hard-coded credentials, SQL injections, and path injections.

To see this in action, in this request to Copilot to create a GitHub workflow file to release a static website to AWS S3, you will get a result with GitHub repository secrets instead of returning hard-coded example strings (see Figure 13.4).

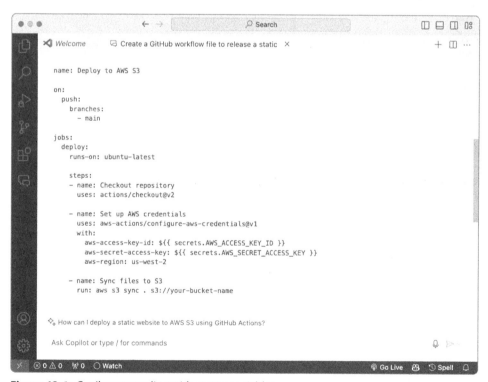

**Figure 13.4:** Copilot responding with secrets variables

In addition to the vulnerability prevention system, GitHub filters out things like personal identifiable information (PII) before it reaches the models. This filtering process assists in the prevention of sensitive data exposure from the model training process.

## Inclusiveness

The principle of inclusiveness establishes the idea that "AI systems should empower everyone and engage people" [6]. One way that GitHub fosters inclusiveness is by providing several options to obtain a license to GitHub Copilot, which works to make the product available for everyone. For students and maintainers of popular open-source projects, Copilot can be completely free. For individuals, the current price is $10 per month or $100 per year. And there are also multiple options for organizations to purchase the plan that fits their needs.

Another example of inclusiveness is that GitHub Copilot does not operate on its own in the background while the programmer works. The tool was never intended to replace programmers or make them obsolete. It partners *with* the programmer, which keeps them included in the work being done. This is great for the labor market, but it also lends to the principle of accountability, which I'll dive into in a moment.

## Transparency

The idea of the principle of transparency is that "AI systems should be understandable." To illustrate this principle, you can ask GitHub Copilot Chat to explain the code that it has written for you (see Figure 13.5). This is an example of transparency in that it allows the user to understand what's being offered in terms of a code suggestion.

Another way you can see this principle show up in practice is in the documentation and explanation of how the product works. GitHub did not create GitHub Copilot to operate in a black box. It was created in a way that lends to transparency and allows users to understand how the product is working, how it is trained, the data it leverages, and the code it produces.

## Accountability

The accountability principle posits that *"People* should be accountable for AI systems." While every principle is important, this is perhaps the most critical. Because of the pace of AI development and the very real impact AI can have—positively and negatively—on human lives, it could be easy to get into a loop of blaming AI for being unsafe, providing unfair responses, or sharing biased views and perspectives.

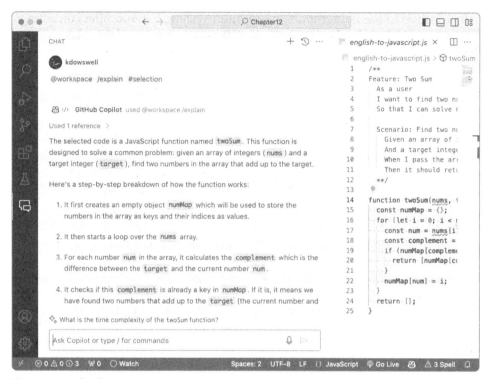

**Figure 13.5:** Copilot `explain` command results

GitHub imbues this principle at multiple points in the process, from development to use and output.

In the development process, GitHub product teams partner with the Microsoft Office to Responsible AI to move the product through the established responsible AI processes. This keeps humans from multiple organizations and perspectives engaged in the process. Should there be a responsible AI challenge with the product, there is accountability at the GitHub and Microsoft levels.

For product use and output, the user is kept in the loop throughout the duration of the process.

An important concept to highlight here is that you are responsible for accepting and reviewing the code and information provided by GitHub Copilot. GitHub Copilot will never "accept" code of its own volition. The concept of "human-in-the-loop" is a core implementation detail in numerous Copilot features. It provides a level of accountability at the user level and drives accountability at varying levels of AI use by requiring active human engagement. As shown in Figure 13.6, when accepting inline code changes, you need to accept or discard the result. This human-in-the-loop activity is vital to ensure safety and adherence to the principles of your software development practice.

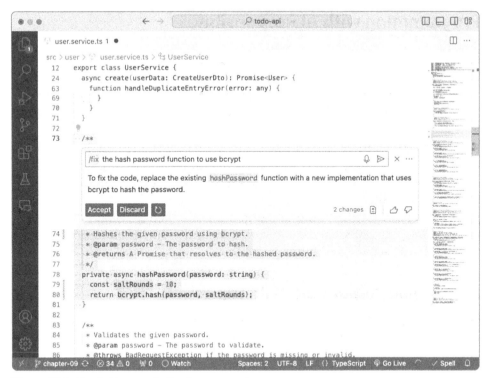

**Figure 13.6:** Copilot human-in-the-loop example

In addition to checking for accuracy, inspecting the generated code for security vulnerabilities is always encouraged. Copilot, like any other programmer, can make mistakes, and you should do your best to validate generated code for security compliance.

Another example of accountability with GitHub Copilot is the Copilot Copyright Commitment from Microsoft. With this commitment, Microsoft has pledged support for business and enterprise Copilot customers [7]. The GitHub Copilot product-specific terms in the "Defense of Third Party Claims" section details the protections offered under this agreement [8].

## Further Research

For full details on these responsible AI principles, please visit the Microsoft Responsible AI website.

```
https://www.microsoft.com/ai/responsible-ai
```

For more details on how GitHub Copilot works and information about responsible AI related to the product, visit the GitHub Copilot Trust Center.

```
https://resources.github.com/copilot-trust-center
```

## Programming with AI Responsibly

When you are programming with AI-powered tooling like GitHub Copilot, it is important to consider the positive impacts as well as the challenges.

There are numerous benefits to using GitHub Copilot. These benefits include increased productivity, enhanced code quality, and improved decision-making, as well as increased developer happiness [9].

While the benefits are awesome, it's important to keep in mind the challenges of adopting AI tooling. Becoming overly reliant on it, injecting negative bias, or neglecting security concerns for the sake of development productivity can set you up for failure.

Individual code contributors and organizations need to balance the benefits of AI tooling with potential risks, ensuring that software development practices remain ethical, secure, and human-centric.

### Researching Responsible AI Principles

When evaluating AI tools, it is important that you do your research to ensure that you are adopting a tool that has a foundation of fairness, safety, inclusiveness, transparency, and accountability.

While doing research to understand how adopting AI tooling like GitHub Copilot will affect you and your organization, know that with technology like generative AI, the landscape is fast moving and ever evolving as new information and advancements are made. So, don't be discouraged if you don't have all the answers to the impacts of these tools, but be sure to understand the available information.

To help you in this journey of discovery, the GitHub Copilot Trust Center is a great resource for Copilot-specific inquiries into these questions.

In addition to understanding the tool and how it is created, I challenge you to also think about what principles you can adopt to solidify the way in which you infuse and leverage AI tools in your workflow. Maybe one of the principles previously discussed resonates with you. Make sure you use the principles you identify as a north star and stay true to that as you navigate this exciting and fast-paced world of AI advancements.

## Conclusion

This chapter provided a high-level exploration of responsible AI, detailing the regulations set forth by governments, the application of responsible AI principles in GitHub Copilot, and considerations for adopting AI-powered tools like GitHub Copilot. You should now have a good starting point to understand and engage with AI technologies ethically and effectively.

# References

[1] EU Artificial Intelligence Act, 2024. "The EU Artificial Intelligence Act," `https://artificialintelligenceact.eu`

[2] The White House, 2023. "Blueprint for an AI Bill of Rights," `https://www.whitehouse.gov/ostp/ai-bill-of-rights`

[3] Microsoft AI, 2024. "Principles and Approach," `https://www.microsoft.com/ai/principles-and-approach`

[4] GitHub, 2024. "GitHub Copilot Trust Center," `https://resources.github.com/copilot-trust-center`

[5] GitHub, 2023. "Nine years of the GitHub Security Bug Bounty program," `https://github.blog/2023-08-14-nine-years-of-the-github-security-bug-bounty-program`

[6] Microsoft AI, 2024. "Empowering responsible AI practices," `https://www.microsoft.com/ai/responsible-ai`

[7] Microsoft, 2023. "Microsoft announces new Copilot Copyright Commitment for customers," `https://blogs.microsoft.com/on-the-issues/2023/09/07/copilot-copyright-commitment-ai-legal-concerns`

[8] GitHub, 2024. "GitHub Copilot Product Specific Terms," `https://github.com/customer-terms/github-copilot-product-specific-terms`

[9] E. Kalliamvakou, 2022. "Research: quantifying GitHub Copilot's impact on developer productivity and happiness," `https://github.blog/2022-09-07-research-quantifying-github-copilots-impact-on-developer-productivity-and-happiness`

# Augmenting the Software Development Life Cycle with GitHub Copilot

In this chapter, we will explore the details of the software development life cycle (SDLC) and how GitHub Copilot can help you each step of the way. We will assess the current adoption statistics of AI tooling in the SDLC and future predictions. Additionally, we will define the levels of AI integration in the SDLC. Finally, this chapter will address potential concerns with ever-increasing AI adoption in software development workflows and what impacts adoption might have on job stability and work dynamics.

- Introducing the SDLC
- Assessing the Adoption of AI in the SDLC
- Detailing Levels of AI Integration in the SDLC
- Showcasing GitHub Copilot in the SDLC
- Addressing Concerns: AI Adoption and the Future of Work

## Introducing the SDLC

The SDLC is a systematic process aimed at producing high-quality software in a cost-efficient manner. It guides development teams through the various phases of software development. Generally, this process consists of the following steps: requirements gathering, system design, testing, deployment, and maintenance (see Figure 14.1) [1].

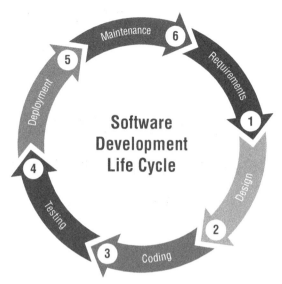

**Figure 14.1:** Adoption of AI in the SDLC

The primary goal of the SDLC is to facilitate the creation of successful software releases. Recognizing the complexities of software development, teams use the SDLC's structured methodology to build, test, and deliver software that is ready for production, ensuring the final product is robust and reliable. Let's detail the activities of each of these phases and how GitHub Copilot can assist in each step of the SDLC.

## Requirements

In the Requirements phase, the primary activities involve gathering and defining requirements, documenting specifications, and prioritizing features. GitHub Copilot can significantly enhance this stage by suggesting documentation templates, assisting in expanding initial requirement needs into features, brainstorming requirements details, and even writing requirement specifications based on your guidance.

## Design

During the Design phase, activities such as creating architectural diagrams, designing user interfaces, and planning system interactions are crucial. GitHub Copilot assists here by generating boilerplate code for design patterns, offering coding alternatives, and suggesting improvements or best practices based on current design trends.

## Coding

The Coding phase is where GitHub Copilot truly excels, helping you write code, review code, and integrate modules. It provides real-time code suggestions, completes lines or blocks of code, and helps you write more efficient, error-free code quickly.

## Testing

In the Testing phase, writing test cases, conducting various types of tests, including unit, integration, and system tests, debugging, and validating are key activities. GitHub Copilot aids by suggesting and generating test cases, helping identify potential edge cases, and providing code for automated testing frameworks to enhance the robustness and coverage of tests.

## Deployment

The Deployment phase involves configuring servers, deploying code to production, and monitoring the deployment process. GitHub Copilot offers guidance on deployment scripts, suggests best practices for CI/CD pipelines, and helps troubleshoot deployment issues by providing relevant code snippets and configurations.

## Maintenance

During the Maintenance phase, activities such as bug fixing, upgrading systems, and optimizing performance are prevalent. GitHub Copilot helps by quickly identifying bugs with suggested potential fixes, offering performance optimization techniques, and assisting in updating documentation or comments within the code to maintain its relevance and readability over time.

# Assessing the Adoption of AI in the SDLC

In recent years, with the rapid advancements of AI-powered development tooling like GitHub Copilot, the development community has been testing the waters to determine how they can incorporate AI into their SDLC.

Gartner forecasts a significant increase in the adoption of machine learning (ML)–powered coding tools among enterprise software engineers, projecting that by 2027, 50% will use these technologies—a substantial rise from the current figure of less than 5% [2]. This represents a 120% change rate for the next three years in adoption rates.

In a separate study conducted by GitHub and Wakefield Research, a survey of 500 enterprise developers working in the United States found that a vast majority (92%) of developers are utilizing AI coding tools for tasks related to their jobs as well as for personal projects [3].

The Gartner and GitHub/Wakefield current usage statistics are very different. GitHub/Wakefield Research resulted in a higher percentage due to the small number of developers surveyed (500) and the hyper-focus on the enterprise developer population. Even though these studies differ in approach and results, both indicate high interest and growth in the use of AI tooling in the SDLC. Gartner refers to this as *AI-augmented software engineering* (AIASE) [2].

As you can see, with surveys such as the one conducted by GitHub and Wakefield Research, the adoption of AI in the SDLC is progressing quickly. Although usage is high in some sectors, the overall market is ripe for growth as tools like GitHub Copilot continue to advance in capabilities and companies begin to adopt AI tooling deeper within their development workflows. Today, we may be within an early adopters phase (see Figure 14.2). But as we progress into the next years, expect AI tooling to be an essential part of software development.

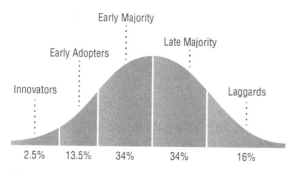

**Figure 14.2:** Adoption of AI in the SDLC

## Detailing Levels of AI Integration in the SDLC

In this section, you will learn the levels of AI integration in the SDLC, starting from level 0 with nonexistent processes in place to level 5, where your organization is optimizing the implementation of AI tooling. Using these levels, you can evaluate the maturity of AI integration into your SDLC.

With the knowledge of where you are within these levels, you can navigate ways to level up your development life cycle with more advanced implementations of AI tooling. Making these advancements will amplify competitive advantages and empower development teams with the knowledge and tools, like GitHub Copilot, that they need to succeed with AI in their development workflow.

This section draws inspiration from capability maturity model integration (CMMI). CMMI is a collection of global best practices designed to enhance business performance by developing and benchmarking essential capabilities [4].

The levels of integration described in this section are nonexistent (0), initial (1), managed (2), defined (3), quantitatively managed (4), and optimizing (5), as shown in Figure 14.3.

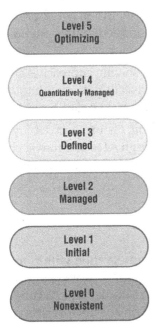

**Figure 14.3:** Levels of adoption of AI in the SDLC

## Level 0: Nonexistent

At level 0, AI integration in the SDLC is virtually absent. This stage is characterized by a complete lack of AI tools and processes within the development framework. Organizations at this level rely solely on traditional software development practices, without the augmentation of AI capabilities.

At this level, there is high potential for misuse of AI tools by engineering teams due to lack of clarity from the organization on proper use and best practices. This lack of clarity and misuse can lead to organizational risk.

As discussed in the previous section, developers surveyed directly are adopting AI tooling at a high rate while organizations are not yet identifying their adoption rates at as high a rate [2, 3]. This indicates that there is most likely a large number of organizations with no guidance on AI integration in the SDLC while their engineering teams are seeking out AI tooling on their own.

### Capabilities Demonstrated

These are the capabilities:

**Traditional Development Approaches**   Development processes are manual and follow conventional methodologies without the support of AI-driven insights, automation, or efficiency enhancements.

**Limited Awareness or Understanding**   There may be little to no organizational awareness of the potential benefits that AI integration could bring to the software development process. This lack of understanding extends to both the managerial level and the development team.

**Reactive Problem-Solving**   Without AI tools, problem-solving approaches are reactive rather than proactive. Issues are addressed as they arise, without the predictive capabilities or data-driven insights that AI could provide.

**No AI-Driven Optimization**   Processes such as coding, testing, and deployment lack optimization that could be achieved through AI techniques such as machine learning models, natural language processing, and automated testing frameworks.

## Level 1: Initial

At level 1, organizations begin their journey toward AI integration within the SDLC by exploring and tentatively adopting AI tools and methodologies. This level is characterized by initial efforts to understand and implement AI capabilities in a limited, experimental fashion, often focused on specific projects or parts of the SDLC.

### Capabilities Demonstrated

These are the capabilities:

**Basic AI Tool Experimentation**   Teams start to experiment with basic AI tools, such as code completers, simple bug detection algorithms, or automated code reviewers, to gain familiarity with AI's potential applications in software development.

**Initial Data Analysis Efforts**   There's an emerging effort to use AI for analyzing development data, such as code repositories or bug reports, to extract insights that could inform development decisions, albeit in a rudimentary form.

**Ad Hoc AI Integration in Projects**   AI integration is sporadic and project-specific, lacking a cohesive strategy across the organization. Projects selected for AI integration serve as pilots to understand the benefits and challenges of using AI in development.

**Awareness Building Among Teams**   A growing awareness of AI technologies and their potential impact on software development practices is fostered within the team, often accompanied by initial training sessions or workshops.

## Level 2: Managed

At level 2, organizations have moved beyond the initial exploration of AI in the SDLC to a phase of managed integration, where AI tools and practices are implemented with specific management oversight and integration into selected development processes. This level is marked by a deliberate approach to AI adoption, driven by targeted objectives and monitored through structured management practices.

### Capabilities Demonstrated

These are the capabilities:

**Targeted AI Implementation**   AI technologies are selected and deployed based on their ability to meet specific development goals or solve identified challenges, such as improving code quality, enhancing efficiency, or automating repetitive tasks.

**Process-Specific AI Integration**   AI tools are integrated into stages of the SDLC where they can provide the most significant benefits, with efforts managed and monitored to ensure alignment with development objectives.

**Management of AI Tools and Processes**   The use of AI in software development is actively managed, with clear roles and responsibilities defined for overseeing AI integration, ensuring that AI tools are used effectively and in accordance with organizational policies.

**Performance Measurement**   The impact of AI integration on development processes are systematically measured against predefined metrics, allowing for the evaluation of AI's contribution to development goals and the identification of areas for improvement.

## Level 3: Defined

At level 3, organizations achieve a phase of defined integration in the adoption of AI within the SDLC. This level signifies a mature approach where AI tools and methodologies are not just managed but are fully integrated into standardized processes across the organization. AI practices are documented, and their integration is characterized by consistency, repeatability, and alignment with the organization's strategic goals.

*Capabilities Demonstrated*

These are the capabilities:

**Standardized AI Processes**   The organization has developed and implemented standardized processes for integrating AI tools across various stages of the SDLC. These processes are documented and shared across teams, ensuring consistency in how AI is leveraged for software development.

**Organization-wide AI Integration**   AI integration extends beyond specific projects or teams and is now a standard part of the development process across the organization. This widespread adoption ensures that all projects benefit from AI's efficiency and innovation potential.

**Comprehensive AI Strategy**   There exists a comprehensive strategy for AI adoption that aligns with the organization's overall business and technology objectives. This strategy guides the selection, implementation, and management of AI tools and processes.

**Advanced AI Use Cases**   The organization is implementing advanced AI use cases, such as deep learning for complex problem-solving, AI-driven user experience personalization, and predictive analytics for strategic planning and decision-making.

## Level 4: Quantitatively Managed

At level 4, organizations reach a stage where AI integration within the SDLC is not only standardized across projects but also closely monitored and controlled through quantitative measures. This level is characterized by the systematic use of metrics and data analytics to manage and optimize AI-driven processes, ensuring that AI integration contributes effectively to the organization's strategic goals.

*Capabilities Demonstrated*

These are the capabilities:

**Advanced Metrics and KPIs**   The organization implements a comprehensive set of metrics and key performance indicators (KPIs) to measure the effectiveness, efficiency, and impact of AI tools and methodologies on the software development process.

**Data-Driven Process Improvement**   AI integration processes are subject to continuous analysis and improvement based on quantitative data. This approach allows for the fine-tuning of AI strategies to maximize development outcomes and organizational objectives.

**Predictive Analytics for Process Optimization**   The use of advanced predictive analytics enables the organization to anticipate process bottlenecks, identify opportunities for efficiency gains, and tailor AI tools to specific project needs proactively.

**Performance Benchmarking**   Regular benchmarking against industry standards and best practices ensures that the organization's AI integration remains at the forefront of technological advancement, driving continuous improvement.

## Level 5: Optimizing

At level 5, organizations have achieved the pinnacle of AI integration within the SDLC, where AI-driven processes are not only quantitatively managed but are also continuously optimized for peak performance and innovation. This stage is characterized by the organization's proactive and strategic use of AI to drive ongoing improvements and achieve competitive advantages in software development and product innovation.

### Capabilities Demonstrated

These are the capabilities:

**Continuous Process Optimization**   AI integration processes are continuously analyzed and refined, with adjustments made in real-time based on performance data, emerging trends, and strategic objectives. This includes optimizing AI tools and methodologies to enhance efficiency, quality, and speed across the SDLC.

**Innovative AI Application**   The organization leverages cutting-edge AI technologies and explores innovative applications of AI in software development, such as advanced machine learning models for predictive development analytics, AI-driven user experience design, and intelligent automation of complex development tasks.

**Strategic AI Evolution**   AI strategies and initiatives are dynamically evolved to align with changing business goals, technology advancements, and market demands. The organization remains agile, adapting its AI capabilities to support strategic pivots or capitalize on new opportunities.

**Enterprise-wide AI Culture**   A culture of innovation and continuous improvement pervades the organization, with AI and data-driven decision-making at the core of not just software development but all business practices. Employees across the organization are engaged in leveraging AI for optimization and innovation.

## Summary

This section described the various levels of AI integration within the SDLC, modeled after CMMI. It outlines a progression from level 0 to 5.

This structured approach of evaluation should help you and your organization assess your current AI maturity level and strategize advancements to enhance development effectiveness and competitive positioning.

# Showcasing GitHub Copilot in the SDLC

Now that we have a great understanding of what different levels of AI-augmented software development looks like from an organizational level, in this section, you will learn how GitHub Copilot can be applied to the phases of the SDLC. This example will showcase how GitHub Copilot can be used in a Scrum sprint at the team level. The Scrum framework is going to be used to provide a practical guide to different touchpoints you can have with GitHub Copilot during your SDLC. From ideation to deployment, Copilot has got your back ready to assist you in every phase of the process.

Scrum is a subset of the Agile methodology, characterized by its iterative and incremental approach to software development and project management. Scrum divides project work into small, manageable chunks known as *sprints*, typically lasting two to four weeks. This approach allows teams to quickly adapt to changes, continuously improve processes, and deliver high-quality software that meets user needs more effectively.

In this section, we will inspect the use cases for GitHub Copilot within a Scrum sprint showcasing several different team members and how they can gain insights and support for GitHub Copilot along the way.

While this section is intended to show the broad use of Copilot in a Scrum development cycle, this is not intended to be an exhaustive list of all the applications that can be made with Copilot but rather an expanded view of the programming-focused tasks that have been demonstrated so far in this book.

## Detailing the Example Scenario

To illustrate this scenario, we will use an example of an ecotech-focused startup dedicated to bringing sustainability into everyday living through smart technology. Their newest offering, FreshFridge, is an eco-friendly smart refrigerator designed to minimize food waste and promote sustainable eating habits. FreshFridge uses advanced sensors and AI to monitor food inventory, track expiration dates, and suggest recipes based on available ingredients. Additionally, it integrates seamlessly with online grocery services to suggest replenishments for low-stock items, favoring local and seasonal products. The FreshFridge app allows users to manage their grocery list, access nutritional information, and receive personalized meal suggestions, all aimed at reducing waste and supporting a healthier lifestyle.

The development team faces the challenge of seamlessly integrating various technologies into FreshFridge, ensuring user-friendliness while incorporating complex AI functionalities. They decide to utilize GitHub Copilot throughout their Scrum process, enhancing efficiency and powering greater creativity from requirements research to release management.

## Requirements Gathering

The product owner, Sofia, uses GitHub Copilot to efficiently draft detailed functional requirements and user stories for the FreshFridge's inventory tracking, recipe suggestion, and grocery replenishment features, ensuring a comprehensive approach to sustainable living.

In this instance, you will see Copilot used within the VS Code IDE. With GitHub Copilot Enterprise, the product owner could use GitHub Copilot Chat within GitHub.com.

Starting with the first requirement that the team has outlined, Sofia opens VS Code and starts a window chat with Copilot. Here she can request that Copilot give a list of potential user stories supporting the inventory tracking requirement (see Figure 14.4).

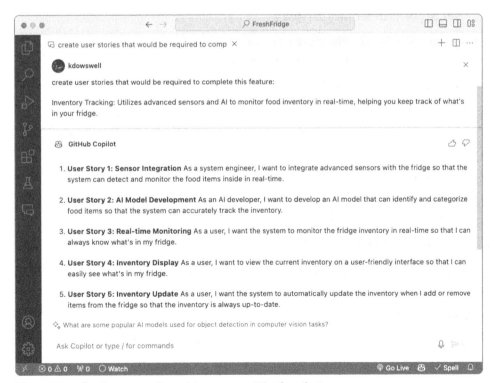

**Figure 14.4:** Copilot responding with user story titles for a feature

Here's the request to Copilot:

```
Create user stories that would be required to complete this feature:

Inventory Tracking: Utilizes advanced sensors and AI to monitor food
inventory in real-time, helping you keep track of what's in your fridge.
```

Let's review the results from Copilot:

**User Story 1: Sensor Integration**

**As a system engineer, I want to integrate advanced sensors with the fridge so that the system can detect and monitor the food items inside in real-time.**

**User Story 2: AI Model Development**

**As an AI developer, I want to develop an AI model that can identify and categorize food items so that the system can accurately track the inventory.**

**User Story 3: Real-time Monitoring**

**As a user, I want the system to monitor the fridge inventory in real-time so that I can always know what's in my fridge.**

**User Story 4: Inventory Display**

**As a user, I want to view the current inventory on a user-friendly interface so that I can easily see what's in my fridge.**

**User Story 5: Inventory Update**

**As a user, I want the system to automatically update the inventory when I add or remove items from the fridge so that the inventory is always up-to-date.**

**User Story 6: Low Inventory Alerts**

**As a user, I want to receive alerts when a food item is running low so that I can restock it in time.**

**User Story 7: Expiry Date Tracking**

**As a user, I want the system to track the expiry dates of food items so that I can consume or dispose of them before they spoil.**

**User Story 8: Data Privacy**

**As a user, I want my inventory data to be stored securely so that my privacy is protected.**

These stories give a great starting point to the Scrum team to be able to iterate quickly on the baseline requirements for the inventory tracking feature.

Let's see how GitHub Copilot can create acceptance criteria for the generated user stories (see Figure 14.5).

**Figure 14.5:** Copilot responding with user story acceptance criteria in gherkin format

Here's the request to Copilot:

```
Write gherkin ac for this story: As an AI developer, I want to develop
an AI model that can identify and categorize food items so that the
system can accurately track the inventory.
```

From here, Sofia can upload these stories and acceptance criteria to the product backlog for her team to review in their product backlog refinement meeting. Or, if there are changes that she would like to make, she can simply ask Copilot to make the adjustment to the acceptance criteria, allowing her and her team to rapidly iterate on the details of the user story.

As you can see from the request made in the example, the prompt simply indicated "ac" instead of fully spelling out "acceptance criteria." Because Copilot is trained on such a large dataset, it can predict the intent of the prompt and still produce a response that meets our needs.

## Refining the Backlog

In Scrum, there is a concept of a *product backlog*, which is a single source of truth for all items that are to be worked by the Scrum team. Here the team should be able to see an ordered list of the items to be worked. The order should be determined by the product owner as they consider several factors like value add, risk, and dependencies.

In the product backlog refinement (PBR) meeting, the Scrum team goes through each item that is not yet groomed to the point that they are ready to build it. These meetings can be long and strenuous. But as we have already seen with the previous example, Copilot can assist in ideation and creation of templated work to be done so that the team can think more creatively and move to solutions faster.

In the PBR meeting, the Scrum team working on the FreshFridge product are all together. Here the team is clarifying requirements, refining items, prioritizing items based on needs and dependencies, estimating, and removing obsolete items if necessary.

The team is reviewing the user story for identifying and categorizing food items. Here is a snippet of that requirement:

*As an AI developer, I want to develop an AI model that can identify and categorize food items so that the system can accurately track the inventory.*

*Scenario: Successful identification and categorization of food items*

- Given the AI model is trained with various food items
- When a new food item is presented to the model
- Then the model should correctly identify the food item
- And categorize it into the correct food category

The acceptance criteria with the scenarios are a great start for the team. During the PBR meeting, the team discusses the story and scenarios to determine if they need to add any detail or change. One important element they need to understand is the AI vision system they will use to complete this work. Knowing this will help them size the work item with accuracy.

Let's examine how Tom, the technical lead, uses Copilot to investigate a vision system that could be used. First, he can ask a question with the story open in his VS Code editor for context (see Figure 14.6).

Here's the request to Copilot:

```
Are there any AI vision system libraries that should be considered to
accomplish this story?
```

In the result options, OpenCV stands out as a good option for the team to try. They determine that they feel confident in their ability to complete the user story based on their research.

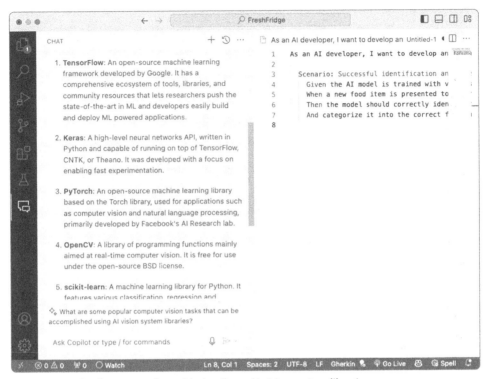

**Figure 14.6:** Copilot responding with details on AI vision system libraries

This is just one example of ideation and a question that you can leverage with Copilot. There are endless options to leverage Copilot in the context of user story discovery and ideation.

With this new information, Tom can make an edit to the scenario by leveraging the Copilot inline chat (see Figure 14.7).

Here's the request to Copilot:

```
Update this scenario to indicate the use of the OpenCV library.
```

As you can see, Copilot is highly capable of editing documentation using the same refactoring techniques used in other sections.

With this tight feedback loop from the discovery to editing of the story, the FreshFridge team can move faster than ever have before with better knowledge and more accurate edits to their requirements.

## Planning with Copilot

After the team has established their sprint backlog, they need to plan their implementation for each of the items in the sprint.

Continuing the example feature scenario, the team can leverage Copilot to create a list of tasks to complete during the sprint. As in the previous example, they will use VS Code with the story in the editor to provide context to the sidebar chat with Copilot (see Figure 14.8).

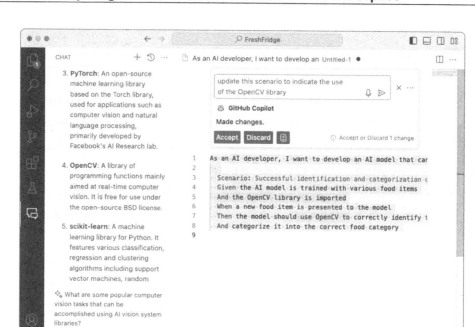

**Figure 14.7:** Copilot inline chat assisting in edits to a user story scenario

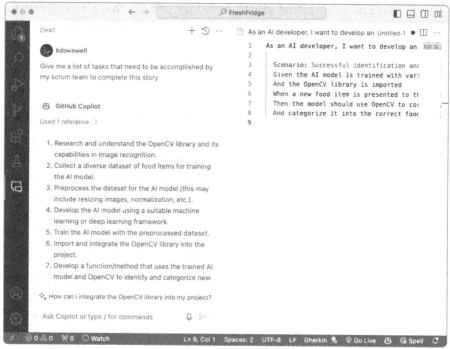

**Figure 14.8:** Copilot inline chat assisting in tasking of work for a user story

Here's the request to Copilot:

```
Give me a list of tasks that need to be accomplished by my scrum team to
complete this story.
```

The results from Copilot are great. They provide a very logical starting point, which the team can build from. See the complete list generated by Copilot here:

- Research and understand the OpenCV library and its capabilities in image recognition.
- Collect a diverse dataset of food items for training the AI model.
- Preprocess the dataset for the AI model (this may include resizing images, normalization, etc.).
- Develop the AI model using a suitable machine learning or deep learning framework.
- Train the AI model with the preprocessed dataset.
- Import and integrate the OpenCV library into the project.
- Develop a function/method that uses the trained AI model and OpenCV to identify and categorize new food items.
- Test the function/method with various food items to ensure it's working as expected.
- Refine and retrain the model as necessary based on test results.
- Document the usage of the function/method and any important details about the AI model.
- Review and refactor the code for clarity, efficiency, and adherence to coding standards.
- Conduct a final review of the user story to ensure all requirements are met.

## Coding with Copilot

After the team has detailed sprint tasks for the items to be worked on, they can leverage Copilot again to implement the code tasks required. In this case, the AI developer, Alexi, has taken the task of importing and integrating the OpenCV library into the project.

The team has a Python project they have created already. Alexi has the project open and is ready to import and integrate OpenCV to the project. They then use Copilot Chat to find the correct installation and import command to run and use the library (see Figure 14.9).

Here's the request to Copilot:

```
Import and integrate the OpenCV library into the project.
```

Now, Alexi can continue to install the required library. With this completed, they can continue to the next task for this sprint item:

*Develop a function/method that uses the trained AI model and OpenCV to identify and categorize new food items.*

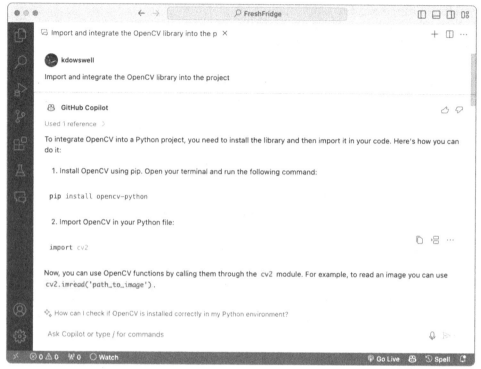

**Figure 14.9:** Copilot inline chat assisting in installing and importing a library

At this point, Alexi can use a variety of Copilot features to complete the work. A top-level comment, window chat, or inline chat would work great here. Let's see how the team can use inline chat to create a great starting point for a function that matches the requirements from the task selected (see Figure 14.10).

Here's the request to Copilot:

```
Develop a function/method that uses the trained AI model and OpenCV to
identify and categorize new food items.
```

As you can see from this example, the team generated an `identify_food` function from the task text. This completion was assisted by the file, file type, import statement, and request text.

From here, the developer can continue to interact with Copilot to implement the missing imports and methods that will finalize the implementation.

## Testing with Copilot

With a baseline function in place, let's explore how Copilot can assist in creating a unit test to help shorten the feedback loop of functionality and stabilize the codebase.

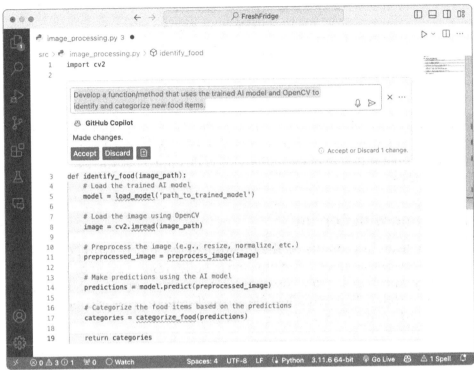

**Figure 14.10:** Copilot inline chat assisting in completing a function for using a trained AI model for item identification and categorization

Using the Copilot inline chat, the developer can select the code within the `image_processing.py` class. After selecting the code and activating inline chat, they can send the `/tests` command to create a test file and baseline test asserts (see Figure 14.11).

Here is the complete test file created by Copilot:

```python
import unittest
from image_processing import identify_food

class TestImageProcessing(unittest.TestCase):
    def test_identify_food(self):
        # Test case 1: Image with a single food item
        image_path = 'path_to_image_with_single_food_item.jpg'
        expected_categories = ['apple']
        self.assertEqual(identify_food(image_path), expected_categories)

        # Test case 2: Image with multiple food items
        image_path = 'path_to_image_with_multiple_food_items.jpg'
        expected_categories = ['apple', 'banana', 'orange']
        self.assertEqual(identify_food(image_path), expected_categories)
```

```
# Test case 3: Image with no food items
image_path = 'path_to_image_with_no_food_items.jpg'
expected_categories = []
self.assertEqual(identify_food(image_path), expected_categories)

if __name__ == '__main__':
    unittest.main()
```

As you can see, this test is a great example of the power and speed that you have at your fingertips with GitHub Copilot. From here, the development team can iterate on the design of the underlying code until it has successfully passed the unit tests.

## Deploying with Copilot

Once the team has completed their feature development work, Copilot can assist in creating an integration pipeline to build, test, and deploy their code.

To accomplish this, a development team member can request that Copilot create a GitHub Actions workflow file to handle pull requests and merge actions in their GitHub repository (see Figure 14.12).

**Figure 14.11:** Copilot inline chat assisting in the creation of unit tests

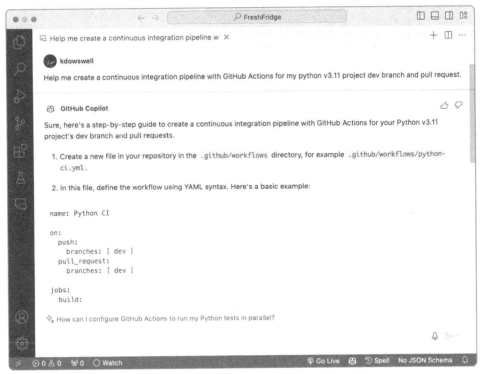

**Figure 14.12:** Copilot Chat response for integration pipeline workflow file

## Here's the request to Copilot:

```
Help me create a continuous integration pipeline with GitHub Actions for
my python v3.11 project dev branch and pull request.
```

## Here is the complete workflow YML file:

```yaml
name: Python CI

on:
  push:
    branches: [ dev ]
  pull_request:
    branches: [ dev ]

jobs:
  build:

    runs-on: ubuntu-latest

    steps:
    - uses: actions/checkout@v2

    - name: Set up Python 3.11
      uses: actions/setup-python@v2
```

```
    with:
      python-version: '3.11'

  - name: Install dependencies
    run: |
      python -m pip install --upgrade pip
      pip install -r requirements.txt

  - name: Lint with flake8
    run: |
      pip install flake8
      flake8 .

  - name: Test with pytest
    run: |
      pip install pytest
      pytest
```

As you can see, Copilot's chat response gives a step-by-step instruction set with a complete workflow file to kick-start the integration of the new feature work from the team. Also, Copilot uses the Python version from the request in the generated result.

These examples showcase how GitHub Copilot can be utilized at every phase of the SDLC. This was just a glimpse at the numerous ways a development team can leverage Copilot while working on sprints.

## Addressing Concerns: AI Adoption and the Future of Work

As you progress through different stages of AI integration within your development workflow, it's natural to have concerns about what AI adoption means for your future in software development. This section aims to directly address the worries you might have about how AI technologies could impact your role, job security, and the nature of your work.

One important point to understand is that AI tools are designed to augment, not replace, your capabilities. By automating repetitive and mundane tasks, AI allows you to focus more on creative, complex problem-solving aspects of software development, potentially making your job more satisfying and fulfilling. This concept of augmentation versus automation is an important part of how GitHub Copilot is engineered. Having a "human-in-the-loop" to accept, reject, or change responses is vital.

After you have worked with AI in your development process, you should see more opportunities to shift toward new skills and competencies and away from mundane or monotonous tasks. It's important to view this as an opportunity for growth and take advantage of the space AI can give you to learn and grow.

Engaging in continuous learning to acquire AI-related skills can open new avenues in your career and increase your value as a developer.

While AI will undoubtedly change the landscape of software development, this transformation is about evolving roles rather than eliminating them. Explore how emerging AI technologies are creating new specializations and roles within the industry and consider how you might position yourself to take advantage of these opportunities.

Furthermore, it is important to familiarize yourself with ethical and responsible AI principles as you navigate this future of work. Responsible AI principles include fairness, reliability and safety, privacy and security, inclusiveness, transparency, and accountability. Understand how these are applied at your organization when AI tooling is used.

In addition, the GitHub Copilot Trust Center highlights more information about the Labor Market and GitHub Copilot [5].

## Conclusion

In this chapter, you learned about the SDLC and how AI can be integrated into a Scrum team's workflow. Copilot can be helpful in every phase of the SDLC.

We explored the current adoption statistics and future predictions detailing what today's development landscape looks like and where we are headed. These statistics and predictions emphasize the upward trajectory of GitHub Copilot in the software industry.

Additionally, you learned about the levels of AI integration in the SDLC. From level 0 to level 5, you should be empowered to address where you are in your organization's adoption of AI in the SDLC and be able to navigate a way forward.

Finally, this chapter addressed potential concerns with ever-increasing AI adoption in software development workflows and the impact that might have on job stability and work dynamics.

## References

[1] GitHub, 2024. "Understanding the SDLC: Software Development Lifecycle Explained," `https://resources.github.com/software-development/what-is-sdlc`

[2] Gartner, 2023. "Gartner Hype Cycle Shows AI Practices and Platform Engineering Will Reach Mainstream Adoption in Software Engineering in Two to Five Years," `https://www.gartner.com/en/newsroom/press-releases/2023-11-28-gartner-hype-cycle-shows-ai-practices-and-platform-engineering-will-reach-mainstream-adoption-in-software-engineering-in-two-to-five-years`

[3] GitHub, 2023. "Survey reveals AI's impact on the developer experience," `https://github.blog/2023-06-13-survey-reveals-ais-impact-on-the-developer-experience`

[4] ISACA, 2024. "What is CMMI?," `https://cmmiinstitute.com/cmmi/intro`

[5] GitHub, 2024. "GitHub Copilot Trust Center," `https://resources.github.com/copilot-trust-center`

# CHAPTER 15

# Exploring Copilot Business
# and Enterprise

This chapter will cover the features within Copilot Business and Copilot Enterprise. Building on the robust offerings of the Copilot experience, Copilot Business enables organizations to leverage Copilot while giving leaders the control they need and ensuring the security of their intellectual property.

In addition to the controls and security that Copilot Business offers, you will learn the advanced capabilities of Copilot Enterprise. These robust features enable your entire organization to get more done. You will learn about chat within `GitHub.com`, indexing repositories, knowledge bases, pull request features, and more.

- Introducing Copilot Business and Enterprise
- Chatting with Copilot in `GitHub.com`
- Indexing Code Repositories to Improve Copilot's Understanding
- Getting Better Answers with the Knowledge Base
- Leveraging Copilot Chat in Code Repository Files
- Enhancing Pull Requests with Copilot
- Managing GitHub Copilot
- Looking Ahead

# Introducing Copilot Business and Enterprise

This section aims to give a short overview of the base-level features of both Copilot Business and Copilot Enterprise. In addition to the base features, this section will cover the additional control and security that Copilot Business offers. Lastly, you will learn the additional features that you get with Copilot Enterprise and references to additional information that will help you get started.

## Detailing Base Features

With Copilot Business and Copilot Enterprise, you get all the base features available in Copilot Individual. This includes code completions in your IDE, Copilot Chat in the IDE, Copilot in the command-line interface (CLI), and more. These base features are the same ones detailed throughout this book.

### Programming with Copilot in Your IDE

A key component of GitHub Copilot is programming in an integrated development environment (IDE). With each plan, Copilot Individual, Copilot Business, and Copilot Enterprise, you can enjoy a full-featured code completion experience enabling you to get fast suggestions from Copilot right within your editor, getting complete variables, functions, and even entire class files.

In addition to code completions, you can leverage the power of Copilot to assist in authoring new code blocks with the use of comment lines and comment blocks. This ability to use natural language, sample data, examples, and more in a comment greatly enhances Copilot's ability to give you accurate results in the code completions within the file (see Figure 15.1).

The Copilot code completions feature is available in Visual Studio Code, Visual Studio, Vim, Neovim, JetBrains IDEs, and Azure Data Studio. Copilot's support for such a large variety of IDEs enables you to do more with Copilot where you feel most productive.

### Chatting with Copilot in Your IDE

Collaborating with Copilot within the editor is great for productively working through targeted problem sets. In addition, you can use Copilot Chat within your IDE to ideate, solution, and get actionable results that keep you in your flow without leaving your development environment (see Figure 15.2).

Copilot Chat is currently supported in Visual Studio Code, Visual Studio, and JetBrains IDEs. At the time of writing, the inline chat feature to make changes directly in your editor is available for Visual Studio Code and Visual Studio only. However, this can change as GitHub rolls out features to more IDEs.

**Figure 15.1:** Copilot code completions

**Figure 15.2:** Copilot sidebar chat

### Leveraging Copilot in the CLI

If you are in the terminal and need assistance to complete a task, GitHub Copilot in the CLI is there to help. Leveraging the GitHub CLI, GitHub Copilot in the CLI is installed as an extension and enables you to get suggestions on how to accomplish tasks or explain a command so that you can keep moving through a task without leaving the terminal (see Figure 15.3).

**Figure 15.3:** Copilot in the CLI

With GitHub Copilot in the CLI, you can interact with Copilot in a whole new way. Assisting with command suggestions and explanations, the ability to gain insights and get executable results from Copilot is a powerful addition to the already highly effective set of tooling in the IDE.

## Highlighting Copilot Business

GitHub Copilot Business builds upon the base features of GitHub Individual allowing your organization to have the control and security you need to confidently roll out the use of Copilot.

In the "Managing GitHub Copilot" section, you will learn the details for how you can do content exclusion, manage access to Copilot, update and refine policies for allowed use, and review audit logs [1].

For a full list of features and extended documentation for Copilot Business, please head to the GitHub Copilot Business feature set documentation page.

```
https://docs.github.com/enterprise-cloud@latest/copilot/
copilot-business/github-copilot-business-feature-set
```

## Presenting Copilot Enterprise

GitHub Copilot Enterprise is a subscription plan designed for organizations using GitHub Enterprise Cloud. It offers enhanced AI features on `GitHub.com`, including the capability to interact with Copilot directly in the browser and access contextual information from across your project repositories [2].

Throughout this chapter, you will get an in-depth look at the features of Copilot Enterprise. If you would like additional information from the GitHub documentation site, head to the features set page.

```
https://docs.github.com/enterprise-cloud@latest/copilot/github-
copilot-enterprise/overview/github-copilot-enterprise-feature-set
```

All the remaining features discussed in this chapter will be exclusive to Copilot Enterprise, except for the GitHub Copilot management features.

## Chatting with Copilot in `GitHub.com`

The Copilot Enterprise feature called Copilot in `GitHub.com` supercharges your experience in `GitHub.com`. In this section, you will discover the Copilot Chat features in `GitHub.com`. Whether you are looking to get insights for general programming-related questions or diving into the functionality of a repository you are viewing, the power of GitHub Copilot is at your fingertips with Copilot in `GitHub.com`.

When chatting with Copilot in `GitHub.com`, you can talk to Copilot about the following:

- Repository-specific questions
- General software questions
- File- or symbol-specific inquiries
- Questions about specific lines within a file
- Knowledge base–related questions
- Pull request diff inquiries

Throughout the remainder of this chapter, you will see examples of all these features in action.

> **NOTE**   Copilot in `GitHub.com` is available for organization members who have been granted access to GitHub Copilot and the organization policy is enabled for Copilot in `GitHub.com`. Details for these settings are in the "Managing GitHub Copilot" section later in this chapter.

## Getting Insights About a Repository

After you have your account set up with GitHub Copilot Enterprise and have the Copilot in `GitHub.com` feature enabled, you can begin having conversations with Copilot right within `GitHub.com`.

After logging in to `GitHub.com`, you will see the Copilot icon at the top right of your screen. Opening Copilot from here will activate a chat window pinned to the bottom right of your screen (see Figure 15.4).

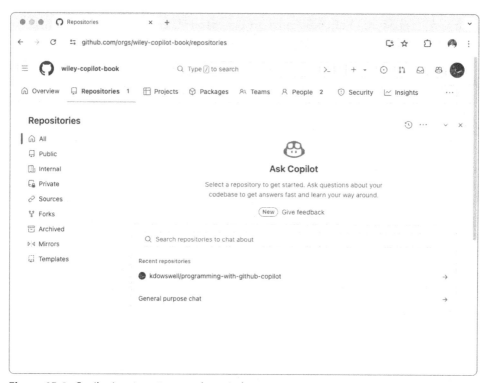

**Figure 15.4:** Copilot in `GitHub.com` chat window

Here you will see an introduction from Copilot with a search field for repositories, a list of your most recently accessed repositories, and an option to start a general-purpose chat.

Let's see how we can chat with Copilot about a specific repository. In the search input field for the repositories, search for "codeql." You should see a list of options to choose from (see Figure 15.5).

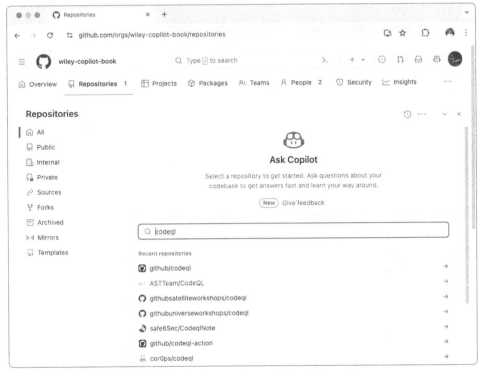

**Figure 15.5:** Copilot in `GitHub.com` chat window with CodeQL results

Select `github/codeql` from the list.

CodeQL is a sophisticated analytics tool designed to detect security vulnerabilities in a codebase by treating code as data. It enables users to write queries that help identify patterns and gain insights into the code. The tool supports multiple programming languages such as C++, Java, JavaScript, TypeScript, and Python. CodeQL is widely used in security research globally and is a key component of code scanning in GitHub Advanced Security.

With the repository selected, Copilot can give specific insights to code files within the repository. Copilot can search code and give you details about what it finds, find a file based on natural language, or retrieve a code reference based on a symbol definition that you provide to Copilot. While this conversation can be about the repository you have selected, you can always ask general programming questions.

The CodeQL project encourages submissions of new security queries that can detect vulnerabilities in the supported languages listed earlier. Let's see what the contribution guidelines are for the CodeQL repository (see Figure 15.6).

Here is the request to Copilot:

```
What are the guidelines for contributing to CodeQL?
```

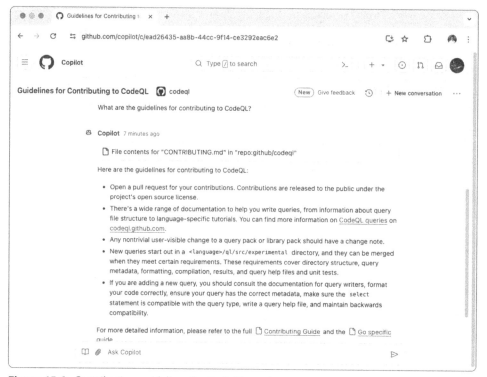

**Figure 15.6:** Contribution guidelines for CodeQL results

Here you can see Copilot has utilized the repository index to find the CONTRIBUTING.md file and embed that result within the reply. There are several great links that point you in the right direction to being a pull request.

Additionally, Figure 15.6 showcases the immersive chat view. This view is accessible from the ellipse menu at the top right of the chat window. You can see that this changes the URL to github.com/copilot and adds the unique identifier for the conversation to the route. This enables you to pin a conversation or the immersive view to your bookmarks if you want to have a quick entry point to Copilot in GitHub.com.

## Asking Copilot General Programming Questions

From the immersive view, start a new chat by clicking the new conversation button located at the top right of the screen. From here, you are presented with the default landing page showing previous repositories and the general purpose chat option. For this section, select the general purpose chat.

After opening this new conversation, you should be presented with a welcome statement from Copilot reminding you to review the output carefully before use; it's always good to take note of. Copilot can and will make mistakes due to the nature of the technology. It is up to you to ensure the quality of the output and help guide Copilot to give quality responses.

In addition to the notification at the top, you should see conversation suggestions at the bottom of the screen. These are useful to help you explore the robust abilities of Copilot. From backend infrastructure as code to front-end frameworks, Copilot can assist you to research, refine, and implement bespoke solutions for your needs (see Figure 15.7).

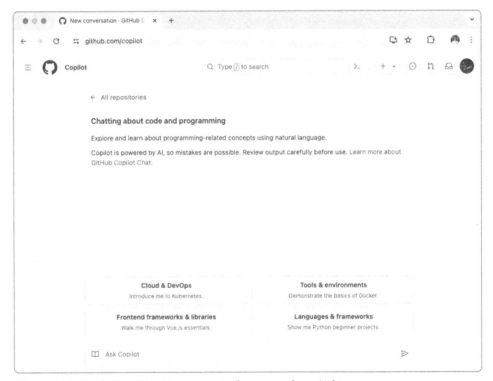

**Figure 15.7:** Copilot in `GitHub.com` general-purpose chat window

While you will have different suggested conversation prompts each time, in this case, I will choose the conversation prompt for a walk-through on Vue.js essentials.

Unlike the previous chat example with a repository referenced, this response is generated from the large language model of GitHub Copilot without the embedded resources of a GitHub repository file (see Figure 15.8).

Copilot has provided a great response with details on a default Vue.js app instance, what critical information you need about directives, general component structure, Vue router, Vuex library, Vue CLI, single-file components,

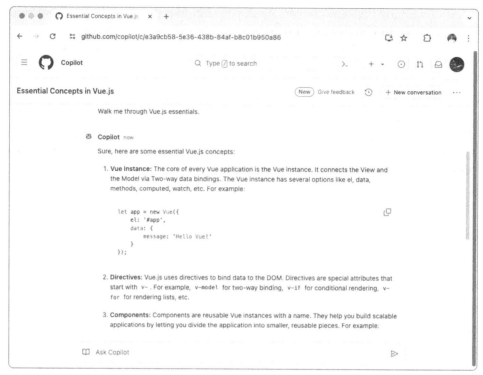

**Figure 15.8:** Copilot in `GitHub.com` conversation about essential concepts in Vue.js

and reactivity. This robust information about Vue.js provides a great starting point to be productive with Vue.js.

You can also ask repository-specific questions that could provide you with more targeted results. This will be covered in the "Indexing Code Repositories to Improve Copilot's Understanding" section. There you will find how you can ask Copilot to assist in specific tasks and knowledge discovery that leverages the index files in a repository in addition to the base model of GitHub Copilot.

# Indexing Code Repositories to Improve Copilot's Understanding

Next, let's look at how you can index a repository. This enables Copilot in `GitHub.com` to have insights about your code and any documentation that you have in your repository.

## Detailing the Example Project

In this section we will be using an example project called eShopOnWeb. This project is a sample ASP.NET Core application with a client app and backend

API [3]. The example project is an ecommerce application allowing users to search products, add them to a cart, and submit an order. It also allows admin users to manage product inventory through an admin web application.

If you would like to access this repository, you can do so here:

```
https://github.com/dotnet-architecture/eShopOnWeb
```

Figure 15.9 shows the main page of the client application with the navigation, header, filters, products, login, and cart (see Figure 15.9).

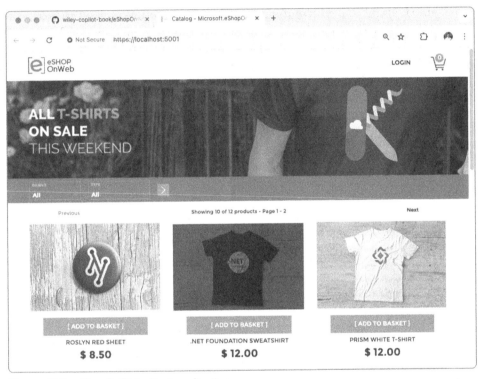

**Figure 15.9:** eShopOnWeb client application

## Introducing Retrieval-Augmented Generation

Retrieval-augmented generation (RAG) allows a large language model (LLM) to extend its capabilities beyond its initial training data by retrieving information from a diverse range of data sources, which can also be customized to specific needs [4].

This technology is used in several scenarios when interacting with Copilot (the referenced article has a wealth of information giving you a better understanding of the intricacies of using RAG within the context of GitHub Copilot).

When you pose a question about an indexed repository using GitHub Copilot Chat in GitHub.com, the RAG in Copilot Enterprise uses the platform's internal search engine to find relevant code or text from indexed files to provide an answer.

This process involves a semantic search where the content of documents in the indexed repository is analyzed, and the documents are then ranked by relevance. GitHub Copilot Chat utilizes RAG to perform a similar semantic search, extracting the most relevant snippets from these top-ranked documents. These snippets are incorporated into the prompt, enabling GitHub Copilot Chat to generate an accurate and relevant response.

## Indexing Your Repository

To enable Copilot to perform the operations discussed, you need to index the repository you would like to be included in Copilot's reasoning and response process. Most likely, this step will be required only for private repositories as most public repositories have been indexed.

To index your repository, all you need to do is open a chat window within GitHub.com and select the repository you would like to index from the search repositories section. With the forked eShopOnWeb repository selected, you will see an alert from Copilot to index the repository to improve Copilot's understanding and response quality (see Figure 15.10).

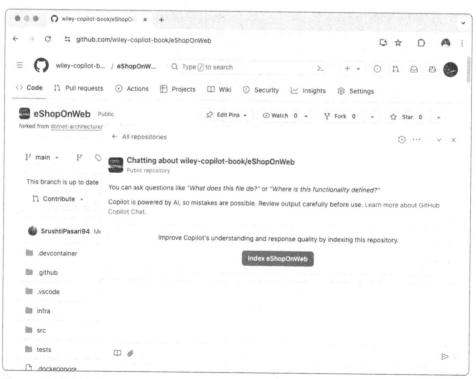

**Figure 15.10:** Indexing your repository for GitHub Copilot in GitHub.com

This indexing process can vary greatly based on the size of the repository being indexed. For small repositories, this can take seconds. For a larger repository like this one with a robust infrastructure including a client app and API, it will take several minutes.

## Asking Repository-Specific Questions

After the indexing process completes, you can ask questions about the repository to Copilot and get bespoke results. The following examples will highlight ways that you can interact with Copilot to gain deep insights into the functionality of a codebase.

These examples assume you have an indexed repository and a chat window with GitHub Copilot in `GitHub.com` open with the indexed repository selected for conversation context.

### How Question

With multiple projects and different ways to run this example project, getting started can be a hard task for new contributors. Let's see how Copilot can assist in gaining knowledge about the specific task we would like to accomplish.

As an example, submit the following request to Copilot:

```
How can I run the API locally?
```

After submitting this question to Copilot, you should get a response like the one in Figure 15.11.

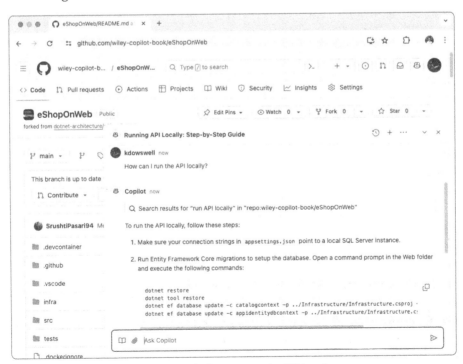

**Figure 15.11:** Copilot Chat response for how to run the API locally

This result is infused with the details from the indexed repository. There are specifics on the type of database connections required, project-specific command-line statements, and alternative dev containers using Docker.

### Where Question

Next, let's see how Copilot can give bespoke results for a specific part of the repository. When you need to know where code is for a specific feature in a larger repository, a simple symbolic or keyword search can leave you with limited understanding. Let's see how Copilot can supercharge your search experience and give you the insights you need to be productive.

With a Copilot Chat window open and the repository selected as context for the conversation, send a request to Copilot to understand where authentication is handled (see Figure 15.12).

Here's the Copilot request:

```
Where is authentication handled in our API?
```

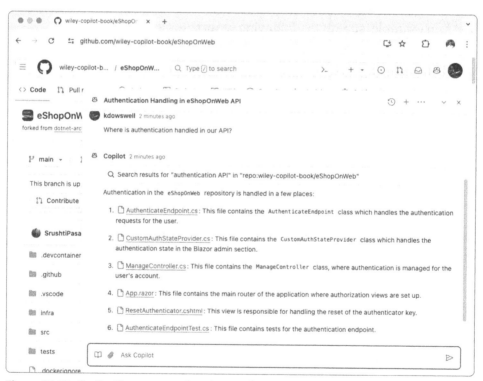

**Figure 15.12:** Copilot Chat response for where authentication is handled in our API

Here Copilot surfaced important files related to our question. Unlike a traditional search, Copilot was able to provide additional context about what the files do and specific attributes that pertain to the authentication question.

As you can see, Copilot excels with the index that was created, enabling you to get insights about your codebase with the power of Copilot to compile logical responses and assets to help you do more.

# Getting Better Answers with the Knowledge Base

Let's explore the GitHub Copilot knowledge base feature. This is available to Copilot Enterprise customers on GitHub.com.

GitHub Copilot knowledge bases are great for the following:

- **Documenting project details:** They can be used to provide comprehensive information about a project, including its purpose, functionality, architecture, setup, and usage instructions.

- **Sharing FAQs:** Common questions and issues encountered by users or developers can be addressed in the knowledge base to provide quick solutions.

- **Onboarding new team members:** It can act as a central source of truth about the project, helping new team members to understand the project faster.

- **Improving code maintainability:** By documenting code-related decisions, practices, and standards, the knowledge base can help in maintaining the codebase.

- **Reducing repetitive communication:** By addressing common queries and issues, it can help in reducing repetitive communication in the project team.

## Creating a Knowledge Base

To create a knowledge base, you need to be an organization owner. As an organization owner, from GitHub.com, click your profile icon at the top right of the screen, and then select your organizations (see Figure 15.13).

From here, you can select settings for the organization that you would like to add a knowledge base to. After selecting the organization settings, you will see Copilot in the left menu. Expand that and select the knowledge bases menu item. You should now see the Knowledge Bases page with a prompt to add a new knowledge base (see Figure 15.14).

Next, click New Knowledge Base. Here you will have the ability to add a name, description, and repositories to reference in your knowledge base.

When creating knowledge bases, consider the best strategy for your organization. One effective way to create knowledge bases is to create one for each

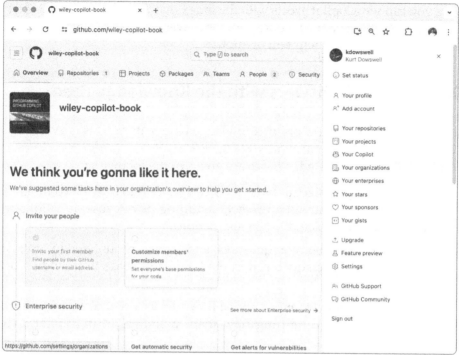

**Figure 15.13:** Your organization settings menu

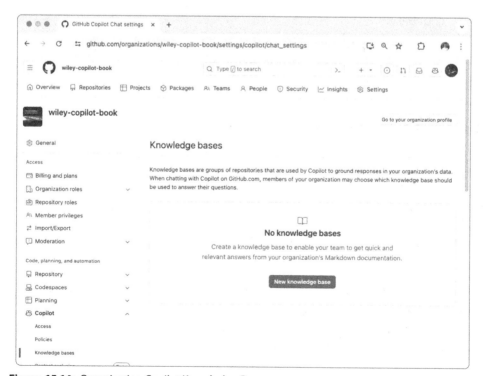

**Figure 15.14:** Organization Copilot Knowledge Bases screen

specific domain of work involved in your software development life cycle (SDLC). Here are some options that you might consider for your knowledge bases:

- **Front-end development**
  - UI/UX design
  - Front-end frameworks (React.js, Angular)
  - Web technologies (HTML, CSS, JavaScript)
  - Performance optimization
  - Accessibility standards
  - Cross-browser compatibility
- **Backend development**
  - Programming languages (Python, Java, Node.js)
  - Server and API development
  - Security practices
  - Scalability and performance
  - Integration with third-party services
- **Database administration**
  - Database management systems (MySQL, MongoDB)
  - Data modeling and normalization
  - Performance tuning
  - Backup and recovery strategies
  - Database security
- **Quality assurance**
  - Testing techniques (unit, integration, system testing)
  - Test automation
  - Bug tracking and management
  - Performance and load testing
  - CI/CD integration
- **Information assurance**
  - Risk management
  - Compliance with security standards (ISO/IEC 27001, GDPR)
  - Encryption and data protection
  - Incident response
  - Security policies and procedures

- **Operations**
  - Monitoring and logging
  - System administration
  - Incident management
  - Deployment and scaling
  - Disaster recovery and business continuity
- **Requirements management**
  - Requirements elicitation and documentation
  - Change management
  - Traceability of requirements
  - Tools and software for managing requirements

These examples are intended to get you started. Make sure you consider your organizational needs and team dynamics when implementing your knowledge bases.

Let's look at an example and focus on front-end development. Start by adding a name and optional description. Then add relevant repositories to the content area like `dotnet/razor`, `twbs/bootstrap`, and `dotnet-architecture/eShopOnWeb` (see Figure 15.15).

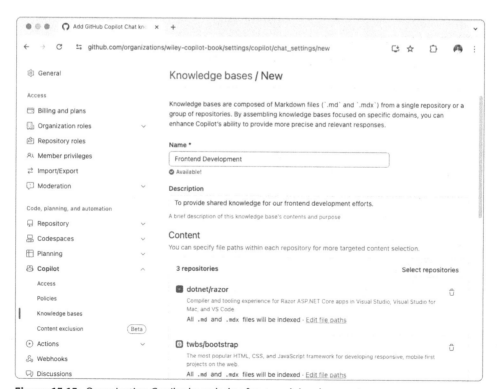

**Figure 15.15:** Organization Copilot knowledge front-end development

After you have selected the repositories, you want for your knowledge base, click Create at the bottom of the page.

You can now use the knowledge base from Copilot Chat in `GitHub.com`. Open a new chat window and click the book icon at the bottom left of the chat window (see Figure 15.16).

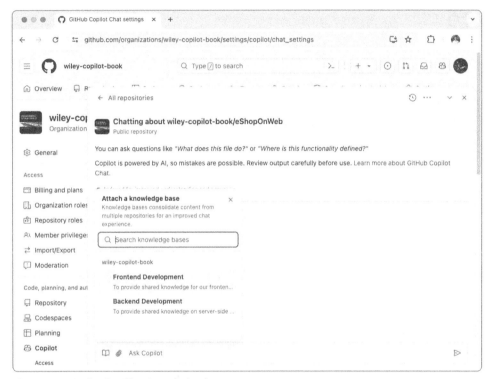

**Figure 15.16:** Copilot Chat knowledge base menu

From here, click Frontend Development. As you can see, I created a second knowledge base for backend development to showcase the menu structure.

Within the Copilot conversation, you will now see a "chatting with frontend development" alert. This will direct Copilot to reference the repository Markdown files when answering questions in this conversation.

Since the front-end development knowledge base is referencing bootstrap, ask Copilot what the latest version of that library is (see Figure 15.17).

```
What is the latest version of bootstrap?
```

You can see Copilot referenced six files to determine the best answer given the question. Copilot responded with the correct, most current version of bootstrap, which is 5.3.3 at the time of writing.

Let's see what other information we can gather regarding version changes for bootstrap. Ask Copilot what you have to change when migrating from version 4 to version 5 (see Figure 15.18).

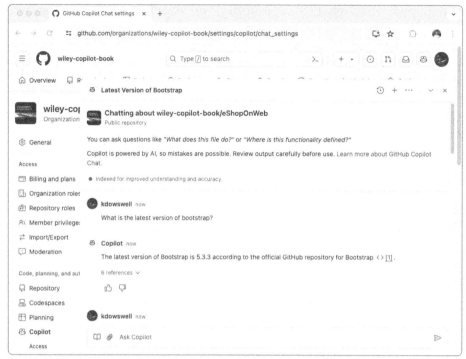

**Figure 15.17:** Copilot Chat bootstrap version question

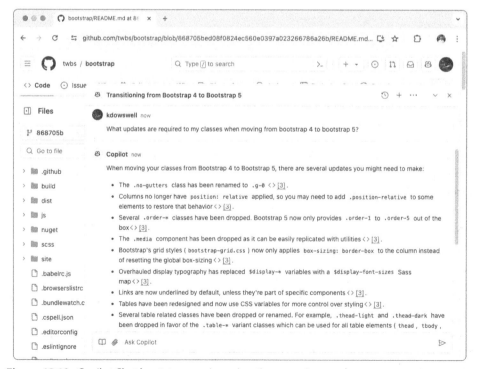

**Figure 15.18:** Copilot Chat bootstrap version migration question result

```
What updates are required to my classes when moving from bootstrap 4 to
bootstrap 5?
```

Here you can see Copilot gathered great information on a migration from version 4 to version 5 of bootstrap with references to the documentation from the official repository.

Also, you might notice in Figure 15.18 that I have navigated to the bootstrap repository and continued my conversation with Copilot. This ability to follow your reference files linked in the chat responses while maintaining your conversation with Copilot offers a great fluid experience. You can always minimize the Copilot Chat window if you would like quick access while navigating around different pages.

## Summary

As you can see from this short example, this is applied across your entire organization to assist in productive conversations with up-to-date authoritative data sources, which is a game-changer. These conversations can quickly uncover company-specific information about internal libraries, tools, or best practices.

With knowledge bases, you and your team can quickly jump into conversations that give you the targeted and best information possible to keep you moving.

# Leveraging Copilot Chat in Code Repository Files

Let's turn our attention to how GitHub Copilot Chat in `GitHub.com` allows us to gain understanding about files within a repository. To initiate this example using the eShopOnWeb example project repository set in Copilot Chat as the context, ask Copilot the following (see Figure 15.19):

```
What files are used when updating a quantity for a basket item?
```

With the specific question about files and a targeted feature within the repository, Copilot has done a great job of identifying the files used in this process. With this result, open the `Basket.cs` class file.

## Explaining Code with Copilot

With the `Basket.cs` file open, here you will find Copilot ready to assist in a couple of places. On the top menu for the file, the Copilot button is there to allow you to add context to this specific file to your conversation with Copilot. Additionally, if you select a line in the file, you will see a Copilot button appear on the right side of the line (see Figure 15.20).

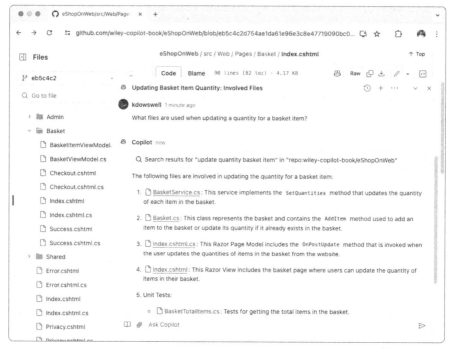

**Figure 15.19:** Copilot Chat response for what files are used when updating a quantity for a basket item

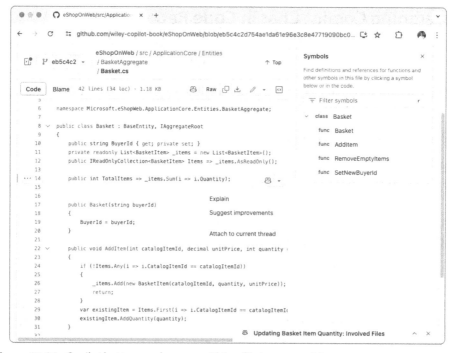

**Figure 15.20:** Copilot buttons and menus within a file in your codebase

With the `TotalItems` property selected, select the Explain Menu option from the inline Copilot menu. This will initiate a new conversation with Copilot with an explanation of the selected code in the file (see Figure 15.21).

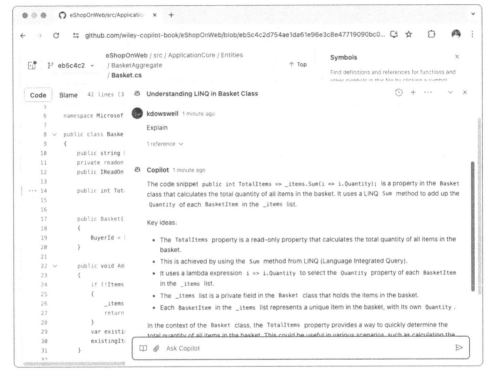

**Figure 15.21:** Copilot conversation about selected code in file

Copilot has given a great explanation of this single line of code, going in-depth on the details of the property type, functions used, and purpose.

## Getting Suggested Improvements from Copilot

Back in the `Basket.cs` file, let's explore what Copilot can help with when we request a suggested improvement to a file function. Start by selecting the code for the `AddItem()` function and choose the inline Copilot menu option Suggest Improvements (see Figure 15.22).

After selecting this option, you will be directed to a new chat conversation with Copilot, which will immediately respond with an analysis of the current code. Then Copilot will proceed to evaluate the code for improvements and provide a final edit of the code if there are any improvements to be made (see Figure 15.23).

Copilot has done a great job evaluating the current code. It has made the following evaluation about the code: redundant check on the item property, lack of exception safety, and use of var reducing readability of data values. While

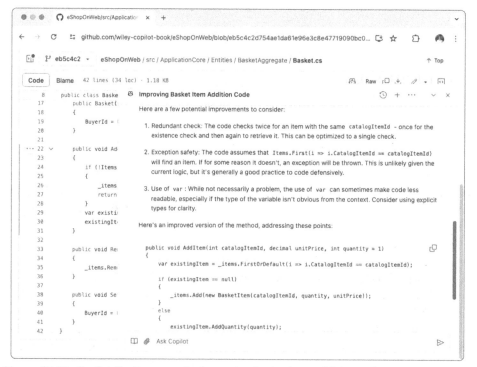

**Figure 15.22:** Copilot inline menu for suggesting improvements

**Figure 15.23:** Copilot Chat response for improving basket item addition code

these are good suggestions to consider, it is always up to you to determine if the suggestions are accurate and adhere to your codebase standards.

## Adding Context with Attach to Current Thread

Lastly, Copilot Chat in `GitHub.com` allows you to attach files and symbols to your conversation with Copilot to add context. From the file view as stated before, you can use the Copilot button at the top of the file to quickly add context to the file in your Copilot Chat. After clicking this button from the `Basket.cs` file, you will see an attachment alert at the bottom of the conversation window (see Figure 15.24).

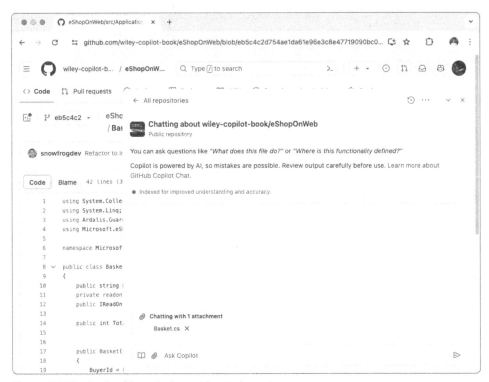

**Figure 15.24:** Copilot Chat window with attachment

With the `Basket.cs` file attached to the chat window, you can have a conversation with Copilot that will be infused with context from the attached file. With the attachment, you can make requests to Copilot that have a more simplistic structure, as shown in Figure 15.25.

```
Explain the purpose of this file.
```

Here you can see that Copilot understands the context of your question and can give you an insightful response with limited work on your behalf.

In addition to a single file attachment, you can click the paperclip icon to select as many files as you need to support your conversation with Copilot (see Figure 15.26).

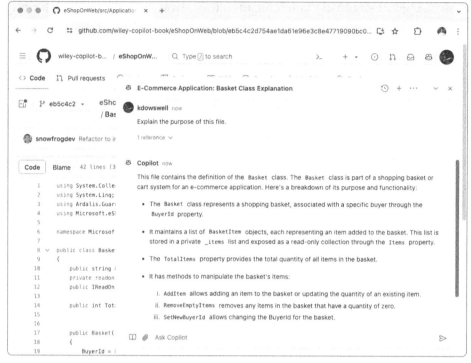

**Figure 15.25:** Copilot Chat window with attachment response

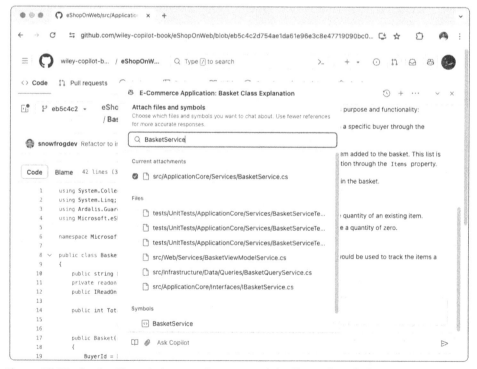

**Figure 15.26:** Copilot Chat window attachment search for files and symbols

Searching and adding files or symbols to your conversation is a simple task with the intuitive search feature. With the `BasketService.cs` added as additional conversation context, you can ask questions targeted at the interaction of these files.

## Enhancing Pull Requests with Copilot

GitHub Copilot has proven to be a valuable companion to assist in learning more about repositories, code files, and general programming questions. In this section, you will learn how Copilot can assist in the process of creating a pull request from ideation to submission.

Let's start with a new chat window with GitHub Copilot in `GitHub.com`, which should be targeted at the repository you would like to modify. In this example, you will see how Copilot can assist in editing the eShopOnWeb example project. In this scenario, you will see the steps required to add a remove item feature to the basket page for product items selected for purchase in the online store.

Figure 15.27 shows the basket page that will be modified with a remove item functionality.

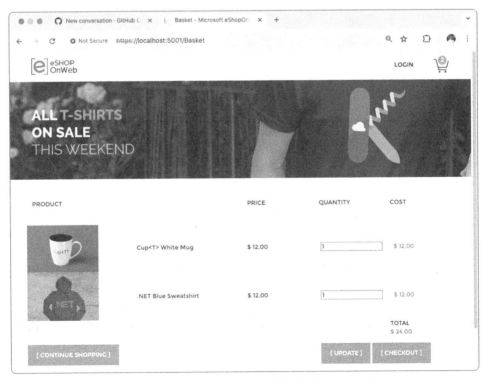

**Figure 15.27:** Web application basket page to be modified with a remove button

Here you can see that the basket page allows users to see their items selected, as well as the title, price, quantity, and cost. The user can continue shopping, update the quantity for an item, or check out.

Currently, a user needs to reduce the quantity of a basket item to zero and click Update to remove an item. To improve this user experience, we will add a remove button to the basket page for each item to give an intuitive way for the user to interact with the basket item.

## Discovering Pull Request Tasks

In your chat window with GitHub Copilot in `GitHub.com`, with the eShopOnWeb repository selected for context, ask Copilot the following (see Figure 15.28):

```
How would I add a remove item feature to the basket page?
```

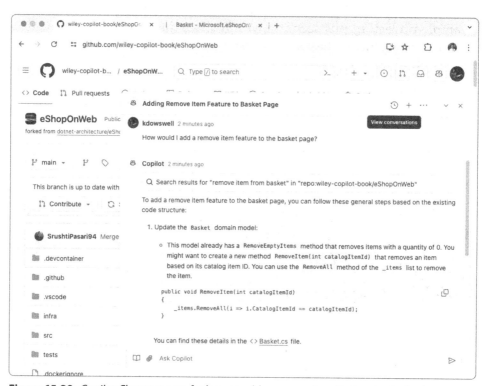

**Figure 15.28:** Copilot Chat response for how to add a remove item feature to the basket page

Copilot has responded with reference to the repository. At the top of the response, you can see that Copilot uses a search term "remove item from basket" against the indexed repository information to gather all of the necessary resources to give a holistic response to our request.

In summary, here are the steps Copilot has outlined for our change:

1. Update the `Basket` domain model.
2. Update the `BasketService` and `BasketViewModelService` to expose the functionality to the web application layer.
3. Update the basket page (`Index.cshtml` and `Index.cshtml.cs`)

## Making a Code Change with Copilot

With your task list generated from Copilot, you can now begin making changes to the source code and validating the results. Start by cloning the repository and creating a branch. In this case, call the branch `feature/remove-item-from-basket`.

To make these changes in VS Code, you will need to follow the `README.md` instructions from the eShopOnWeb repository. Specifically, review the guide under the heading "Running the sample locally." In addition to the steps outlined, for me to get the application to run, I needed to set the default value of `useOnlyInMemoryDatabase = true` within the `Dependencies.Configure Services()` method.

To assist in a better developer experience, I highly suggest using the C# Dev Kit extension for VS Code to give you several language services and native testing support for unit tests. Get the extension here:

```
https://marketplace.visualstudio.com/items?itemName=ms-dotnettools
.csdevkit
```

After following the steps for running locally and installing all the required dependencies, you can run the following dotnet CLI commands.

From the project root, open a terminal and execute the following to run the API:

```
cd src/PublicApi
dotnet watch
```

Open a second terminal at the project root and execute the following to run the client application:

```
cd src/Web
dotnet watch
```

With the API and web projects running in watch mode, you can now make the edits outlined in the previous section.

### Update the Basket Domain Model

In my case, Copilot responded with a `RemoveItem()` function within the initial chat response for adding the remove functionality to the basket page. You can work with Copilot in several ways to create this method. Whether you prompt

Copilot for a code completion via an inline comment, start a new chat within VS Code, or use Copilot Chat in GitHub.com, you should end up with a function like this added to your Basket.cs file:

```
public void RemoveItem(int catalogItemId)
{
    _items.RemoveAll(i => i.CatalogItemId == catalogItemId);
}
```

After adding this code to your Basket.cs file, you can then add a test using Copilot Chat to ensure the functionality. Do this by selecting the RemoveItem() function in the editor. Open a new chat with Copilot in the side menu. From this chat, send a request to Copilot like this (see Figure 15.29):

```
@workspace /tests #selection #file:BasketAddItem.cs XUnit
```

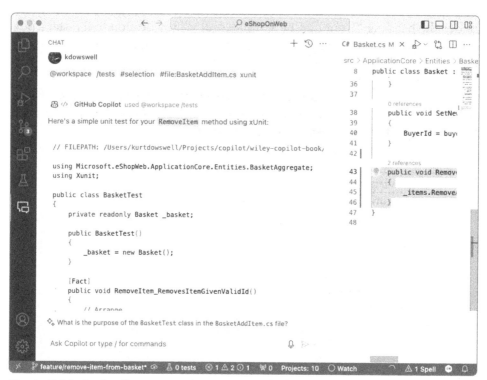

**Figure 15.29:** Copilot Chat response for creating tests for the new method

The test result from Copilot needed additional guidance to generate an XUnit test. Additionally, the using statements, namespace, and class name all needed to be adjusted. The unit tests themselves were in good standing, but it is important to always review the output critically from Copilot and refine as needed.

### Update the Basket Service

First, because the `BasketService` uses an interface `IBasketService`, we should update this interface file to help drive our code completion for this step. Open the `IBasketService.cs` file and add the following interface method declaration to the bottom of the file:

```
Task<Result<Basket>> RemoveItemFromBasket(int basketId, string
username, int catalogItemId);
```

Next, with the `IBasketService.cs` file open for context, open the `Basket Service.cs` file and go to the bottom of the file. Since you have a context of the interface file, Copilot should be able to discern your intent when adding new lines to the bottom of the class. If not, you can add an inline comment to drive the code suggestion from Copilot (see Figure 15.30).

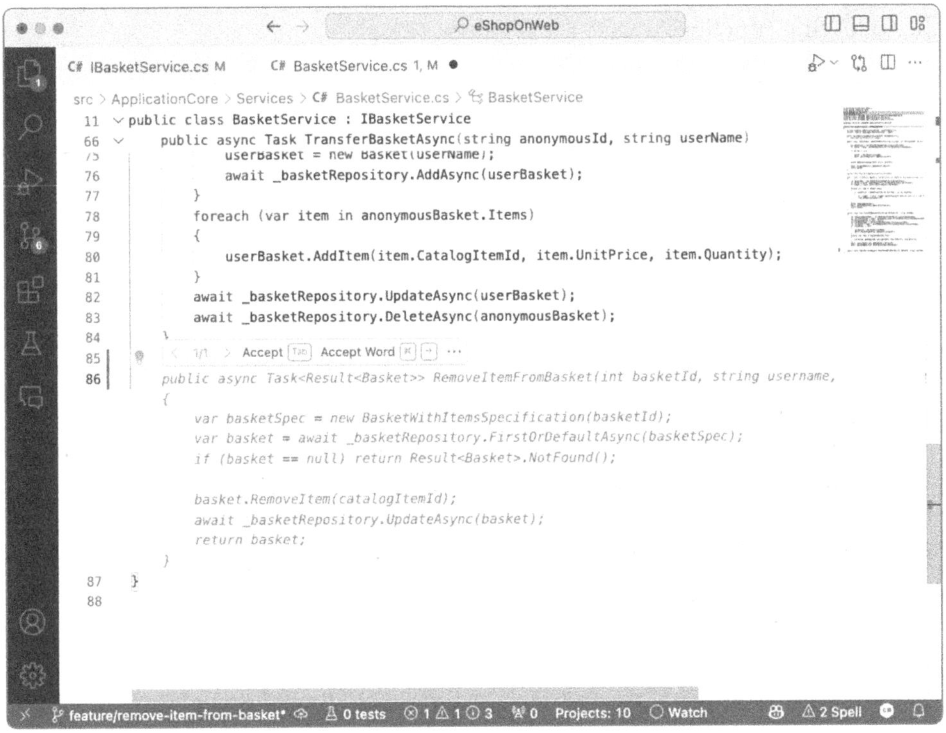

**Figure 15.30:** Copilot function creation for remove item from basket function

Here you can see Copilot creating the function with the necessary interactions with the basket specification class, basket repository, and basket class with the assistance of the interface file context. Here is the complete method for reference:

```
public async Task<Result<Basket>> RemoveItemFromBasket(int basketId,
string username, int catalogItemId)
```

```
    {
        var basketSpec = new BasketWithItemsSpecification(basketId);
        var basket = await _basketRepository.FirstOrDefaultAsync
(basketSpec);
        if (basket == null) return Result<Basket>.NotFound();

        basket.RemoveItem(catalogItemId);
        await _basketRepository.UpdateAsync(basket);
        return basket;
    }
```

### *Update the Basket Page*

Now, let's update the basket page allowing the user to remove an item from the basket.

Within the `Index.cshtml.cs` file in the `src/web/pages/basket` folder, add the following function:

```
    public async Task OnPostRemove(int id)
    {
        var basketView = await _basketViewModelService.GetOrCreateBasket
ForUser(GetOrSetBasketCookieAndUserName());
        var username = GetOrSetBasketCookieAndUserName();
        var basket = await _basketService.RemoveItemFromBasket
(basketView.Id, username, id);
        BasketModel = await _basketViewModelService.Map(basket);
    }
```

With this function in place, which can use the new basket service `Remove ItemFromBasket` function, you will also need to adjust the `Index.cshtml` page. For my edit, I added a `btn btn-link` button to the right of the other basket item table row fields. Additionally, I adjusted some alignment of the grid rows to be aligned with the new remove button. Here is a snippet of the button that was added to the `cshtml` file:

```
<section class="esh-basket-item esh-basket-item--middle col-xs-1">
    <button class="btn btn-link" name="removebutton" asp-route-id="@
item.CatalogItemId" type="submit" asp-page-handler="Remove">
        Remove
    </button>
</section>
```

With all these changes in place, the remove button is now functioning. The output you should have after making the edits for layout and adding the button as described earlier should look like Figure 15.31.

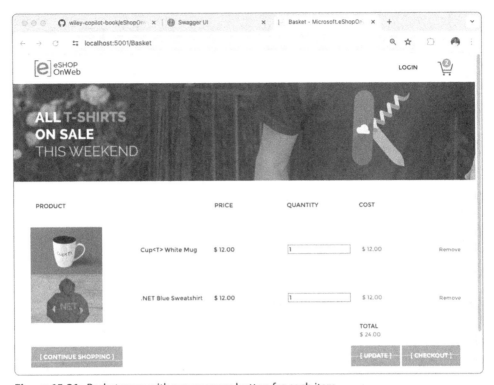

**Figure 15.31:** Basket page with new remove button for each item

With the remove button in place and functioning, you are ready to commit to the local branch and submit the pull request.

## Committing to the Feature Branch

When committing code to your feature branch, Copilot can assist in creating a commit message for you. This feature is available to all plans of Copilot. It is a great way to be descriptive of your changes without taking up precious time crafting the perfect message.

You will find this feature identified by the sparkle icon. This sparkle icon is used to indicate an intelligent action that can be taken by Copilot within VS Code (see Figure 15.32).

**NOTE**   The GitHub Copilot generate commit message feature is available to all GitHub Copilot plans.

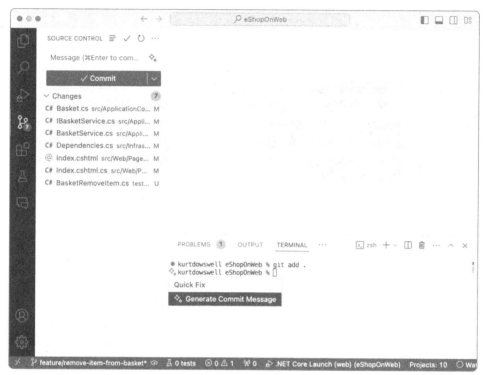

**Figure 15.32:** GitHub Copilot commit message help feature

## Leveraging Copilot to Summarize Your Pull Request

After you return to your repository in `GitHub.com`, you should see a prompt at the top of the repository to compare and pull request the changes you just committed. Proceed to the Create Pull Request screen for these changes.

Here you will find the Copilot icon in the top menu bar for the pull request description. Clicking this icon displays an option to generate a summary of the changes in the pull request. Click this menu and wait for Copilot to generate a description (see Figure 15.33).

After Copilot completes the summary, you should review the output and make sure it aligns with the changes you have made in the feature branch. After reviewing the changes and making any necessary adjustments, you should have an output with detailed functionality adjustments with links to files that were changed in the feature branch (see Figure 15.34).

With this pull request summary from Copilot, team members will have clear insights into the changes made and be able to investigate each update to ensure that it is acceptable.

And while reviewing the pull request code diffs, you can leverage Copilot to explain the code you are reviewing, giving you the insights you need to evaluate the best updates made to the repository.

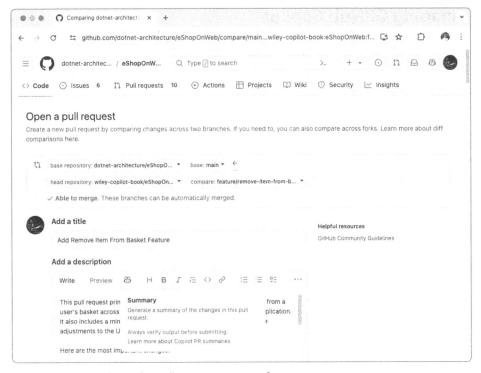

**Figure 15.33:** GitHub Copilot pull request summary feature

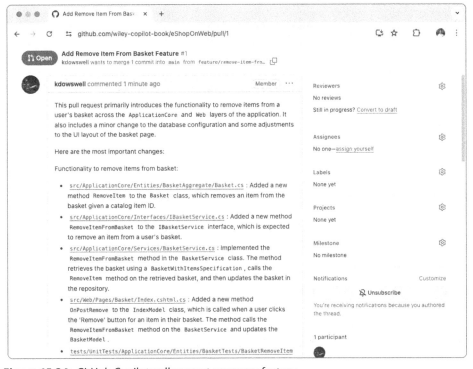

**Figure 15.34:** GitHub Copilot pull request summary feature

## Managing GitHub Copilot

GitHub organization admins that have active plans for Copilot Business or Copilot Enterprise can manage access, policies, knowledge bases, content exclusions, and audit logs.

To access these Copilot management settings, go to your profile menu in the top `GitHub.com` menu and click your organizations. From the organizations page, click the settings button for the organization to manage Copilot settings. Once you are on the organization settings page, you will find the Copilot menu item on the left under the "Code, planning, and automation" section header.

### Managing Access

In the Copilot menu in your organization settings, select the Access menu item. This will enable you to see your Copilot seat count, estimated monthly cost, access control settings for your organization, and a list of all individuals with access (see Figure 15.35).

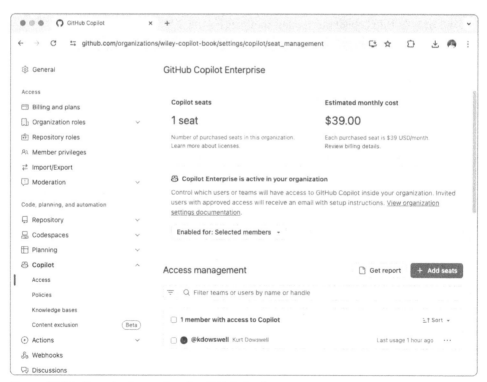

**Figure 15.35:** Organization settings for GitHub Copilot access

As you can see from Figure 15.35, you can enable, disable, or enable settings for selected members. Once you have selected an option, you can add seats via a search utility. This feature allows you to select teams or individual organization members.

## Managing Policies

The next option you can manage is the policies for GitHub Copilot, encompassing the following:

- Suggestions matching public code
- Copilot in `GitHub.com`
- Copilot Chat in the IDE
- Copilot in the CLI

Figure 15.36 shows a view of this page as an organization member with the settings and their indicators of enabled and disabled status.

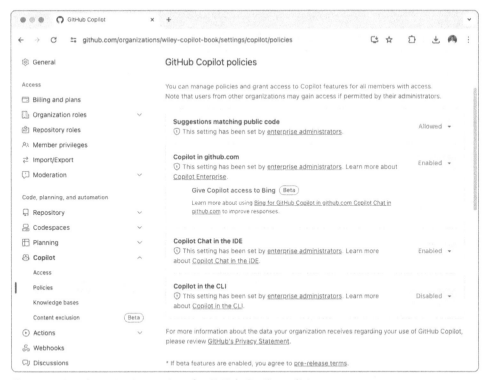

**Figure 15.36:** Organization settings for GitHub Copilot policies

Controlling these settings enables you to roll out Copilot in your organization in a thoughtful and strategic way.

At the enterprise level, policies may be centrally established for the entire enterprise, or alternatively, the decision-making authority may be delegated to the owners of individual organizations to tailor the policy as appropriate for their specific contexts.

## Content Exclusion

Content exclusions can be set to ensure you don't expose sensitive information. Currently, these exclusions only affect code completions and do not affect Copilot Chat. Additionally, Copilot will prevent directly accessing excluded files and folders that you specify (see Figure 15.37).

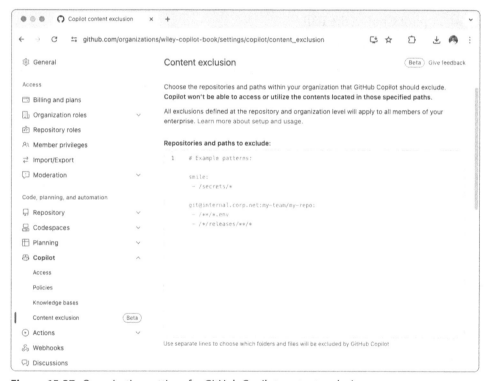

**Figure 15.37:** Organization settings for GitHub Copilot content exclusions

When specifying exclusions, you need to follow the formatting guidelines as follows:

```
# Ignore file path
- "/path/to/exclude/*"

# Ignore specific file
- "/path/to/file/file_name.json"
```

```
# Ignore file type
- "*.log"

# Ignore file for a specific repository folder
git@wiley.corp.com:copilot-team/book-repo:
    - "*"
```

For more information on the allowable syntax and more examples, head to the official documentation at the following URL:

```
https://docs.github.com/copilot/managing-github-copilot-in-your-
organization/configuring-content-exclusions-for-github-copilot
```

## Reviewing Audit Logs

Accessible from the Archive menu in your organization settings page, you can review the audit logs for events specific to GitHub Copilot activity (see Figure 15.38).

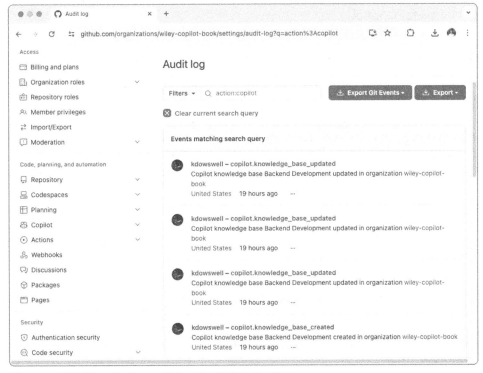

**Figure 15.38:** Organization audit logs for GitHub Copilot

Here you can see the audit logs with a filter for `action:copilot`, which allows you to see all Copilot activity against the organization settings.

# Looking Ahead

Today, Copilot Enterprise provides the tools you need to be much more productive and empowered in the SDLC. GitHub is moving at a rapid pace to enhance the developer experience across a wide spectrum of developer tooling and services. The following sections are development areas that are of interest for the 2024 calendar year.

These product features might change or might not be released after their alpha and beta testing rounds. Regardless, there are some very compelling features on the horizon, and I'd like to share them with you.

## Augmenting Results with Web Search Powered by Bing

Like the embeddings you have seen in the examples where repository files are referenced by Copilot in a response, GitHub Copilot is rolling out web search powered by Bing. This feature is currently in Beta at the time of writing.

The Copilot Enterprise administrator will need to enable this under the Policies area for Copilot.

## Customizing Copilot with Fine-Tuned Models

Fine-tuned models will allow for Copilot to respond with information specific to your organization directly in the responses from the large language model.

This process takes the base model for Copilot and fine-tunes it to your organization's specific repositories. Code standards, packages, documentation, and more can all be directly returned in your Copilot responses.

This feature is currently in internal development based on the GitHub Copilot landing page:

```
https://github.com/features/copilot
```

Also, it is worth noting that this feature is exclusive to Copilot Enterprise and will be an add-on service.

## Supercharging Copilot with Workspace

Copilot Workspace looks to take Copilot's abilities in `GitHub.com` to a whole new level. This project appears under the GitHub Next website in the research prototype phase.

```
https://githubnext.com/projects/copilot-workspace
```

Copilot Workspace is intended to help with "simplifying the process of making repo-wide edits, using verifiable AI-generated plans and code" [5].

## Conclusion

This chapter provided a comprehensive overview of GitHub Copilot's capabilities for Copilot Business and Copilot Enterprise applications. It began with an introduction to Copilot's functionalities on `GitHub.com` and progressed through advanced features like retrieval augmented generation and the benefits of indexing code repositories to enhance Copilot's understanding.

The use of Copilot Chat within code repository files and its application in enhancing pull requests were highlighted as methods to streamline development processes and improve collaboration. Strategies for managing GitHub Copilot effectively were also discussed, along with a look toward future advancements in the tool.

The insights from this chapter should equip you to assess and integrate AI-powered tools like GitHub Copilot within your organization's SDLC addressing both the potential and the challenges of increased AI adoption in professional workflows.

## References

[1] GitHub, 2024. "GitHub Copilot Business," `https://docs.github.com/enterprise-cloud@latest/copilot/copilot-business`

[2] GitHub, 2024. "GitHub Copilot Enterprise," `https://docs.github.com/enterprise-cloud@latest/copilot/github-copilot-enterprise`

[3] .NET Foundation and Contributors, 2024. "dotnet-architecture/eShopOnWeb," `https://github.com/dotnet-architecture/eShopOnWeb`

[4] Choi N., 2024. "What is retrieval-augmented generation, and what does it do for generative AI?," `https://github.blog/2024-04-04-what-is-retrieval-augmented-generation-and-what-does-it-do-for-generative-ai`

[5] GitHub, 2024. "Copilot Workspace," `https://githubnext.com/projects/copilot-workspace`

# Conclusion

As this exploration of GitHub Copilot concludes, it's clear that the landscape of software development is undergoing a significant transformation. GitHub Copilot has introduced a new paradigm of programming, one where artificial intelligence acts not just as a tool but as a collaborator, enhancing software development capabilities and workflows far beyond traditional developer tooling.

Throughout this book, you have encountered many aspects of GitHub Copilot, from basic code completions to its role in learning new programming languages, writing robust tests, refactoring code, and even navigating the complexities of CI/CD processes. You've seen how Copilot can act as a universal converter, diagnose and resolve bugs, and help ensure code security.

As technology evolves, so will GitHub Copilot, and with it, its applications in the software development life cycle (SDLC) will continue to expand. Future advancements will drive deeper integration of AI tools in the SDLC, potentially reshaping job roles and industry standards. Embracing these tools can lead to unprecedented productivity and innovation.

Encouraging responsible use of AI and understanding its implications on privacy, security, and employment are essential as you move forward. As you integrate GitHub Copilot into your development practices, please continue to engage with the community, share insights, and contribute to the progression of this transformative tool.

Thank you for joining me on this educational journey through the features, capabilities, and applications of GitHub Copilot. The knowledge and strategies shared here will help you harness the full potential of GitHub Copilot in your development workflow.

# Resources for Further Learning

This appendix is a curated list of resources designed to help you understand and navigate the various aspects of GitHub Copilot. This guide includes everything from getting started with the tool to detailed information about subscription plans, community support, and legal guidelines. Whether you are a new user looking to integrate GitHub Copilot into your workflow or seeking deeper insights into its impact and ethical considerations, these resources provide valuable information to enhance your knowledge and use of this innovative tool.

- GitHub Copilot Overview and Subscription Plans
- Community Engagement and Support
- Legal and Ethical Considerations
- Research and Insights

## GitHub Copilot Overview and Subscription Plans

This section offers a collection of essential resources for those looking to explore GitHub Copilot. It covers everything from initial setup and usage to choosing the right subscription plan that fits your development environment. These resources are ideal for enhancing your understanding and utilization of GitHub Copilot, whether you're an individual or managing a team within an organization.

## Getting Started with GitHub Copilot

Learn how to begin using GitHub Copilot by installing its extension in your preferred development environment, configuring GitHub Copilot within supported IDEs, or adjusting settings for GitHub Copilot on `GitHub.com`.

```
https://docs.github.com/copilot
```

## GitHub Copilot Individual

Explore the features and benefits of the Copilot Individual plan for solo developers.

```
https://docs.github.com/enterprise-cloud@latest/copilot/
copilot-individual
```

## GitHub Copilot Business

Find details on the GitHub Copilot Business plan, tailored for small to medium-sized enterprises.

```
https://docs.github.com/enterprise-cloud@latest/copilot/
copilot-business
```

## GitHub Copilot Enterprise

Learn about the extensive features offered in the GitHub Copilot Enterprise plan.

```
https://docs.github.com/enterprise-cloud@latest/copilot/github-
copilot-enterprise
```

## Managing Billing for GitHub Copilot

Access a guide on choosing the right billing plan for GitHub Copilot, including eligibility for free licenses.

```
https://docs.github.com/enterprise-cloud@latest/billing/
managing-billing-for-github-copilot/about-billing-for-github-copilot
```

## GitHub Copilot Product-Specific Terms

Review the specific terms and conditions applicable to GitHub Copilot users.

```
https://github.com/customer-terms/github-copilot-product-specific-
terms
```

## GitHub Copilot FAQs

Get the answers to frequently asked questions covering general concerns, privacy, responsible AI, and upcoming features and offerings.

```
https://github.com/features/copilot#faq
```

# Community Engagement and Support

This section provides resources focused on community engagement and support mechanisms for GitHub Copilot users. It includes links to community discussions where users can share insights, seek help, and access the GitHub Copilot Trust Center to address specific concerns about using the tool in development processes.

## GitHub Community Discussions on Copilot

Engage with the GitHub Community to discuss educational resources and support related to GitHub Copilot.

```
https://github.com/orgs/community/discussions/categories/copilot
```

## GitHub Copilot Trust Center

Find answers to questions about using GitHub Copilot in development processes.

```
https://resources.github.com/copilot-trust-center
```

# Legal and Ethical Considerations

This section addresses the legal and ethical considerations associated with the use of GitHub Copilot and AI technologies in general. It features resources from Microsoft and governmental entities outlining copyright concerns, responsible AI practices, and regulatory frameworks designed to ensure the ethical deployment of AI systems. These documents are essential for understanding the broader implications and responsibilities of integrating AI into professional environments.

## Microsoft Copilot Copyright Commitment

Microsoft's commitment details copyright concerns with using Copilot.

```
https://blogs.microsoft.com/on-the-issues/2023/09/07/copilot-
copyright-commitment-ai-legal-concerns
```

## Empowering Responsible AI Practices

Microsoft discusses its efforts and policies to promote responsible AI use.

```
https://www.microsoft.com/ai/responsible-ai
```

## Blueprint for an AI Bill of Rights

This is the U.S. government's framework to ensure safe and fair use of AI technologies.

```
https://www.whitehouse.gov/ostp/ai-bill-of-rights
```

## The EU Artificial Intelligence Act

This details the EU legislation aimed at regulating artificial intelligence applications.

```
https://artificialintelligenceact.eu
```

# Research and Insights

This section delves into various research and insights related to GitHub Copilot and generative AI. It includes studies on the impact of GitHub Copilot on developer productivity, insights into the use of large language models (LLMs) in its development, and an introduction to OpenAI Codex. These resources offer valuable perspectives on how advanced AI technologies shape software development practices.

## What Is Retrieval-Augmented Generation?

This is an overview of how retrieval-augmented generation impacts generative AI.

```
https://github.blog/2024-04-04-what-is-retrieval-augmented-
generation-and-what-does-it-do-for-generative-ai
```

## Quantifying GitHub Copilot's Impact on Productivity

Read the research findings on how GitHub Copilot has influenced developer productivity and satisfaction.

```
https://github.blog/2022-09-07-research-quantifying-github-copilots-
impact-on-developer-productivity-and-happiness
```

## AI's Impact on the Developer Experience

Delve into survey results discussing the influence of AI on developers' work routines and experiences.

```
https://github.blog/2023-06-13-survey-reveals-ais-impact-on-the-
developer-experience
```

## Inside GitHub: Working with LLMs

Get insights from GitHub engineers on their experiences working with large language models during the development of GitHub Copilot.

```
https://github.blog/2023-05-17-inside-github-working-with-the-llms-
behind-github-copilot
```

## OpenAI Codex

Get an introduction to Codex, the AI model behind GitHub Copilot, which is capable of interpreting and executing commands in several programming languages.

```
https://openai.com/blog/openai-codex
```

# Glossary

**AI (artificial intelligence)** — The simulation of human intelligence processes by machines, especially computer systems.

**AI Bill of Rights** — A nonbinding document proposed by the White House outlining the rights citizens should have in the AI-enhanced world, emphasizing privacy, transparency, and fairness.

**AI Executive Order** — A directive by the U.S. President mandating federal agencies to incorporate and monitor responsible AI practices in their operations.

**Angular** — A platform and framework for building client-side, single-page web applications using HTML and TypeScript.

**@terminal agent** — An agent in Copilot Chat focused on assisting with terminal-related tasks and queries, optimizing the use of the terminal within the development workflow.

**@vscode agent** — A keyword used in Copilot Chat to inquire about or interact with features specific to the Visual Studio Code environment.

**@workspace agent** — A keyword in Copilot Chat allowing users to interact with their entire workspace, enabling the AI to fetch context from all files in the project for generating responses.

**Azure Data Studio** — A cross-platform database tool by Microsoft designed for data professionals to manage SQL Server, Azure SQL Database, and Azure SQL Data Warehouse from Windows, macOS, and Linux.

**Behavior-Driven Development (BDD)** — A software development approach that involves specifications written in plain language, forming a common understanding among development, QA, and nontechnical stakeholders. BDD focuses on the behavioral specification of software units.

**Bootstrap** — A free and open-source CSS framework directed at responsive, mobile-first, front-end web development.

**C#** — A modern, object-oriented, and type-safe programming language developed by Microsoft, designed to enable developers to build a variety of secure and robust applications that run on the .NET ecosystem.

**capability maturity model integration (CMMI)** — A process-level improvement training and appraisal program administered by the CMMI Institute, which provides organizations with the essential elements of effective processes that ultimately improve their performance.

**code refactoring** — The process of restructuring existing computer code—changing the factoring—without changing its external behavior. It is aimed at improving code readability and reducing complexity to enhance the maintainability and extensibility of the code base.

**code security** — The practices and processes put in place to protect code from vulnerabilities, unauthorized access, and other threats, ensuring that software behaves as intended without any unintended or malicious activities.

**CodeQL** — A tool for code analysis, used within platforms like GitHub Actions and Azure DevOps pipelines to automatically identify vulnerabilities in code before it is merged and deployed.

**contextual prompting** — Techniques used in Copilot Chat to enhance the AI's understanding of the user's coding environment and intentions, such as the use of tags like #editor and #file.

**continuous deployment (CD)** — A strategy for software release where code changes are automatically prepared and deployed to a production environment without explicit approval from developers, ensuring a fast and automated way to release.

**continuous integration (CI)** — A software development practice where developers frequently merge code changes into a central repository. After this, automated builds and tests are run.

**CSRF protection** — Measures to protect against Cross-Site Request Forgery, a type of malicious website exploitation where unauthorized commands are transmitted from a user that the web application trusts.

**data encryption** — The method of converting plaintext data into a coded form to prevent unauthorized access.

**DevSecOps** — Short for Development, Security, and Operations, it integrates security practices into the DevOps process. It emphasizes security at every phase of the software development lifecycle to minimize vulnerabilities and ensure continuous delivery of high-quality software.

**Dockerfile** — A text document that contains all the commands a user could call on the command line to assemble an image. Docker can build images automatically by reading the instructions from a Dockerfile.

**dotnet CLI** — The command-line interface for .NET used to create, run, and manage .NET applications from the command line or terminal.

**#editor context variable** — A tag used in prompts to give GitHub Copilot context about the visible code in the editor window, aiding in relevant and accurate code suggestions.

**end-to-end tests** — Comprehensive testing that validates every process along with the flow of an application from start to finish. It ensures the system's components function together as expected from the user's perspective.

**Entity Framework** — An open-source object-relational mapping framework that is part of the .NET Framework.

**ESLint** — A pluggable and configurable linter tool for identifying and reporting on patterns in JavaScript, helping to make code more consistent and avoiding bugs.

**EU AI Act** — European Union legislation aimed at regulating AI applications by setting standards for ethical practices, risk assessment, and compliance for AI systems used within the EU.

**/explain command** — A command used in Copilot Chat to request detailed explanations or discussions about specific pieces of code or concepts.

**#file context variable** — A tag that allows users to specify which file(s) should be considered by GitHub Copilot during the conversation, even if the file is not currently open.

**FIPS (Federal Information Processing Standards)** — Publicly announced standards developed by the United States federal government for use in computer systems.

**/fix command** — A command in Copilot Chat where GitHub Copilot provides suggestions to correct errors in code based on the context of the error.

**Gartner Hype Cycle** — A methodology used by Gartner, an IT research and advisory firm, to represent the maturity, adoption, and social application of specific technologies.

**generative AI models** — Artificial intelligence models that can generate new content based on their training data.

**Gherkin syntax** — A business readable, domain-specific language that lets you describe software's behavior without detailing how that behavior is implemented. Gherkin is primarily used to write structured tests for BDD.

**GitHub** — A platform for version control and collaboration, allowing developers to work together on projects from anywhere.

**GitHub Actions** — GitHub's CI/CD platform that enables automation of all software workflows, now with world-class CI/CD. Build, test, and deploy code right from GitHub.

**GitHub Advanced Security** — A feature set for GitHub that provides tools for secure code development, such as code scanning for vulnerabilities.

**GitHub Classroom** — A tool provided by GitHub to automate the use of GitHub for educational purposes, which can be used to distribute and collect assignments.

**GitHub CLI** — Command-line tools provided by GitHub that facilitate GitHub operations like cloning repositories, managing issues, and handling pull requests directly from the command line.

**GitHub Copilot** — An AI-powered tool designed to assist developers by suggesting code snippets and entire functions while programming. It acts as an artificial pair programming partner.

**GitHub Copilot Business** — A subscription plan that builds upon the functionalities available in Copilot Individual by providing additional control and security features. This plan allows organizations to manage how GitHub Copilot is used within their teams, ensuring that the integration of this tool aligns with their security policies and operational needs.

**GitHub Copilot Chat within `GitHub.com`** — A feature in Copilot Enterprise that allows users to interact with GitHub Copilot directly through the GitHub.com interface, facilitating code-related discussions and queries.

**GitHub Copilot Enterprise** — The most advanced subscription plan, designed for large organizations using GitHub Enterprise Cloud. This plan includes all the features of Copilot Business and adds exclusive capabilities such as direct interaction with GitHub Copilot in the browser, access to advanced AI features on GitHub.com, and more extensive control over how Copilot interacts with the organization's codebases and data. Copilot Enterprise is tailored to enhance productivity across the entire organization by integrating deeply with GitHub's ecosystem.

**GitHub Copilot knowledge base** — A feature in GitHub Copilot Enterprise that allows organizations to create and maintain a centralized repository of knowledge, documentation, and FAQs to enhance the contextual understanding and response accuracy of GitHub Copilot.

**GitHub Copilot Vulnerability Prevention System** — A feature of GitHub Copilot designed to enhance security by proactively identifying and blocking insecure coding patterns in real-time. This mechanism ensures that the code suggestions provided by GitHub Copilot adhere to best security practices, thereby helping developers avoid common security pitfalls while coding.

**GPT-3 (Generative Pre-trained Transformer 3)** — The third iteration of OpenAI's generative pre-trained transformer series of large language models released in 2020.

**GPT-4 (Generative Pre-trained Transformer 4)** — The fourth iteration of OpenAI's generative pre-trained transformer series of large language models released in 2023.

**HTTPS (Hypertext Transfer Protocol Secure)** — An extension of the hypertext transfer protocol (HTTP) used for secure communication over a computer network.

**integration testing** — A level of software testing where individual units are combined and tested as a group. The purpose is to expose faults in the interaction between integrated units.

**JavaScript** — A high-level, interpreted programming language that conforms to the ECMAScript specification. JavaScript is one of the core technologies of the Web, alongside HTML and CSS, and enables interactive web pages.

**JetBrains IntelliJ IDEA** — An IDE by JetBrains primarily focused on Java development but also supports a wide range of other programming languages and technologies through plugins.

**legacy system** — An old method, technology, computer system, or application program that continues to be used despite its age.

**modernization** — The process of refactoring, re-architecting, or replacing legacy software systems to align them more closely with current business needs.

**Neovim** — An extended version of Vim, an open-source text editor designed to improve Vim's functionality and ease of use for more complex editing and development tasks.

**NestJS** — A progressive Node.js framework for building efficient, reliable, and scalable server-side applications.

**.NET** — A free, cross-platform, open-source developer platform for building many different types of applications, known for its robustness and wide range of capabilities.

**.NET Core SDK** — A software development kit (SDK) used to develop applications with .NET, which includes the runtime and command-line tools for creating .NET applications.

**/new command** — A command used to initiate the scaffolding of a new project or codebase in a specific programming context, guided by the user's specifications.

**/newNotebook command** — A command that triggers the creation of a structured Jupyter Notebook for tasks such as exploratory data analysis, leveraging Copilot's ability to scaffold code.

**NIST (National Institute of Standards and Technology)** — An agency of the U.S. Department of Commerce, responsible for developing standards, including those for data encryption.

**Node.js** — An open-source, cross-platform, JavaScript runtime environment that executes JavaScript code outside a web browser.

**OpenAI Codex** — A descendant of the GPT-3 model, trained specifically to understand and generate code across various programming languages.

**OWASP (Open Web Application Security Project)** — An online community that produces freely available articles, methodologies, documentation, tools, and technologies in the field of web application security.

**OWASP Top 10** — A standard awareness document for developers and web application security. It represents a broad consensus about web applications' most critical security risks.

**pair programming** — A software development technique where two programmers work together. One, the driver, writes code while the other, the observer or navigator, reviews each line of code as it is typed in. The roles are frequently switched.

**Pandas** — Pandas is an open-source Python library used for data analysis and machine learning, built on Numpy, which supports multi-dimensional arrays.

**Polars** — A high-performance data manipulation library, providing a DataFrame object similar to Pandas but with better performance.

**prompt engineering** — The practice of crafting precise and effective prompts to improve the quality of responses from AI systems, crucial in working with tools like GitHub Copilot.

**React.js** — A JavaScript library for building user interfaces, particularly for single-page applications where you need to interact quickly with the user.

**red teaming** — A strategy where teams actively try to find and exploit new vulnerabilities in a system, helping to identify and mitigate potential security issues.

**responsible AI** — Practices that ensure artificial intelligence technologies are developed and implemented in a safe, ethical, and reliable manner, adhering to principles like fairness, transparency, and accountability.

**retrieval-augmented generation (RAG)** — A process used to enhance the output of large language models by incorporating real-time data retrieval from an external knowledge base, ensuring the generated content is accurate, relevant, and informed by the latest information.

**Scrum** — An agile process framework for managing complex knowledge work, with an initial emphasis on software development, although it has been used in other fields and is slowly starting to be explored for other complex projects, too.

**security scanning** — The process of scanning software for security vulnerabilities, typically integrated into the CI/CD pipeline to ensure that vulnerabilities are caught and remedied before deployment.

**#selection context variable** — A tag indicating to GitHub Copilot that the selected text in the editor should be considered as context for the conversation.

**shift left on security** — A practice in DevSecOps of integrating security measures early in the software development lifecycle rather than at the end to catch vulnerabilities earlier when they are typically less costly to fix.

**software development life cycle (SDLC)** — A systematic process used by development teams to create high-quality software efficiently. It includes phases such as requirements gathering, system design, implementation, testing, deployment, and maintenance.

**Swift** — A powerful and intuitive programming language created by Apple for building apps for iOS, Mac, Apple TV, and Apple Watch, designed to work with Apple's Cocoa and Cocoa Touch frameworks.

**Tailwind CSS** — A utility-first CSS framework for rapidly building custom designs.

**Terraform** — An open-source infrastructure as code (IaC) software tool that provides a consistent CLI workflow to manage hundreds of cloud services. Terraform codifies cloud APIs into declarative configuration files.

**/tests command** — A command that instructs GitHub Copilot to generate unit tests for a specified method or function, helping to streamline test development.

**TLS (Transport Layer Security)** — A cryptographic protocol designed to provide communications security over a computer network.

**TypeORM** — An ORM (object-relational mapper) for TypeScript and JavaScript that facilitates interactions with databases by abstracting database interactions into easily manageable objects.

**TypeScript** — A superset of JavaScript that compiles to plain JavaScript, known for its optional static typing features.

**unit tests** — Tests that validate the functionality of a specific section of code, usually at the function level, allowing developers to verify that each part of the system operates as expected independently.

**Visual Studio** — An IDE developed by Microsoft that supports a multitude of programming languages and tools for developing and managing complex software projects.

**VS Code (Visual Studio Code)** — A free source-code editor made by Microsoft for Windows, Linux, and macOS. Features include support for debugging, syntax highlighting, intelligent code completion, snippets, and code refactoring.

# Index